HOOLIGAN WARS

£9·99

i

EDITED BY **MARK** PERRYMAN

HOoLigAN WArS

CAUSES AND EFFECTS OF FOOTBALL VIOLENCE

published in association with

PHILOSOPHY FOOTBALL

MAINSTREAM
PUBLISHING

EDINBURGH AND LONDON

First published in Great Britain in 2001 by
MAINSTREAM PUBLISHING COMPANY
(EDINBURGH) LTD
7 Albany Street
Edinburgh EH1 3UG

ISBN 1 84018 421 3

A catalogue record for this book is available
from the British Library

Typeset in Bembo
Printed and bound in Great Britain by
Mackays of Chatham

CONTENTS

ACKNOWLEDGEMENTS

Hooligan Wars presents a range of answers to what causes football violence and seeks to account for its effects. The writers don't all agree and it isn't the point of this collection to offer one single explanation or solution, because there almost certainly isn't such a thing. Most of the authors are active football fans, but not all of them, because one of the problems with much of what passes for considered comment on this subject is a refusal to put football hooliganism into a broader context.

In developing this book I've been lucky enough to test out the ideas on a sometimes unsuspecting public. I am grateful to Ian Woods at BSkyB, Jonathan Wills at Carlton TV's *London Tonight*, Michel Peremans of VRT TV in Belgium, Pete Stevens at BBC Radio London Live, and Adam Gilchrist at British Forces Broadcasting Service in particular for providing me with TV and radio opportunities to put across a fan's point of view when 'Ingerland comes to town'. Michael Gove at *The Times* and David Leigh at *The Guardian*; Andy Lyons, Editor of *When Saturday Comes*, Gary Tipp, Editor of *Total Football* and Jason Cowley, Literary Editor of the *New Statesman* have all been more than generous with their word counts when my articles on this subject have had a tendency to spill over the agreed limit. In February 2001 I was appointed Research Fellow at The Chelsea School, Brighton University, where staff and students have been extraordinarily forthcoming in helping to challenge, develop and more often than not change how I approached the subject of this book. Stephen Parrott at Birkbeck College continues to invite me to lecture on his 'Football, Culture and Society' summer extra-mural course, where an unrivalled mix of opinions is always guaranteed to lift me from the muddle my word-processor can get me into.

In 1994 I co-founded the self-styled 'sporting outfitters of intellectual distinction', *Philosophy Football* with Hugh Tisdale. Sometimes described as a 'fanzine for the chest' the footballing thoughts of Camus, Guevara, Cruyff and others are emblazoned across a 100 per cent cotton top in Hugh's stunning designs. Our partnership and friendship has helped me through many a season, not to mention two European Championships and one World Cup. It never ceases to amaze me how a day spent stuffing our T-shirts into bio-degradable plastic envelopes can help stimulate the thought bugs, but somehow it does.

One of our ventures which has nothing to do with T-shirts but a lot to do with a patriotism without the prejudice is 'Raise the Flag'. Now acknowledged as an England fans' tradition it was my idea and Hugh's planning that turned thousands of red and white cards into a fans' St George Cross flag whenever England play. Thanks are due to Peta Dee of the FA Commercial Department, the Nationwide Building Society, the England Team Sponsor and Adam Stebbing of Forrest Press for helping to make it happen. The volunteers who lay the cards out on all those seats include Tony Dekanski, Geraldine Ford, Ken Jackson, Nicola Everatt, Paul Jonson as well as many more.

As an active member of *englandfans*, the official England Supporters Club, I have learnt a lot from the process of seeking to develop a supporters' organisation that could make a significant contribution towards a positive England. Fans with whom I have sometimes agreed, sometimes disagreed but always enjoyed the discussion with include Dave Tomlinson, Karen Hutton, Duncan White, Pete Ryan, Mark Dodd, Alan Lee, Mark Raven, Laura Allen, Craig Brewin, Daniel Buckingham, and others too many to mention. Many of these discussions have taken place via e-mail. A massive thank you to all England fans on the London England Fans' e-loop. The FA takes a lot of criticism for its dealings with England fans, some of it deserved, some of it not; James Worrall, Alan Barnard, Mark Sudbury, Adrian Bevington, Ian Murphy, Nick Barron are amongst those FA staff who have taken the trouble to listen – thanks.

In 2000 the Home Office set up a Working Group on Football Disorder. Having complained bitterly that no England fan representative had been invited to join the Working Group's discussions I was pleasantly surprised not only to be asked to join in but also to see that at least some of the fans' input did make a difference. I am grateful to David Bohanan, Kevin Parker and Lord Bassam from the Home Office for the invite, and in particular to the thoughtful contributions that I heard from Billy Bragg, Kevin Miles, Cathy Long, Andy Walsh, Piara Powar, Adam Brown, Tim Crabbe, Ron Hogg and Clifford Stott. I am also grateful to Glyn Ford MEP and Chris Heaton-Harris MEP for asking me to take part in an EU hearing on the problem of football violence.

Dan Murrell played about with a computer and helped to turn Tony Davis's great photograph of a football I'd mysteriously asked him to paint black into an amazing image. At Mainstream Publishing Tina Hudson turned all of this into a tremendous cover while Jess Thompson, Alison Provan and Clive Hewat did a grand job on the editorial production side, and Bill Campbell stumped up the advance. Thanks for showing faith Bill, again. Stefan Howald helped me out of my pig-ignorant hole when one author expected me to be able to read German. Andy Smith helped me track down David Shayler's account of being a Boro fan on the run in the fanzine *Middlesbrough Supporters South*.

The greatest debt of all is to what I like to think of still as the 'beautiful game'. My club team Spurs has been a source of constant, well I can't say joy, not yet anyway, but at least inspiration. And as for England, well the away trips have never been far short of enjoyable, even if the results haven't always been all we dreamt of. Philip Cornwall has on more than one occasion proved to be a great travelling companion. At Euro 2000 I was lucky enough to be put up by hosts including Harry Zevenbergen, The Thuburns, Thierry and Helene Lacasse, Peter Slabbynck and Luc Maton, while through the World Cup 2002 qualifying campaign the hospitality of Paavo, Liisa, Heini and Janne Löppönen in Helsinki, Bujar Bashar in Tirana and Claus Melchior in Munich, made football and travel the kind of ideal mix I would wish it to be for everyone – a mix that has been made so much more pleasurable for me thanks to the love of Anne Coddington, home and away. Her endless energetic exploration of far-flung markets and shops can sometimes tire me out on matchdays when all I can think of is who will be in the team and when kick-off is, but that scarcely matters, not really. Following England not to mention my entire world (plus or minus the football) just wouldn't be the same without her.

None of the aforementioned can be blamed for what follows. That's down to me, and the individual contributors. But perhaps out of this untidy combination of conversations, arguments, study, politicking, activism, cheering and despairing a fan culture we can all be proud of will emerge. And you never know it might just coincide with Sven-Goran leading us to some silverware. England dreaming? Yes please.

THE GOOD, THE BAD AND THE BEAUTIFUL GAME

HOOLIGAN WARS

Mark Perryman

> One observer compared the atmosphere surrounding the England
> support for the recent match against France as being akin to 'watching
> a football match during a Nuremburg rally'.
> *Home Office Working Group on Football Disorder Discussion Paper, October
> 2000*

Travelling to watch England can on occasion be an unpleasant experience,
few would deny that. But to compare sitting in the stands at the Stade de
France in September 2000 for France versus England to one of Adolf Hitler's
choreographed party pieces seems just a tad over the top. But this is how the
Home Office Working Group on Football Disorder chose to open its first
published deliberations, though thankfully by the time the group's final
report was published in March 2001 this particular description of the
atmosphere fans generate at an England game had been removed.

The mood in the Stade de France was much like it always is when
following England. The sightlines were better than Wembley's where it is
near-impossible to watch a game without standing up. At a stroke a major
cause for tension was removed. But a laddish crowd of latecomers filled up
the gangway and, refusing to budge, obscured others' views. They were all
Stone Island jackets, baseball caps pulled down tight over the eyes, and
expensive-looking designer jeans, and from the look of them it would be a
brave fan to ask them to move aside. 'Le Marsellaise' received a lusty booing,
and 'God Save the Queen' was bawled out. As bad as it gets as good it gets
with England abroad.

When the French team paraded their two trophies a fair smattering in the
England end respectfully cheered them on; the love of football for some
crosses borders. The England end itself had a better representation of women
than usual, and children too. The location and date were ideal for this: a
weekend game, in sunny Paris, just a stop or two down the line thanks to
Eurostar, and at the tail end of the summer holidays. After the team had
earned a creditable draw against the World and European champions the fans
streamed back to central Paris. Around the Gare de Nord the lads continued
their drinking, turning the square into their own patch of little England as

they waited for the dawn train back home. The scene was intimidating, menacing even, but if you chose to avoid it the rest of Paris was a hugely pleasurable place to be, for the French and their English visitors alike.

The French Riot Police, the CRS, know all about trouble, they've got a gruesome pedigree going back to Paris May 1968. They were certainly up for a confrontation with any English lads who fancied their chances. Outside the stadium the CRS were held back in reserve while the tension rose with more than the odd England fan becoming abusively louder and louder as he (invariably it was a he) vented his anger at having to queue on the young, brightly jacketed stewards. You didn't have to speak French to be able to read their faces: 'C'mon its only a game, just wait your turn like everyone else, don't make my life a misery, *s'il vous plâit*' . . . And when the abuse didn't stop, not unreasonably the offenders were removed. But as the kick-off approached larger and larger numbers of impatient England fans were building up the pressure on the hard-pressed turnstile operators. Maybe they should have had the sense to arrive early but navigating the Metro in good order isn't such an easy task and with the huge stadium a near sell-out and the temptation to see the odd sight before heading off to the match, kick-off time can catch up on you before you know it. With the scene starting to turn frantic the CRS waded in, batons drawn and flailing. Not a pretty sight.

The picture could be the same at almost any England game – home and more especially away. If a trip on the wild side is what takes your fancy it's easy enough to find the spaces and places where things have a habit of turning nasty. If you're more of a voyeur, a thrill-seeker who wants to come home with the sniff of tear gas in your clothes but not the scars of a bruising encounter or three, then stand on the edge of the crowd and escape any serious retribution. Though, if the police have a habit of sweeping entire areas free of anyone looking remotely like an England fan, the chances of getting away with it are significantly reduced. For those whose preference is a milder slice of life, the sights, the restaurants and bars off the soon to be beaten-up track are easy enough to locate with a *Rough Guide* to hand, and after taking a few sensible precautions – like avoiding large squares with bars all around the perimeter, getting to the game early, and knowing where you're going after the game (preferably in a taxi you've already booked) – the likelihood of seeing trouble is probably less than chucking-out time in any large English town or city.

A month or so after the trip to France, England took on Germany at Wembley. The match would mark the end of an era for the Twin Towers, though few sitting under them for what they thought would be the last time could have dreamt they'd still be standing twelve months later. And as for the opposition, they'd taken a 2–4 hammering in Wembley's greatest-ever moment and after 34 years of subsequent hurt, in June we'd finally triumphed over them again. A repeat performance however wasn't to be.

Losing 0–1 on a freezing cold October Saturday with near constant rain put paid to any celebrations. Worse than that, against a poor German side our team looked disorganised and clueless. Dreams of World Cup qualification had taken a knock and Wembley's final game would go down in memory as a day of drizzle and defeat. The afternoon had begun brightly enough. The opening bars of 'God Save the Queen' were the cue for some 60,000 red-and-white cards all around the stadium to be held up by the fans. Creating four huge St George Cross flags it was a great moment – our national flag transformed into a fans' flag. And uniquely the hundred or so England supporters who had laid these cards out on the seats to be occupied by the home fans had also gone to the trouble to lay out cards in the colours of the German flag with a welcome in German, in the away section too: fan ambassadorship of which we should be proud. No, it didn't stop the booing of the German national anthem, but like Rome, the new Jerusalem won't be built in a day, or 90 minutes come to that. It would have been nice if somebody, somewhere, might have picked up on this fan-led initiative, though of course Keegan's resignation in the end overshadowed everything connected with that fateful Saturday afternoon. But even in the more measured Monday comment pieces the occasion was used to engage in yet another bout of overblown national self-hatred, 'That bunch of cretins in *News of the World* plastic bowler hats, the dark underbelly of Euroscepticism' was how Richard Williams described a large portion of the crowd in *The Guardian*. Williams had been horrified by the number of England fans who had taunted the Germans by singing 'Stand Up if You Won the War'. An encore of the Dam Busters' March, with accompanying aeroplane gestures'. His estimation that this involved a significant proportion of the crowd was undoubtedly correct, though of course it would take a crack squad of mass observationists to account for those many silent voices who didn't join in. But that's by the statistical by. Nevertheless the widespread singing of such ditties can surely be connected to a more widespread europhobia, which, lashed together with imperial decline, footballing lack of success, and Seaman's failure to hold on to Dietmar Hamann's soft-touch free kick doesn't excuse a bit of oral mischief-making but at least helps to contextualise it. Meanwhile another England, passionate but positive, once again gets sidelined. The German fans, ironically, seemed more aware than many of our own of this side of English fan culture – the commitment, the wit and the banter – for which we are rightly renowned. On going 1–0 up they stunned the England fans hemmed in on both sides of them with a perfectly executed rendition of 'You're Not Singing Any More' in English. Who says the Germans don't have a sense of humour?

The curious bi-polarity of England fans' culture is rarely commented on. They are huge in number, highly committed, yet contain within their ranks a brand of thuggery that few other national teams' support can match.

During Euro 2000 *The Observer* sports section printed an editorial on precisely this phenomenon, and it is well worth quoting at length precisely because of its rarity value:

> There's no doubt about it: England has the worst football fans in the world . . . Gary Lineker called for passport confiscation on a grand scale. Were such a scheme put into operation it would have rid the Championship of its *best* supporters, The English . . . Passionate, knowledgeable, peaceful supporters happy to sit and talk with anyone and everyone . . . Stop off for a beer or a coffee in Tilburg, or Breda, or Antwerp, or Ghent and you'll bump into friendly, knowledgeable English fans who will help with tickets, and advice on restaurants and accommodation . . . But this is no surprise. The English watch football, and love watching football, like no other nation . . . Yes, England has the worst football fans in the world. But it also has the best.

For some random evidence of the depth of commitment of our fans, take Saturday, 24 March 2001. Across Europe national teams were battling their way through the World Cup 2002 qualifying groups. England attracted a sell-out crowd of 44,262 to Anfield for their encounter with Finland. Sweden had 22,106 at their game: Turkey 25,000; Scotland 37,480; Spain 35,000 and Hungary 20,000. Germany could only attract a lowly 22,500 for their match with Albania. England's game with Albania in September 2001 had *already* sold out St James' Park's 51,000 capacity. The previous October 30,155 had turned out for England's Under-21 game against Germany, while in May 2001 30,000 were at St James' Park for a European Championship Under-16 semi-final, England versus France – crowds few other countries in Europe could match even for a Senior International!

Before we turn up the volume on the national tub-thumper a look down the attendance charts for 24 March does reveal that the Ukraine versus Belarus crowd numbered a staggering 75,000. However unless the Ukraine economy is about to go into overdrive the Ukrainian travelling support will remain a tiny fraction of this impressive home support. Here is the other crucial difference between us and our continental footballing neighbours. Certainly since the early 1980s the size of England's away following has been large, expanding, and for key matches at easy-to-reach locations likely to dwarf any other country's. The mix of two extremes; friendly passion and nasty disorder make for not such an unlikely pairing under such conditions.

But the conditions should not be allowed to excuse away a 'victim culture' that sees the buck flying by so fast when it comes to accounting for football violence. There is a pervasive tendency to blame everybody else. The usual suspects are, and remain: the media, the police, the football authorities and the opposing fans. In almost every case some, if not all, of this lot will have at least some bearing on the events that surround the mayhem associated with England coming to town. But what about ourselves as England fans taking our fair share of the responsibility? If, as is so often claimed, those who have nothing to do with the violence are in a majority why are we so apparently incapable of having any effect on what happens? The position, rightly put by fans, is that we are part of the solution; then we have to make ourselves part of it while at the same time marginalising the minority who are so obviously a part of the problem. Without that clear and unquestionable distinction criminalisation of us all will be the consequence. The organisations and agencies which seek to control the situation almost always hanker after criminalisation as their tactic. We have to convince them by any means necessary that their emphasis is all wrong, that the stick is no good without the carrot.

Creating the context where an anti-violence culture emerges around England fans requires a recognition of three related factors. The first of these is the need to recognise that relatively small numbers are involved in the actuality of violence. On the day of England versus Germany in Charleroi estimates of the numbers of England fans in the town circled around the 15,000 mark. The number involved in the town square confrontation, even at its peak, scarcely topped the 1,000, and far fewer than that actually chucked a chair or threw a punch.

Charlie Whelan wrote an impassioned piece in *The Guardian* denouncing the way that the trouble in Charleroi had been blown out of all proportion. Whelan has made himself somewhat notorious for describing, in his own inimitable words, England fans as 'racist scum, plankton and pond life' so his view can hardly be described as supporter partisan, rather he was writing as a BBC Radio 5 Live presenter shocked by the recklessness of media colleagues:

> Waiting in the main square were the world's media. I counted at least 50 TV cameras ready to witness the inevitable. On the radio, our team reported the events from 6 a.m. No chairs had been cleared, strong beer was readily available and the police let gangs of Germans into the square. They obligingly tipped the TV crews that they were going in to arrest some Germans and the rest is history. Gordon Farquhar, the experienced 5 Live sports news reporter, scored the level of violence as three out of ten, but who cared about the radio? The incident with the water cannon actually lasted no more than ten minutes, while 15,000 England fans enjoying themselves with Germans in the hundreds of bars around the square received no coverage. ITN reported the water cannon scenes as effective policing, so effective that their reporter Bill Neely got hit in the face by a fan. Those nutters in the square loved every minute of it and even cheered when the water cannon returned.

After the game few England fans stayed the night in Charleroi. Those who did remain might have been surprised to flick the TV on the next morning to hear the French-speaking Mayor of Charleroi calmly assert that the previous day had 'hardly been World War Three' and that the damage amounting to a 'handful of broken windows' was less than the town centre was used to putting up with after most Saturday nights. Even more perplexing for those who harbour a hard-bitten belief that all England fans leave behind them is ill-will, debris and a wish never to return, is the theme tune RCS Charleroi played each time they scored a goal in the 2000–2001 season – 'The Great Escape'. Not quite the legacy that you'd expect if England coming to town is the most unpleasant memory you can imagine, is it?

But the smallish numbers involved and mainly modest collateral impact of the damage caused must be measured against a second factor. The events feed off a set of attitudes and accompanying mood that in large measure legitimise the actions. The violent minority is precisely that, small in number compared to the huge travelling support. The anti-violent minority is equally small in number and quite possibly less well-organised. For the majority violence simply isn't an issue. There is little or no sense of the menace or the intimidation that large voiciferous crowds might pose, rather this is offered as a natural form of solidarity; togetherness in a foreign culture. Of course this is precisely the attraction of being a fan, that sense of community, so simply denouncing all this as 'the other' is singularly inappropriate. But with little or no articulation from within the fan culture associated with England of an anti-racist and anti-violence voice, it is no surprise that the togetherness of the unruly crowd can so easily transgress and transform into a baying mob egging on others to smash, fight and abuse.

England is not an easy pole of attraction for those who distinguish pride from prejudice. Though if *The Sun* can paint a picture of England in a 2001 St George's Day editorial as 'a country of tolerance – peopled largely by gentle, good-natured men and women' then maybe it's not such an impossible task as some too often suggest. The same editorial offered a tour through the usual martial history, offering up England, and generously the USA too, as the countries that 'defeated the great threat of our time, totalitarian communism'. But the editorial also listed 'creativity, humour, culture' as other national attributes along with 'Chaucer, Shakespeare, Milton and Tennyson'. These are the resources of hope around which a positive Englishness can be built. For every Jim Davidson there's a Lenny Henry or Meera Syal; for every 'Rule Britannia' there's homegrown reggae, soul, garage or jungle and it doesn't take a genius to guess which is the more popular. For all the incidents of lager-loutery on the Costa del Sol there's a youth culture that generated a transcontinental book like Alex Garland's *The Beach* or turned Ibiza into the anglicised dance capital of Europe. Engaging with the network of attitudes that the violence feeds off by posing a great variety of alternative ways of celebrating our Englishness should be at the core of any strategy to isolate the violent minority.

Hackett, the upmarket clothing company that unwittingly dressed many of those who made the front pages and filled the TV cameras as they charged towards police lines or opposing fans came to a very clear commercial conclusion. According to Chief Executive Sven Gaede, the St George Cross symbol is to be phased out from their fashion range following events at Euro 2000. For Hackett it's easy enough to drop what for them is just another logo; for a national culture that's no option at all. Turn St George into meaning something quite different, soften its hard edges, rob it of its unwanted associations and another identity for England fans will soon be in the making. A failure to take a softened patriotism as our starting point would be flying in the face of reality, to ditch the English question that refuses to go away. Of course football culture cannot on its own conjure up a new national identity, and it's not a cosmetic make-over that we want in any case but something much more deep-rooted. But it is at an England game that more St George Cross flags are flown than on any other occasion, including our national day. The shirt that has come to symbolise England is a football shirt, now complete in the latest design with a subliminal St George Cross.

The broader network of largely uncontested negative values associated with following England away help to explain the significance of a violence relatively few are involved in. But the small numbers do not equate with the third factor, the huge impact of what is perceived virtually as a national trait, 'football hooliganism'. One England fan reports a conversation from when he was in Italy for a game and was visiting a bank to change some travellers' cheques for Lira. The cashier received his passport and spotting the nationality and knowing a game was on, cheerily suggested 'Ah English . . . football hooligan?' To which the fan instantly retorted 'Ah Italian . . . Mafiosi?' The ludicrousness of each other's stereotype was hopefully not lost in the translation. But this representation of what it means to be English is extraordinarily common. A British Council November 2000 report *Through Other Eyes 2: How The World Sees the United Kingdom* specified that 'Britons' (the report's description, though the text makes it obvious enough we're talking about the English) are perceived by young people in other countries as 'arrogant, xenophobic and frequently drunk.' David Green, the British Council Director explained he was concerned: 'by the high proportion of young people who associate us British (*sic*) with an arrogant and condescending view of other countries. Anyone who watched, for instance, the scenes at Charleroi during Euro 2000 can understand how these perceptions arise.' And the perception (whether it's true or false is immaterial), isn't only held by those overseas. A poll in the *The Observer* of

18 March 2001 revealed that the feature that most made Britons embarrassed of Britain was hooligans or lager louts, scoring 33 per cent, three times higher than the runner-up in the embarassment stakes, litter at 11 per cent. The images that the violence sets in place have an impact on FIFA, UEFA, future host nations and cities with attendant media and police forces, our own government, the FA, and the general population, home and abroad. This isn't simply the product of hyped-up media coverage and an ingrained reputation for causing trouble, it is also because of the sport the violence has become associated with. In terms of global appeal nothing comes even close to football and so anything connected to it has, in its wake, a tendency to become similarly overblown. Football hooliganism is regarded by these contintental youngsters as a negative of Englishness, yet ironically football is also used by the British Tourist Authority to promote tourism. At opposite ends of the spectrum, the effect is the same. Football is becoming more, not less, integral to our national bank of symbols.

The fourth factor is the key to unlocking the entire problem. Currently there is a lack of a travelling fan culture associated with England. With this emerging we would begin to witness the marginalisation and isolation of the violent minority and attendant attitudes while being able to identify with the positive majority. Friday night in Derby, 25 May 2001, England versus Mexico. The word on some fans' electronic grapevines is that there will be trouble between Derby supporters and their hated rivals from Nottingham Forest in town for the England game. Outside the city centre pubs there's a heavy police presence in anticipation of fighting while on the road to the game there are snatches of 'No Surrender' to be heard. But this is the side show. All around are kids with painted faces, mums, dads and lads are queuing up to be kitted out in Sombreros courtesy of *The Sun*, there are pictures to be had with the Mexican band strumming their guitars outside the stadium. The mood is friendly, celebratory, and with a dash of sunshine it might not even be stretching things too far even to describe it as 'carnivalesque'. Inside the ground as England take a 3–0, and finally a 4–0 lead it's the England stands that initiate round after round of the 'Mexican Wave' and barely a body in the place fails to jump up and join in joyfully. Away, almost entirely the opposite is true. The mood of impending trouble affects us all, even those who have absolutely no intention of getting caught up in it. Security and personal safety are major concerns, the support is much, much narrower than at home, the celebration is largely left on the shores of good old blighty. England expects? To get home safely, we hope. Until all of this is reversed the actuality of the violence will persist, the initiatives focussed on control will fail and the consequences of this failure will magnify.

To travel away following England should be an adventure we can all at some stage in our career of fandom look forward to. Sun, sights to see, unfamiliar food and drink to savour, and a football match that will have the nation talking for perhaps decades to come – this is what we might be able reasonably to expect. What spoils much of this for many of us, and deters so many more from travelling, is the expectation that there will also be trouble. Of course there are exceptions, but the England games where there's no football violence rarely get remembered for the fans, though the cultural capital gained each time the widely-predicted trouble fails to break out perhaps shouldn't be underestimated. The Helsinki tabloid *Iltalehti* splashed across its front page the day after the 11 October 2000 Finland versus England game 'WHAT DID WE HAVE TO FEAR – ENGLAND FANS ARE LAMBS' backed up by the incontrovertible evidence: 11 arrests, of which 10 were Finns. And notions of an exclusively 'English disease' look less conclusive after a French policeman is put into a coma by a pack of German fans in Lens during France '98. Sometimes the focus on England is simply a force of certain circumstances being drawn against us. Suppose Holland had ended up playing Germany on that fateful Saturday in Euro 2000 while we had to settle with, say, Belgium. Would England fans have gone home then as the sole culprits? Almost certainly not.

But no championship organising committee plan or qualifying group draw should have to be made simply to sanitise the English risk. So what we have to prepare for instead are the consequences of the self-fulfilling prophecy. If it is widely predicted that England away is a mad, bad and dangerous place to be is it any wonder that the mad, the bad and the dangerous turn up for precisely those reasons while countless others choose not to go? Of course we're not sheep, but the absence of almost any positive messages, images or information to encourage a more balanced sense of what travelling with England is like will inevitably narrow the away support. The potential breadth of England's away support is obvious at any England home game. Lots of families, plenty of women, fans of all ages – though still few black and Asian supporters. Yes, away support is almost always more 'hard core' than the home support, in lots of ways that is its defining characteristic. But England's away support is significantly more hard core compared to how the away support of a club side or another country relates to its corresponding home support. Bringing our home and away support closer together must involve unpicking the self-fulfilling prophecy of England abroad. When *The Observer* with their 'Hooligans Link up on the Net to Plot Mayhem at Euro 2000' headline and accompanying full-page feature, or *The Independent* with 'Euro 2000 Braced for the Wired-Up Hooligan', complete with maps and diagrams – are the more cool, calm and collected end of the pre-match build up then it is hardly any surprise that those looking for trouble made their way in large numbers to Charleroi and Brussels during Euro 2000. Meanwhile many of those who had enjoyed England's home qualifiers but feared for their safety having read these reports thought twice and didn't bother travelling. And then, when the championships are over, you've missed all the trouble, had a great time and you travel home only to be greeted by Steven Howard in *The Sun* as: 'the fans who had once again brought disgrace to the oldest footballing nation in the world and contempt to the lips of everyone else' and read of 'the base, sordid behaviour of the pond-life that accompanies England everywhere they travel.' Not exactly the words to encourage anyone to sign up for England's away trips are they? Until we start reading some words that actively encourage the kind of away support all England fans can be proud of then Steven Howard will be left with the excuse to write the same nauseating copy after every major championship that England has the good fortune to qualify for.

Is all this concern about football violence just a case of middle-class morality being imposed on a working-class culture? Alistair Macsporran had a neat answer in the Scottish fanzine *The Absolute Game* writing a review of two of the latest offerings in 'hoolie-lit', *Down the Copland Road* by Ronnie Esplin and *Hearts are Here* by C.S. Ferguson:

> Some pretended intellectual justification is painted on this loathsome project by suggesting that this is a valid part of 'working class culture' which is being swamped by the new culture of plastic seats and replica strips. Now, I'm with them when they feel threatened by the current over-commercialised direction in which football has been travelling for some years. But violent troublemakers are not, and never have been, a valid or admirable part of working class culture, and to suggest otherwise is quite contemptible.

Socialist Worker meanwhile found a different explanation for England's football violence. Under a banner headline 'Winding Up Frankenstein' Martin Smith commented on the trouble at Euro 2000:

> English football thugs hammered anyone they could get their hands on . . . The fighting by English fans is a direct result of the frenzy of nationalism whipped up by politicians and the media. . . The nationalism and the racism of the English hooligans is the mirror image of the racism being whipped up by Tory thugs like William Hague and Ann Widdecombe . . . Tony Blair condems the football violence, claiming it brings 'shame on England'. But new Labour does nothing to counter nationalism . . . It has been more than happy to drape itself in the English flag.

The Left writing off all who follow England as racist thugs spurred on by a violent nationalism is just as inappropriate as 'hoolie-lit' writers romanticising crowd violence as a heritage trail through working-class culture. It could be argued that what is required is to disentangle the football from the flag. That is an admirable enough viewpoint, and in other countries the national stakes are clearly not nearly as high as when England plays. But for a sizeable chunk of both our population and our media it is as if the entire national past, present and future depends on eleven blokes squeezing a spherical bit of leather between three sticks of wood. However we rationalise it, football *is* an inextricably huge part of our national identity. In fact currently there's precious little else. The Scots have their own parliament, the Welsh and Northern Irish an assembly, which leaves England as the one country in any World Cup or European Championship without this most obvious symbol of statehood. None of this mattered while Britishness could be easily transposed for Englishness, though in every single instance this has always been executed at the expense of the Scots, Welsh and Northern Irish. Devolution has changed all that, forever. Throw in resurgent and modernised celtic cultures in the shape of Travis and *Trainspotting*, Catatonia and *Human Traffic* plus *The Fleadh* music festivals and all things Irish and it is not hard to see how the English seem like a little nation lost. This is the rich irony of English nationalism. We lorded it over the rest as Great Britain for such a long time we've forgotten how to calibrate, let alone celebrate, our own nationhood. All we're left with is the odd beer promotion. In 2001 Bombardier beer pulled out all the creative stops with their advert declaring 'Once more unto the Office, dear Friends' adding the explanation 'Because St. George's Day still isn't a national holiday' just in case anyone missed the point of the advert, the national day passes by unnoticed. Which leaves Peter Dobbie in the *Daily Mail* to bemoan the fact, 'Tomorrow in England St George will be ignored instead of celebrated in the same way that the Irish, Scots and Welsh value and trumpet their own icons and identity'. And thus football is left, almost alone, to bear more than its fair share of our emotional investment in national identity and flag-waving. In an era of globalisation local identities are becoming more, not less, important. Shunning our own while filling ourselves up with an unhealthy dose of national self-hatred and do-nothingness in the face of what we sometimes allow Englishness to become adds nothing to the solution and a whole lot more to the problem.

Diktat – do this, don't do that – won't deliver the changes required. It ignores why we go to football in the first place. In large part it is to escape from regulations, instructions, serving on committees and the like. We all want to get out of control, be unruly, shout words and behave in a way unacceptable at work or at home. This doesn't have to involve intimidation, offence or violence, and for the vast majority of us it never does. Consideration for others isn't such a rare virtue in a football crowd. But escape from the everyday is a vital part of football's appeal. J.B. Priestley summed this up brilliantly in his 1929 account of English life *The Good Companions*. His language is a touch antiquated, gender roles have changed a lot (though in football still not enough) since Priestley's day, but his point remains a powerful one:

For a shilling the Bruddersford United AFC offered you conflict and art; it turned you into a critic, happy in your judgement of fine points, ready in a second to estimate the worth of a well-judged pass, a run down the touch line, a lightning shot, a clearance kick by back or goalkeeper; it turned you into a partisan, holding your breath when the ball came sailing into your own goalmouth, ecstatic when your forwards raced away towards the opposite goal, elated, downcast, bitter, triumphant by turns at the fortunes of your side, watching a ball shape Illiads and Odysseys for you; and what is more, it turned you into a member of a new community, all brothers together for an hour and a half, for not only had you escaped from the clanking machinery of this lesser life, from work, wages, rent, dole, sick pay, insurance cards, nagging wives, ailing children, bad bosses, idle workmen, but you had escaped with most of your mates and neighbours, with half the town, and there you were, cheering together, thumping one another on the shoulders, swapping judgements like lords of the earth, having pushed your way through a turnstile into another and altogether more splendid kind of life, hurtling with conflict and yet passionate and beautiful in its art.

Nick Hornby couldn't, and hasn't, put it better. Strong leadership from the football authorities against football violence, while welcome, will only be effective if it is conducted in partnership with the fans who still seek this escape that Priestley so vividly portrays, but buy into this escape being inclusive, not exclusive by virtue of either violence or the attitudes it feeds off.

The initiatives concerned with football violence since Euro 2000 have been largely concerned with control, mixed with a dose of demonisation. In July 2000 *The Guardian* front page headline announced 'Straw to Rush Through Hooligan Crackdown'. And when the legislation was passed later that same month the emphasis was clear enough: to identify known troublemakers in advance of a tournament or high-profile game and prevent them from travelling. Sounds great in theory, but what about the practice? If the bans are limited to those with a conviction in the preceding five years for a football-related, or indeed other, violent offence the numbers are probably manageable enough to detect and detain under a banning order. But of course, as has been pointed out time and time again, many, if not most, of those who end up caught causing violence abroad have no previous convictions. So control becomes focused more and more on either suspicion or distribution of tickets through official channels. 'Innocent until proven guilty' should be the kind of tradition that makes up our national fabric so how far are we willing to go in tearing it up? If a group of lads turns up at the Waterloo Eurostar terminal and start singing 'I'd rather be a Paki than a Turk' then the police have perfectly legitimate grounds to prevent them from travelling under a number of current laws. If, however, they just happen to have shaven heads, are covered in tattoos, and have a liking for expensive designer gear, is that legitimate cause to stop them from leaving the country? Hopefully not. Nobody in their right minds would argue with effective forms of deterrence but the evidence of the past 20 years and more is that these control solutions on their own simply will not work and end up being used to justify increasingly draconian measures. The events on Mayday 2001 in Oxford Circus have been the most high-profile use of legislation in this way. To prevent the day's anti-capitalist demonstration taking place, section 60 of the 1994 Criminal Justice Act was used. This allows:

> Where a police officer of or above the rank of superintendent reasonably believes that incidents involving serious violence may take place in any locality in his area and it is expedient to do so to prevent their occurrence he may give an authorisation that the powers to stop and search persons and vehicles conferred by this section shall be exercisable at any place within that locality for a period not exceeding twenty four hours.

The build-up to the Mayday protest was remarkably similar to that for any high-profile game involving England. The same self-fulfilling prophecy: Oxford Street was set to be a risky place for shoppers and shopkeepers alike, the need for a heavy police presence was promoted, well-organised mayhem was predicted, anybody who joined the protest would only have themselves to blame for the consequences. Demonisation spilled over into widespread criminalisation. Over 2,500 hemmed in by row after row of riot police for eight hours plus. And *The Mirror*'s headline the next day?' One Nil to the Bill', it doesn't take a semiotician to read the signs does it? On the inside pages of the same paper Paul Routledge, *The Mirror*'s Chief Political Commentator denounced the consequences of overkill police tactics: 'Democracy survived in London yesterday. Not in the hands of baton-wielding police, but in the hearts of kids in anoraks taking on the system. Yesterday's real heroes were not the fat blue line, but the anonymous brats of democracy.' Routledge's view ran starkly counter to the *The Mirror* editorial in the same day's paper: 'The May Day 2001 Battle of London was another proud day for the British police'. While the *Daily Mail* splashed across their front page an enormous photo of a policeman hitting a protester on the head with his truncheon accompanied by the banner headline, 'The Day The Law Fought Back.' The previous day Tony Blair added to the criminalisation of the protests in a speech to the London Press Club: 'It is not protest − it is crime pure and simple.'

What has all this to do with football? Demonisation and criminalisation of the majority because of the actions of the minority, that's what. Some would say that draconian policing is a price they are willing to pay to eliminate football violence, many would beg to differ while others will counter that it doesn't work anyway – never has, never will. Section 21 of the Football (Disorder) Act 2000 provides summary detention measures for police constables who have: 'reasonable grounds to believe that making a banning order would help to prevent violence or disorder at or in connection with regulated football matches'. This allows for four hours detention, extended to six hours with the approval of a policeman with the rank of Inspector or above. This period however can go on longer if further information is required. These measures surely can only be expected to work if they are extended ever more widely. That is their logic – treat as suspicious, vet and detain for questioning every person travelling to a country where England is due to play, throw in adjoining countries too, for say a week beforehand, that should just about do it, or not. Having demonised England football fans, we'll throw in foreign travellers too. The expense and impact of such an operation would be huge. So the air of suspicion settles, and the demonisation takes on an ugly edge. Fashion sense, haircut, accent, age and tattoos all become signs of trouble. Meanwhile with all this talk of security sweeps, body searches and covert surveillance, how many fans who've already read that mayhem is ensured when they arrive anyway will once again think twice about travelling? Demonisation leads to criminalisation which produces another form of exclusion every time it is practised. And when it fails to prevent outbreaks of trouble the inexorable logic is for more and more police powers with wider and wider application.

Alongside sweeping legislation and extensive police powers the principal target for action has been the official supporters organisation of the England national team, the England Members Club (EMC). At the October 2000 launch of the Home Office Working Group on Football Disorder, Home Office Minister Lord Bassam singled out the EMC: 'There's a lot of unpleasant racism within that quarter of the crowd. It does greatly disturb us, it's something we want to root out.' He described the EMC as 'a profoundly white, 20–40 year olds supporters' club.' Yet the EMC; now *englandfans*, remains the best hope the government and football authorities have for a meaningful dialogue with the active England fans who detest and abhor the violent reputation others have saddled them with. Demonising all England fans, and the EMC in particular is a big mistake and fails to contribute to dialogue with supporters. (The launch of the working group was reported in the *Daily Mail* with the headline 'Racist Core at Official England Soccer Fan Club'.) This doesn't mean going soft on racism and xenophobia, ignoring the violence of some of our own – anything but. What it does mean though is actively listening to, engaging with, and providing an effective platform for the majority of fans who suffer most from the negatives associated with supporting England.

Parallel to the Home Office initiatives aimed at the EMC, the FA themselves had already committed to wholesale restructuring of the club. Since its formation in time for Italia '90 as the 'England Travel Club' the organisation had effectively functioned as a ticket distribution agency, controlling the official allocation of tickets for England away games and providing priority booking for home games. With qualification for World Cup '98 the first ventures towards a broader role began, taking in the need to improve relations with England fans and cleaning up their reputation abroad. It started slowly, cautiously, conservatively at first but nevertheless with an admirable degree of commitment from the fans and officials involved. Charlie Whelan however was one of those not impressed, writing in *The Observer* four months before Euro 2000 opened: 'This year we are told that England fans are to go on a charm offensive. Are they trying to insult our intelligence?' And he certainly didn't warm to the *England Fans Travel Guide* produced by the EMC for the championships: 'The fans going to Euro 2000 will be given a guide to restaurants, museums and other cultural attractions. This, we are told, will encourage them to sample life in the towns and cities they visit. Who are they kidding?' Whelan denounced the entire initiative as 'utterly offensive', a non-starter before it even had the chance to begin. Of course he was right if the test of its success was the wholesale prevention of any outbreaks of trouble associated with England's support. But alongside the events in Charleroi and around La Bourse in Brussels something had changed since France '98. A different story about England fans abroad ran for the first five days of the championships. England fans were popping up in almost every available media outlet telling their travellers' tales, stories that were such a welcome change to the ones we were used to reading about what it took to be an England supporter. Of course as soon as the trouble began on the weekend of the Germany match all of this was pushed to one side. Does that mean these efforts were in vain? Well if they were we might as well ban all England away travel immediately. And in the wake of Charleroi there were many influential voices who would propose precisely that. In an editorial after Euro 2000, 'Play Games Behind Closed Doors,' the traditionally left-liberal-leaning *New Statesman* proposed: 'What the authorities should have done from the moment the first beer-bellied lout stepped onto Continental soil to give his two-fingered salute: send the English ingloriously home.'

The new regime at the FA charged with seeing through the post-Charleroi modernisation of the EMC is one that is drawn principally from a business background. The FA Director of Marketing, Paul Barber, was appointed in the immediate aftermath of Euro 2000 and in a December 2000 interview with the magazine *Marketing* he described his ambition as being 'to capitalise on the massive interest in the England team'. Matching commercial ambitions with a sense of service and purpose is a difficult balancing act but it is quite wrong to presume it can't be done. The key issue is to avoid reducing any identification with England to nothing more than a merchandising operation. This would certainly miss out on any potential for remaking a positive England. Creating a positive England depends on a number of simple interlocking factors. The first of these is to expand to the maximum the ways in which England fans can become active supporters of the team. The closure of Wembley is a fantastic opportunity for this, with England Senior Internationals for the first time since Wembley was built being played on a regular basis around the country. The chance to see England easily is now open to those living in the Midlands, Merseyside, Manchester, Yorkshire, the North-East and elsewhere. Instead of involving that long trek to reach Wembley, an England International is becoming a local game. However if the match sells out a couple of hours after the telephone booking lines have opened this isn't much help. We need a pro-active 'conveyor belt' offering the widest-possible opportunity for people to become active England fans. The Under-21 game on the night before the Senior International is an increasingly popular alternative, but why not make a Saturday game the climax to a festival week of internationals – at Under-18, Under-16 and Senior Women's levels? Play these in stadiums with plenty of capacity, offer the tickets for free with financial support from sponsors to bus in schools, youth and community groups. Promote the entire six days as a carnival of international football. If that results in more Nationwide mortgages, packets of Walker's crisps or Yorkie bars being sold, fine. The bigger project, though, would be to create an environment where all can feel that, should they want to support, not only is England their team but that being a supporter can be defined in a great variety of ways. Yes, it would take organisational investment but the payback could be considerable in terms of what we come to think of what it means to be an England supporter. We shouldn't be deriding 'armchair supporters' as active fans are wont to do, but instead we should be finding ways to enable them to get into a stadium to support the team. The fan-base for England is potentially huge, it needs to be accommodated in the most inclusive ways possible, not just limiting it to those lucky enough to get hold of a precious match ticket for one of a handful of home Senior Internationals each year. Unlike a club, where support – Manchester United notwithstanding – is largely restricted to one city, or at most a region, England's support is nationwide. Matches are played irregularly, five or six times a year, not like a club that plays once a week, or more, throughout the season. The support is therefore large but dispersed, and lacks the rhythm that naturally forms around a club culture. All who choose England as 'our' team need a great variety of ways to reinforce that identification. This must be done formally, informally, by commercial, emotional, and cultural transactions. We must actively attract all those who want to share in this identity – black and white, men and women, young and old, wherever we come from, whatever we do. This message runs starkly counter to the fallacious argument that the English are born not made. Football becomes part of the making of, not merely the merchandising of, the nation, breaking the link between race and nation that fuels much of the prejudice masquerading as patriotism.

The second of these factors needed to create this positive England is that the connection between being a home England supporter and an away supporter needs to be far more fluid than the current set-up allows. The major concern for the fan organisations (most notably the Football Supporters Association and the Fans' Red Card campaign) with the restructuring of the EMC was the loyalty points system. In brief this is a formula by which fans who travel across Europe for a qualifying campaign go straight to the front of the queue for the tournament tickets when England make it through. It is similar in principle to the well-worn tradition of collecting match vouchers in order to qualify for an FA Cup Final ticket. This is equitable, but not necessarily for those committed England fans who by force of circumstance, work or family commitments can't give up the time to follow England through the qualifying rounds. Similarly if all away-match allocations are made solely on a loyalty point basis then it becomes nigh on impossible ever to become an away fan, and a self-perpetuating group mops up all available tickets. The most loyal fans should be at the front of the queue, but they can't be the whole queue. The compromise made was an obvious one: a higher proportion of tournament and away tickets to be allocated on the basis of loyalty points, with a substantial proportion also available for all-comers.

But this structural device hardly even begins to engage with the question of why some travel away and others don't. It is almost as if away fans are a necessary evil which we'd rather do without and we'll do all we can to discourage – yet another aspect of the self-fulfilling prophecy. An away trip has to be planned months in advance, time booked off work, holidays arranged around it. Those going for the first time would expect detailed and professional travel advice and support. While security cannot be guaranteed it may be reasonable to have the option of pre-booking a place on a coach that will take you safely back to the area in which you are staying, and bi-lingual stewards could be provided to help diffuse any problems between fans and stadium security. Without any of this at present is it any surprise that England's away support has a certain narrrowness about it, and that the exclusivity breeds a siege mentality where the atmosphere so easily turns from the friendliness of an England home game to the menace of an away game? The potential of something quite different to this situation was highlighted by the football magazine *When Saturday Comes* following Euro 2000: 'It now seems there is a distinct travelling fan culture developing which has little to do with the mind-numbing nationalism of England's hooligan and sub-hooligan followers.' Nobody is actively 'selling' the idea of travelling away with England, not turning it into a downmarket hospitality junket, but providing the very real support that those who have spent hundreds of pounds to get to the other side of the continent to cheer England on should be able to expect. So long as we have to whisper that this or that trip might be a bit 'iffy' and lack the information to actually go out and enjoy our travels abroad with England, very little will change from our current sorry predicament.

Thirdly, there must be the spaces for England fans to acquire and articulate a real sense of ownership of a positive England identity. The FA's 2001 survey of EMC members, in which 28 per cent of the membership participated, recorded an astonishing 86 per cent either 'agreed strongly' or 'agreed' with the statement, 'Members of the EMC are ambassadors for English football.' While 91 per cent 'agreed strongly' or 'agreed' that 'Membership of the EMC brings with it a responsibility to behave well.' The negative images most England fans who have nothing to do with the trouble are nevertheless labelled with leaves them on the slippery slope to thinking that surely they must be the minority – nothing is more empowering than realising you're not. The FA cannot 'create' a fan culture for England supporters but it could provide the meeting points, on the web, the week before an International match in Newcastle, Manchester, Leeds or London, for ticketholders as they plan their trips to a World Cup or European Championship, out of which a no-longer-silent majority might emerge, and make it absolutely clear that the FA backs and supports such a process.

Three simple points. Not necessarily in contradiction with some of the necessary legislation and policing which most would accept must accompany any event involving large numbers of moving bodies. But the emphasis is here quite different. This is the 'carrot' that those so ready to wield the 'stick' always seem to forget. Broadening the means by which we can become part of England's support – turning away trips into something people can look forward to as a holiday of a lifetime rather than an excuse for another hooligan war-story, providing the space and the means for those opposed to the violence to shape an England fan culture. This is the three-pointed strategy that would significantly aid the process of marginalising and isolating the violent minority. It is to be hoped it will heavily inform the development of the new national team supporters' organisation, *englandfans*, launched by the FA in July 2001. This does not account for the many thousands of England fans who will travel to high-profile away games or tournament matches unofficially, with or without tickets – hence the limited impact of more careful vetting of those who apply for tickets via the FA. But a real and dramatic shift towards an inclusive, fan-led travelling culture around the official supporters' organisation would provide a realistic possibility of having a positive impact on this broader, often bigger, disorganised support.

Such a strategy, welcome as it would be, would remain ineffective if it failed to connect with the bigger picture which shapes the football violence associated with England. This is vital. Marginalising football violence is a process dependent for its success much more upon cultural shifts than a smarter use of administrative devices. Our sense of splendid isolation is there to be read every day in our national press. And there's no finer example of this than all the pontificating about England's football troubles. Why doesn't it occur to those responsible for football in this country to travel a few hundred miles northwards and converse with a people who speak the same language and who have managed in less than 20 years to turn the same god-awful reputation for visiting vile violations on towns when their national team's supporters arrive. Ian Black, author of *Tales of the Tartan Army* was somewhat surprised when the Home Office had the wit to invite him to join one of their Working Group meetings. His report in *The Herald* betrayed an unmistakeable generosity of spirit towards his south-of-the-border rivals:

> We all know that the majority of the England support are decent folk, there to support their team, anxious to avoid trouble. How do we empower them? How do we focus the headline makers on merriment rather than mayhem? I've thought about this long and hard because I really would like to help, even the English.

But this isolationism isn't just about football is it? *The Daily Mail's* headlining a piece by columnist Stephen Glover 'It's Bonkers Not to Be Beastly to the Germans' portrayed an attitude so commonplace that it barely raised a comment. And so it goes on. The attitudes which the violence feeds off, therefore, stretch well past the gates to football stadiums. Paul Wilson in *The Observer* put the point succinctly in his review of Euro 2000's fans:

> Boorish English behaviour does not begin on the cross-channel ferry or at the commencement of a football tournament. Its existence and tolerance at home is the unwritten story of every time the government or UEFA wring their hands over the latest shaming example of non-assimilation with more civilised cultures.

Boorishness is an easy enough label to pin on somebody else. But how do we go about unpicking its causes and effects? On 28 March 2001 England were due to play Albania in the Albanian capital, Tirana, in a crucial World Cup qualifier. In *The Observer* Simon Kuper had spelt out the blood-curdling scenes that the travelling fans could expect: 'Gunmen walked into a café under the National Stadium and shot dead the club president and Albania's top referee . . . Throwing a plastic chair at a car – in Belgium you'll get away with it. But here you'll probably get a bullet in the head.' Kuper has just about single-handedly pioneered a genre of football-travel writing; a vital tool in this project of generating a travelling fan culture around England. But with Albania he got things badly wrong. Of the couple of thousand England fans who travelled, almost all reported a splendidly friendly and receptive people; near legendary lock-ins which took their drinking well past closing time; great food, sunshine, and more than a handful of decent -enough sights to satisfy the tourist. No signs of any gun-toting gangsters were reported, nor trigger-happy police ready to spray the crowd with lead. Yes, the accommodation was basic but then the prices were low too. And the roads were famously potholed, as was endlessly pointed out by almost every journalist filing his report home and looking for a touch of local colour. On match-day *The Guardian* splashed out on a seven-point guide to Albania. It reported men wielding huge axes in hotel lobbies, non-existent nightlife, pillboxes and bunkers in every field, the pungent smell of pollution and the like. Elsewhere in the paper, not the uncommon event of an escalator on the London Underground being out of action for eighteen months was reported. Do they mean us? Meanwhile the *Albanian Daily News* the day before the game announced: 'Albania Fears Foot-and-Mouth from English Fans'. Being body-searched for cheese sarnies certainly proved a new experience for some and provided an unusual inkling of how others might see the state of England. And then there was the racist booing of the England Under-21 side by Albanian fans. David Mellor gave them his all in the *Evening Standard*, 'poor white-trash society' was what he thought of them. This was a country where a black face is almost never seen, and anti-racist campaigns are unheard of; couldn't this have informed our response? Stones and glass-houses come to mind when the 2001 Premier League Survey reveals that in multicultural Britain only 1.6 per cent of football supporters attending Premiership matches are black.

Peaceful majority, violent minority: these distinctions are often disingenuous. The same emotions frame both, the 'hooligan' is not our 'other', he is us, because a little or large bit of him is to be found in us all. The English carnivalesque will be the product of a culture not so dissimilar to the one that also produces the chaos and mayhem we are more familiar with. We can help direct the outcome – towards the optimistic, the positive, to provide the kind of picture Martin Samuels reported on from Albania in the *Daily Express*:

> There are English fans, quite a few of them, who have come, not to fight, but to watch a game of football, who are staying in hotels that do not shield them from Albanian life, who are spending their own money to travel and whose only reward is to be slandered when 'England fans' are held responsible for chaos abroad. The BBC is showing a programme called *The Men Who Changed Football* and each time I turn it on there is a different talking head in a suit who really only changed his bank balance for the better. They should make a follow up – *The Men Who Make Football*. It would include the name

of every man, woman or child who has come to third-world Europe this week to watch a game in peace. Whatever the result for Sven-Goran Eriksson's side, they are the real heroes.

We recruit. We travel. We represent England in the stands and the streets while the team represents the nation on the pitch. All of this could be read as a manifesto for a future fan culture full to the brim with the ugly inside of Englishness. But it can be read in another way. Fans as ambassadors not invaders. Enjoying rather than enduring. Pride without prejudice. War is over.

THE BIG PICTURE:
REACTIONS, RESPONSIBILITIES AND
FOOTBALL VIOLENCE

WHO YOU CALLING A HOOLIGAN?

John Williams

Up until quite recently, attendances at football matches in Britain had actually been in steady decline since the heady 'mass society' days of huge, orderly, crowds crammed into cavernous and ramshackle grounds just after the Second World War. This decline was offset a little by the rise of a number of new knock-out cup competitions and the crowds brought by European club competitions, but many fewer people pay to watch professional football these days than in the 1940s or 1950s. Football crowds fell fairly consistently from just after the Second World War high (41 million aggregate), through the early 1960s (27 million), and right up to the post-war 'slump' season of 1985–6, following the Heysel Stadium tragedy (16.5 million). Since then football crowds in England have tended to rise again, pretty much year-on-year, closing in on early 1960s levels again, especially as the FA Premier League took hold (around 25 million today). These days it is generally estimated that 5–6 million people attend at least *one* football match in England and Wales every year (mainly men) though it is difficult to be precise with these figures.

There are many reasons, of course, why crowds declined at football in England over the four decades immediately after the Second World War. Social habits changed and there are many more leisure options available to most people today. Some equalisation of power relations between males and females has also meant that the family has slowly become more of a focus for leisure than it was in the 1950s. Households have become more 'privatised' and much more entertainment takes place these days in the home, for example through the role of television and video, especially in the provision of sports coverage. Local football clubs are also not followed as they used to be, irrespective of their standing or performances, as the rhythms and loyalties of working-class life have changed. This, coupled with ease of travel, and the role of television and merchandising in promoting top, glamorous and successful football clubs, is also one of the reasons why many smaller English clubs now have very low attendances. Crowds in the top division have fallen by around one third since 1948–9, Division Three equivalents by closer to 60 per cent. Moreover, until recently the general standards of facilities at some football grounds arguably failed to keep pace with general improvements in social standards and standards of leisure provision elsewhere. This probably also deflected some potential fans away from the game and into a day out with the family, DIY or into other sports and leisure. But one other key factor helps to account for declining football crowds in the 1970s and '80s in England: the general perceptions, and the experience among fans, of football hooliganism.

Hooliganism at football was not popularly identified as a serious social problem in this country until the 1960s – a long time after football's crowds began to fall – so it certainly cannot account on its own for the game's long-term declining popularity after the war. But there seems little doubt that, increasingly, the experience and particularly the *fear* of, hooliganism did deter at least some older and middle-aged fans from 'respectable' working-class and lower-middle-class backgrounds from attending football matches in England between the late '60s and the early '90s. Indeed, surveys and interviews with fans who have recently 'returned' to the sport often identify hooliganism as *the* central reason why they stopped watching football, and its relative disappearance from larger English grounds later as one of the main reasons why they have since returned as football supporters.

Two other features are particularly interesting about the '70s and '80s. One is actually the strong *nostalgia*, in some quarters, for football culture in this earlier period. There has been a recent re-discovery of this era as a sort of lost golden age, a pre-commercial phase of the sport, which offered an authenticity and a bond to football clubs, grounds and to mates, a bond which is supposed to be quite lacking in the culture today. Partly this is about the lost world of terraces and the rise of alienating football business. But this sense of regret is especially apparent, of course if in a rather extreme sense, in the rise of popular 'hooligan' books and websites about the period, in which 'lads' fondly recall their various escapades and stories of fighting at football, and in which supporter camaraderie and adventure are successfully sealed off in these accounts from the sorts of predatory and de-masculinising influences – older fans, females and middle-class and 'consumer' fans, for example – which are supposedly more common at FA Premier League clubs today.

It is always useful to remember, of course, the ways in which social problems are carefully framed by powerful institutions and definers for purposes of public regulation, consumption, and debate. But one of the very obvious failures of these sorts of approaches to conceptualising social problems and public responses to them, is their often extreme social constructionism. Thus, Geoffrey Pearson recently remarked on the slippery issue of *defining* hooliganism: 'If we remove the layers of meaning surrounding the "object" of football hooliganism we will not be left with a residue that is recognisable as the singular, threatening phenomenon which it has been socially constructed as.' Yes, of course. But are we then, in the mind of the above author, left with *anything* at all to examine? Or does football hooliganism, and the social anxiety which is focused upon it, simply melt into air? Sadly, hooliganism is not simply, in the final outcome, the result of a panic constructed and shaped by an authoritarian State, but is, rather, a highly complex and serious social phenomenon that is reflective of the inter-weavings of the social formation of *both* the very real 'troubled' situation of late-modern English masculinities – a sort of 'protest masculinity' according to the sociologist, Robert Connell, – *and* the reflexive power of the labelling processes of media and State institutions.

The second feature which is interesting here in terms of how we relate to these periods is the general public response to the presentation of data on recent apparently declining levels of hooliganism at football matches, comparing these earlier 'hooligan' decades to the possibly more peaceful 1990s. At a time when police capacities to apply sanctions against hooligans and to investigate and track hooligan offenders (via the use of new legislation, undercover policing, and video and other technologies) have all increased significantly, and when tiny falls in officially measured incidences of other kinds of criminal offences usually herald clarion calls and media overload, the apparent transformation of the domestic football hooligan problem in England has been treated much more suspiciously. Counter-intuitively perhaps, as crowds at English football have increased, markedly, over the past 15 years or so (by more than 40 per cent), so officially recorded numbers of arrests have decreased quite remarkably too (by more than 50 per cent).

The usual approach among those who believe hooliganism has *really* declined is to link its fall in England with a number of concurrent things including: shifts in youth cultures, especially around the rise of dance and drug cultures; stadium reconstruction post- Taylor report, and especially after the arrival of all-seater grounds; new intelligence-led policing initiatives and increasing penal tariffs for hooligan offenders; a cultural transformation of the sport, informally via events such as the media presentation of the 1990 World Cup finals in Italy, and commercially via the new pricing and marketing strategies of football in England in the 1990s and beyond; and lastly the emergence of a (sometimes overpowering) new focus on promoting crowd management and public safety, and an appeal to a more disciplined family audience at major venues.

All of these factors have probably had their effect, though directly addressing the deeper, social causes of football hooligan behaviour has not been a major focus in the shaping of the current version of the sport in England. But not all academics, and certainly not all those writers who now make a good living out of producing hooligan texts, even agree that the official picture – of hooliganism in apparent decline – reflects anything like what is actually going on at football matches in England today.

There is, indeed, a hard core of writers and researchers about the hooligan phenomenon who have convinced themselves that, actually, very little has changed around the game in England in this respect – save perhaps the media's relative lack of interest in today's hooligan incidents. This particular sort of social constructionist perspective often draws for evidence for its case on notions of hooligan 'displacement' and on Rupert Murdoch's satellite BSkyB channel's new involvement in promoting the sport in England, and Murdoch's control over large swathes of the British press which now, it is alleged, have a brief to ignore or underplay hooliganism in order to protect Murdoch's vital TV investments in football.

Some of these accounts contend that very little has changed in the football crowd, and that in the partisan football 'ends' it is business as usual for English hooligans. Others argue that hooligan stories are simply being suppressed in order to maintain the game's links with its new and prized affluent audience. Others still, argue that it is actually the social and cultural anxiety and uncertainty of middle England itself which continues to give hooliganism – especially when it involves England fans abroad – its undeservedly high public profile.

So, what would seem to be a legitimate 'success' story of sorts, in a sea of otherwise offending troubles and 'nothing works' social policy hand-wringing, is converted, instead, in these critiques into a non-story about a non-event, namely the purported recent decline of football hooliganism in England. I would differ here. I would argue that although hooliganism has far from disappeared, the experience of going to a Premier League game for most people has changed quite dramatically. I travel home and away, in and around most of the larger grounds especially, and unlike the 1970s and '80s, you really have to look for serious fan action today – it's no longer a case of habitually stepping around danger spots, watching your back, or hastily crossing the road. In my own experience and in the experience of most of the people I know who go to these games, regular fans have to try quite hard – or to be unlucky – to find serious hooliganism at top clubs today. Interest in, and opportunities for, fighting in other contexts in England have not diminished much, of course, but Premier League football has become rather less of a focus than it used to be for this sort of satisfying, collective excitement and identity testing.

On this basis I would suggest that the *routine* place of the serious hooligan encounter, as an obvious and intrusive part of the main football event, on a near-weekly basis at larger football grounds in England 20 years ago, now seems ruptured, possibly for good. Surveys of fans – for example, the FA Premier League National Fan Surveys – and some accounts from 'hooligan' writers, such as Colin Ward and Martin King, would seem to back up these official trends and personal reflections. Routinely, these days, seven out of ten Premier League fans in surveys claim never to witness fighting or missile throwing in connection with football, though the experience of some travelling fans is different. Today, specific smaller clubs or matches, usually involving well-known offenders, or particular club combinations based on geography, or on some other source of rivalry, seem to be the main (if more irregular) hooligan focus.

Police responses to these apparently positive, if rather uneven, hooligan shifts have also been cautious in the extreme. Cynics might suggest that expensive and well-resourced police units which have been set up specially to deal with hooliganism have little interest in reporting on, or predicting, its imminent demise. But there is rather more to the police case than this.

As I have implied, hooliganism has not been quelled at all football venues and certainly not to the same extent everywhere. Perhaps routine conflicts in and around the stadiums of larger clubs have been 'managed away' more effectively than they have been at some smaller grounds – and especially in the more impacted and 'closed' social milieus where prized hooligan reputations are still fashionable and still persist. But it is harder to take seriously some police claims that they are simply suppressing hooliganism at football today – just 'keeping the lid on'. In fact, the condition of most English stadia – and the arrangements for policing inside and outside them – are by no stretch of the imagination as overtly embattled as those of the recent past. 'Police-free' matches are now even possible at some larger clubs, though it is also worth pointing out that concerns over the behaviour of some professional stewards now increasingly figure in supporters' critiques of the sometimes oppressive new management of football fans in England.

Local town tribalisms – especially where modernising influences on fan cultures and stadium facilities have also been slower to have an effect – are still vibrant, however. Indeed, these can also be sparked into new life as clubs drawn from particular areas are thrown together once more by the twin tides of promotion and relegation, so that after years apart satisfying local enmities can be resumed. Recent hooligan struggles in Lancashire, around the clubs in Preston, Blackburn, Burnley and Blackpool, are good examples here.

The situation at some larger clubs is also complex. In the 1970s and early '80s, for example, as Dave Robins and Phil Cohen point out in their book *Knuckle Sandwich*, clubs such as Manchester United and Leeds United, and Chelsea in the South of England, were certainly regional and national attractors for hooliganism and hooligans. Access to Manchester United's away matches was relatively open, and travelling with the club's 'Red Army' was often labelled – and was – an exciting hooligan outing and far removed from the routines at home. 'Lads' from smaller towns were drawn to some larger hooligan clubs at this time precisely for these reasons. Today, United away matches – though far from hooligan-free affairs in an era when the Manchester club attracts new sorts of envy and hostility – tend to be a little more exclusive and are probably rather less compelling than they used to be to large numbers of 'town' hooligans drawn from the Manchester region and beyond.

At the same time, of course, travel with a club such as Manchester United these days is also likely to be invested more strongly by a section of the club's male followers with 'traditional' football values and perhaps more hooligan intent, in order to contrast the experience away from Old Trafford with the alleged extreme passivity of home games. The terracotta and prawn sandwich army of 'consumer' fans at home matches, coupled with prohibitive stewarding, is supposedly firmly in residence at the new Old Trafford and other venues like it. Recent focus group research for the Football Task Force on 'excluded' Newcastle United supporters, for example, also seems to suggest that the attractions of watching live football in a highly managed stadium like the new St James' Park, where the identifiable, partisan 'ends' of the ground have effectively disappeared, now compares rather poorly, for some, with the collective experience of watching TV coverage of matches in the more raucous atmosphere of working men's clubs or pubs. Perhaps these 'virtual' football venues are the new terraces, places where older traditions of watching football survive rather more easily than they do in the comfortable new disciplinary regimes established at some English football grounds today?

It is certainly true, too, that some hooligan displacement – the relocation of incidents away from grounds and out of the range of cameras or police – has also occurred, with hooligan rivalries now being played out on a smaller, but perhaps more focused, scale usually some way from the grounds which host the more symbolic conflict of the match and the, essentially, non-hooligan fan rivalries which are played out there. As Chip Rowe pointed out recently in *When Saturday Comes* (June 2001), NCIS (National Criminal Intelligence Service) data on hooligan incidents suggests a very different picture from earlier periods:

> The NCIS website has a list of 83 'incidents' from the 1999/2000 season. Most came at train stations and pubs. The names that keep cropping up are not Premiership clubs but the likes of Rotherham, Stoke, Wigan, Cardiff and Swansea. Violence has trickled into the Divisions without CCTV or many stewards.

Arguably, some hooliganism displacement also occurred back in the 1970s, when fan disorder involving English supporters abroad became a new and troubling focus for public concern. Certainly today, while followers of English club sides abroad have rather revised their self-identity, largely rejecting large-scale hooliganism (if not always the routine incivilities which tend to mark out many English football travellers overseas) followers of the England national team have changed rather more slowly.

In part, this is because although England abroad attracts quite a wide range of followers today, it is still a magnet for small-town adventurers and sometimes violent metropolitan patriots, in the face of wider national decline. On top of this, the exploits of the England football team are often portrayed by the popular press in England as a metaphor for the nation itself. In this sort of environment, as England declines economically, has shed its empire and faces up to the new world order, the English tabloids speak as if a still 'great' nation is also being betrayed by its bungling and unsuccessful footballers and their managers – and, of course, by its riotous fans. Some followers of England abroad also seem especially unwilling to accept the country's new international positioning – beaten by 'minor' footballing nations; economically outstripped by other emerging nations and by defeated war enemies – especially when the rhetoric of the Thatcherite government in the '80s revived images of empire and famous triumphs in war. The solution? Kick ass in football adventures abroad and rehearse Second World War ideologies. The Scots, with rather less of this identity baggage, and with the English to model themselves conveniently *against*, have reaped the rewards. The Scottish hooliganism which does occur abroad is barely reported on now, as cod-Scottish tartanry takes centre stage instead. Meanwhile, police reinforcements, cameras and international news crews line up for the arrival of the English, whose response is now a complex mix of hostility and, for some, an irresistible desire to perform.

These excursions abroad confirm that displacement has actually been a feature of the development of hooligan conflicts for some time, but an important wider point is that domestic hooligan displacement also seems to be a much more central issue today, as policing and other control strategies (segregation, seating, stewarding and CCTV in and around the larger English football grounds) have become more comprehensive, and especially as sentences for hooliganism have become much more forbidding.

Hooligan displacement is also connected to the alleged rise of new technologies – mobile phones, the internet for example – in organising hooligan confrontations. Here the police view seems rather more ambivalent – at one moment criticising the media for its alarmist focus on the 'military precision' and the supposed complex, sometime trans-national structures and lines of communication of hooligan gangs, and on the other filling the airwaves and newspaper columns with their own ominous messages about 'hooligan summits' and the escalating capacity of hooligans to outwit the authorities at home and abroad. The reality, of course, is that much hooligan activity remains only loosely organised, and opportunistic, and that even when rudimentary strategies for battle are devised by hooligan 'leaders' they remain just that: rudimentary.

Some criminologists might describe the general trend in this changing shape and location of hooligan incidents described above as a form of 'positive displacement' – that is, the relocation of a crime or public disorder problem to a context or place where its scale, effects and consequences are likely to be less damaging. Thus, large numbers of non-hooligan football fans and potential hooliganism sympathisers at matches are no longer liable routinely to witness serious outbreaks of violence or to come into regular contact with it in quite the same way as they would, say, 15 years ago (though, admittedly, some shoppers or unlucky customers in pubs might). Football fans are also less liable to be 'entertained', seduced or to be endangered by its effects as they might have been then. And 'non-hooligans' are rather less likely than they would have been in earlier times to be the subject of forms of hard policing and punitive crowd management inside and outside grounds aimed at controlling hooliganism.

All this means that the inertia or even the tacit support among sections of crowds at matches for the routine activities of core hooligans and of the many more supporters on the fringes of the action, began to shift as English football grounds themselves began to change in the early 1990s, and as supporter cultures and the audience for football also began to show more variety around this time. It is certainly true, too, that exclusion had a role to play here, especially as it applied to younger working-class teenagers, many of whom began to be effectively sealed off from regular live attendance at football in England in the 1990s. This exclusion was secured by the effect of rising prices and by oppressive crowd management, or else by the relative decline of the identifiable, atmospheric and participatory football ends at many of the major league grounds in England, and also the street-wise youth football cultures they nurtured.

These approaches to policing football back in the 1980s – and especially to policing away supporters – which were designed, primarily, to prevent hooliganism or to deal with its outcomes, but which often placed the police, in the eyes of some spectators at least, in the role of just another, official, football 'gang' – reached their climax in 1989. The Hillsborough disaster was only the worst instance of what the sociologist Ian Taylor called this 'overdetermined' focus on producing fan *order* at English football at the expense of supporter safety in the '80s. It would be a mistake, of course, to read Hillsborough as simply the outcome of the police mismanagement of fans of a kind that undoubtedly contributed directly to the deaths of 96 Liverpool supporters on that day. To do so would be to lose sight of the complex circumstances – including real, existing supporter fears about hooliganism in this period – which actually helped *produce* the embattled Hillsborough Stadium as an apparently modernised English football ground of its day, one which was palpably designed to contain rival fans, thus contributing more generally to an increasingly brutalised supporter culture.

It is also true that in considering the persistence of particular (though more limited) forms of hooliganism associated with English football today, we actually often deflect attention from England. This is despite our still unparalleled record in exporting hooliganism; the fact that tournaments in Europe without English participation can usually proceed virtually hooligan-free, and despite the extraordinary fact that no foreign supporters have ever caused serious disturbances on British shores in 40 years of international competition. We look now, instead, to countries such as Italy, Greece and Turkey in Europe, and perhaps towards hooligan problems in Argentina in South America for some sort of ghoulish comfort concerning our own progress.

Usually, the distinction drawn here is between the typically non-lethal hooligan traditions in England, where fists alone are largely still used for fighting, and the weapons-based combat which is sometimes featured more alarmingly abroad. The generally higher levels of reported personal violence in the UK – in street fights, assaults, and in violence in the home – is a useful marker for the general tendency towards high levels of 'normative', non-lethal violence in social relationships here. But the more important point involved in globalising the discussion of the hooligan phenomenon, of course, is the implicit identification in hooligan behaviour across cultures of some common anthropological strands as part of a near-universalistic theme – young men, nature, aggression, honour – which then necessarily overrides or subordinates more localised cultural and structural influences. The latter might usefully include: historical and cultural specificity; power, and relations of class and ethnicity; local structures of feeling; the social construction of kinship and family networks; the recent marketisation of community relations in Britain; and societal-specific patterns of gender identity construction – just for starters.

In fact, this more universalistic approach to thinking about football hooliganism makes mapping what are actually very different spatial and temporal trajectories of the phenomenon in different societies – or marking its relative seriousness and shape in different cultures, *or* launching societal explorations for traces of motive or as guides to policy – at best ill-advised and at worst a waste of resources and energy. It also rules out the prospect for effective government action against hooliganism, at least beyond the usual trappings of prevention and punishment. Instead, this sort of universalism acts, effectively, to normalise hooliganism for young men almost everywhere, so policy intervention is actually unnecessary and even counter-productive. This is even in the face of a welter of countervailing evidence about changes in masculinities over time, and the wide range of relatively culture-specific and complex ways in which young men in different societies – and within the same society – actually display their masculinity.

So, who are the hooligans and why do they do it? Good questions. In fact, there is no useful precise definition of 'football hooliganism' available, nor much agreement among UK academics about its seriousness or even its causes. However, despite bitter disputes over the issue of the social make-up of core hooligans, most of the evidence on hooligan offenders in England (for example from police arrest figures, the work of the Leicester School of sociologists, and from the anthropologist, Gary Armstrong) still seems to suggest that they are aged from their late teens through to their 30s (though some hooligan 'leaders' can be older); that they are mainly in manual or lower clerical occupations (or, to a lesser extent, are unemployed or working in the informal or illegal 'grey' economy) and that they come mainly from working-class backgrounds. Some of those involved, certainly, are street sharp, have perhaps 'settled down' and are in 'good' jobs. The sociologist, Garry Robson, makes the important point that conventional class analysis finds it hard to classify, for example, the upwardly mobile and re-located Millwall-supporting homeowners of Kent, whose material circumstances suggest incorporation but whose attachments to the aggressive aesthetics of working-class masculinity at football and elsewhere seem undiminished. But relatively few – if any – of these fans are obviously 'middle class' in the way implied by alarmist stories about hooligan bank managers or yob stockbrokers, carried by newspapers such as the *Daily Mail*, or in some of the more fanciful dramatisations about the hooligan phenomenon on TV.

Sociologists, unsurprisingly, have tended to stress some of the structural features of hooliganism more than situational or socio-psychological triggers. However, in a more textured approach in looking at the genesis of specific hooligan incidents abroad, the sociologist Tony King has also usefully looked at the combined effects of pre-disposing factors and the important situational issues and triggers which might predict the circumstances under which hooligan incidents may, or may not, occur.

The so-called Leicester sociological school of the 1980s, led by Eric Dunning and best known for two books, *The Roots of Football Hooliganism* and *Hooligans Abroad*, laid emphasis on explanations on the long, if patchy, history of hooliganism at football matches in England and the generation and reproduction of a particular form of aggressive masculinity, especially in lower-class communities. Thus, their main research focus is outside football. In these 'rough' neighbourhoods young males are socialised at home, at work, and in peer-group gangs into standards that value and reward publicly assertive, openly aggressive and violent expressions of masculinity. Young men are expected to be able to 'look after themselves'. Fights can be anticipated and enjoyed, not just because of the challenges they offer, but also because of physiological and psychological arousal – of how they make the protagonists *feel*. Some of those involved, for example, describe the football action as being 'better than sex' (by now a media cliché). Such groups also have strong spatial and locational attachments to neighbourhood, town, region and nation, which are differentially activated on the basis of the nature and level of external challenges.

Club football, as the site for symbolic struggles between representatives of rival working-class communities, is an appropriate and attractive venue for testing masculine identities – particularly at the level of town or city affiliation, but also at the national level. A network of spectator rivalries, with its own traditions and folk memories thus grew up around football and especially around the ritual of travelling to matches away from home. Much of this engagement is about 'running' opposing fans, but core hooligans also enjoy a fight whenever and usually wherever they can get one. As well as the manly status rewards involved in such activities, the camaraderie, loyalty and 'entertainment' value of hooligan involvement is also prized by young men whose opportunities for status and excitement via other channels is relatively limited.

Garry Robson's important and detailed recent work on Millwall fans, *No-One Likes Us, We Don't Care*, seems to have some approaches in common with aspects of the analysis in Leicester, especially in his focus on the sorts of values which are produced out of a durable core of practices, sensibilities and orientations in working-class communities, and on the 'striking historical continuities' in patterns of masculine London working-class identities and practices which are revealed in male spectator codes in following 'the Lions'. But he also argues, returning in fact to an earlier sociological tradition, that the practices of hooliganism – and racism – among some of the club's fans should also be read as a form of resistance to the intrusion into the sport and local cultures of more middle-class sensibilities. He contends, especially, that the ferocious performative manliness of 'Millwallism' is a particular and historically grounded form of social awareness built around concerns for masculinist authenticity and the ridicule of outsiders for their lack of toughness and/or metropolitan Londonness. But at football, these expressive forms are also mobilised in opposition to the new, more disciplined, family and consumer-oriented audiences and practices which are now increasingly favoured by the sport's new marketing elites. Here, being Millwall still sustains a rootedness and a satisfyingly alarming everyday identity in all contexts for south-London men.

The lower-class 'aggressive masculinity' thesis of the Leicester School has itself been criticised in England on a number of counts and by other sociologists. Ian Taylor, for example, argued that the class fraction identified by the Leicester research as the main production ground for hooliganism cannot account for the rise of the high-spending and fashionable football 'casual' who was at the heart of English hooliganism in Europe and elsewhere in the 1980s and '90s. Taylor argued that the recent violence by English fans abroad is the specific product less of impacted forms of socialisation and gang cultures than of an upwardly mobile and 'detached' fraction of the Thatcherised working class which has a certain residual solidarity born of neighbourhood and gender, but is generally individualistic, chauvinistic and sometimes racist.

Aspects of this 'in-your-face' or 'market' masculinism in England Taylor also later connects with the disruption of taken-for-granted transitions from childhood to adulthood. As labour markets have transformed and fragmented, thus demolishing the established systems of socialisation of young men – including the family and the disciplines of local occupational hierarchies – contemporary generations of young working-class men in England grow up outside these disciplinary codes, lacking important symbolic affirmation. Taylor thus favours processes of marketisation, the contemporary troubled state of English masculinity, and the disruption of 'traditional' class practices as the key to understanding the current hooligan problem. Many of those caught up by hooliganism, he argues, now have no real class affiliation or tradition to draw upon at all; instead, they express the values of a contemporary and unregulated kind of masculine brutishness of late-modern England.

As an anthropologist, Gary Armstrong's important ethnographic work, *Football Hooligans: Knowing the Score*, has little truck with sociologists or their work. On hooliganism he argues that the stress on social class is much overdone in the Leicester approach, and he is crudely dismissive of Taylor's approach. He also seems far less interested than sociologists generally in stressing the importance of historically grounded work on the production of gender and class identities. He asserts, instead, that members of 'The Blades' firm at Sheffield United (Armstrong comes from Sheffield and his research focuses on a group he clearly knows well) in fact come from a wide range of locations and backgrounds and are involved in hooliganism primarily because of its attractions as 'social drama' and because of the opportunity it provides for offering a sense of belonging, for competition, achieving 'honour' and inflicting shame on opponents.

These seemingly timeless and borderless concerns for young men, for Armstrong, are relatively harmless. For him, hooligan groups are, in fact, very diverse in their make up and beliefs – they include fans drawn from across classes and explicit anti-racists, for example – they exhibit negligible levels of organisation, and they mainly seek out and enjoy the rituals of confrontation rather than violence itself. Thus, for Armstrong, hooliganism is best understood through anthropology, the study of humankind, and biography rather than through sociology and structure. The social dramas enacted by 'The Blades' achieve, he says, 'communion between disparate individuals pursuing achievement and selfhood'.

Social-psychological perspectives on hooliganism offer different explanations again, but, like Armstrong, their focus is more directly on the meaning of the activity itself rather than on the social background of those involved. Gerry Finn, for example, in an important article from 1994 called, 'Football Hooliganism: A Societal Psychological Perspective', sees the phenomenon as an example of the search for a 'flow' or 'peak' experience; an intense, emotional experience not usually encountered in everyday life. Flow experiences allow for an open expression of shared, collective emotionality: an outpouring of joy or sadness, and a strengthening of a common social identity. Hooligans, like other fans, seek 'peak' or 'flow' experiences through their involvement in football; unlike other fans, however, they reject the 'mediated' role of a football supporter in favour of a more directly active and rewarding role as a direct participant in spectator confrontations. Finn points to the quasi-violent culture of the match itself and to the similarities between the emotional goals of hooligans and non-hooligans.

From all these accounts it should be clear that risk and excitement are central to the hooligan phenomenon. The sociologist Paul Willis also talks about the 'buzz', the frisson, involved in fight situations and about the attractiveness to young working-class men of risk contexts in which 'anything might happen'. But, importantly, these assertions are sociologically grounded. What seems to be missing from these 'situational' accounts is any real sense of why some young men, but not others, might find this sort of activity attractive and rewarding. Nor is it always clear from the more 'situational' accounts why, at particular times and in particular kinds of societies or in particular places, hooliganism of this kind should become so attractive. This is obviously a strength, especially, of Ian Taylor's approach, which at least tries to contextualise recent trends, using history, gender identity construction and structural shifts in the experiences of young working-class Englishmen, as his key themes. Tony King has also recently argued for looking, from a sociological perspective, at the inter-group dynamics of particular incidents as well as at the structural underpinnings of hooliganism. Other sociologists, such as Garry Robson, have usefully focussed more strongly on the cultural and historical legacies of specific localities (in South-East London, for example), or at the specificities of the various constructions of 'Englishness' in trying to explain hooligan traditions around following the England national team.

In short, situational explanations seem to work at a high level of abstraction – 'humanity at large', as Finn puts it – and also seems strongly aimed at connecting hooligan behaviour with the social mainstream. Gary Armstrong, himself, confesses at one point that he sees his job mainly as one of *describing* hooliganism rather than trying to explain it. These accounts of hooliganism as universal 'honour contests' or as part of a normative search for excitement, also read as if 'masculinity' is a given: something common to all cultures, unchanging, and not subject to crucial local and national interpretations and negotiations. In fact, of course, the social reproduction of gender relations and masculinities is always located in particular spaces or places. Some of these accounts from anthropology and psychology seem to find it barely important to mention at all that it is mainly young *men* in particular places and societies, and at specific moments who are the key players in the hooliganism phenomenon.

At a policy level, the Labour government's own responses to the causes of hooliganism have been as inconclusive as those of academics and, in the end, its overall approach has been disappointingly similar to the narrow and punitive stance of previous Tory administrations. At first there was some promise of a radical new agenda, but it was soon dashed. The 2000/01 Home Office Working Group on Football Disorder which offered, initially at least, the possibility of exploring some of the causal roots of the sort of masculinist identity construction which seems to be at the heart of the hooliganism project, instead rapidly emerged with a tired and largely unimaginative agenda aimed mainly at tightening up hooliganism controls once more and reconfiguring the England Members Club.

The Blair government's new Football (Disorder) Act 2000 effectively abandons domestic banning orders for football in favour of what the civil liberty group Liberty described as: 'hopelessly over-inclusive . . . longer lasting and more intrusive international football banning orders'. This initiative followed publicly embarrassing disorder involving England football fans in Belgium during Euro 2000. In the public row in Britain which followed, the Labour administration was accused by the English football authorities and by the Conservative opposition of failing to act with appropriate legislation before the tournament in order to restrict the travel abroad of 'known hooligans' from England. Now it was determined to produce complex legislation within just six weeks in the summer of 2000 in order to cover the potentially volatile visit of England to Paris on 2 September.

In fact, claims were made by England fans following Euro 2000, sometimes over-simplistically, that different styles of *policing* in Eindhoven, Brussels and Charleroi were also in part responsible for outbreaks of England-connected disorder in Belgium, and the lack of them in Holland. Also, crucially, evidence from football disturbances involving England supporters in Marseilles during the World Cup Finals in France in 1998 showed that 82 per cent of those arrested from England were *not*, in fact, previously known to the British police – at least not for their football activities.

The new threshold for the imposition of an international banning order on fans from England was thus extended in the new Act to allow courts to ban fans from football matches (for up to ten years in cases of those with previous convictions) on the basis of the vague 'reasonable grounds' for believing that making such an order would help prevent violence. This was as opposed to the September 1999 position of being satisfied to the criminal standard that such an order would prevent violence. The prior involvement of suspects in violent and criminal activities not at football would also now be included within the banning criteria, as would evidence that 'the respondent has at any time caused or contributed to any violence or disorder in the United Kingdom or elsewhere'.

This latter addition seems to be an extraordinarily wide-ranging condition – which does not require proof of any offence, football or otherwise, committed by the subject. This led some critics to reason that police might initially and lawfully detain, for up to 24 hours, departing football supporters whom they felt *looked* like they may be hooligans, pending further investigations. Such new discretionary powers led the national Football Supporters' Association (FSA) to claim that real English hooligans would now travel to matches abroad in suits and with briefcases, while perhaps brawny and tattooed 'non-hooligan', fans would be more likely to be held by the police at ports.

The group Liberty has also pointed out that professional footballers themselves might now be subject to international banning orders, given their own records of violence at football and also we might see the convictions of some of them for football-related drinking and driving offences. In a broadly supportive (of the government) editorial on 15 July 2000, 'MPs Play a Blinder, But Hooligan Bill Should Go Into Extra Time', *The Guardian*, however, robustly congratulated the government on abolishing the distinction between domestic and international orders, and on the controversial issue, for civil libertarians at least, of the mandatory submission of passports for those subject to banning orders at the time of international matches. The newspaper also apparently approved of the widening of criminal grounds upon which previous offenders could be prevented from travelling abroad. But *The Guardian* also raised serious questions about the vague wording of the then Bill relating to bans for behaviour which fell *short* of criminal conviction, and also on the trigger which would allow the police to detain suspects for up to 24 hours.

Early claims by Conservative politicians – not usually known for their concerns about the rights of suspected offenders, perhaps – that the rushed legislation, in the words of MP Eric Forth, threatened to take away 'some of the most ancient and precious civil liberties' of British citizens (*The Times*, 8 July 2000) had relatively little effect on the Act which finally emerged at the end of July 2000 and which came into force on 28 August. On 30 August, a 21-year-old Swindon Town supporter, who had been deported from Euro 2000 but had not been charged with a specific offence, became the first fan to be banned from all football matches for two years under the new legislation and he is now required to surrender his passport at least five days before England play abroad during this period (*The Guardian*, 31 August, 2000). The FSA, meanwhile, dealt with a stack of cases of supporters who claimed they were wrongly deported from the Low Countries during the 2000 championships. All of them could now be banned from football travel and football grounds under the new legislation.

In some important senses, football banning orders of this kind operate under the same regime as the new Anti-Social Behaviour Orders (ASBO) –

or recent government approaches to the rights of the mentally ill, in that they allow for bans and constraints on subjects on the basis of criminal law but, crucially, without the requirement that subjects be found guilty of a criminal offence, and without any of the normal safeguards associated with individual rights legislation or proper criminal procedure. Then Home Secretary, Jack Straw, urged the police to make more use of ASBOs, arguing that they: 'should be used swiftly where circumstances demand it, not just against the very hard cases of unacceptable behaviour'. (*The Guardian*, 26 June 2000). Moreover, the civil standard of proof required for *football* bans – the balance of probabilities – seems seriously out of step with the punishments now available for any breach of a football banning order. These proposals come dangerously close, in fact, to asserting that the rights of individuals to travel to watch football matches rest only with the permission and judgement of the British police and the State, and they would also seem to run counter to key provisions of the Human Rights Act 1998, which came into force in the UK on 2 October 2000.

This example from football has a wider relevance, as I have suggested above. In the past few years it has become clear that approaches to offending have been subject to a considerable refiguring; crime itself and real and perceived risks from crime and public disorder no longer seem manageable within the established arrangements of modern penality. Conceptions of 'dangerousness' in this new regime, call for both the increased 'responsibil-isation' of active citizens in fighting crime and public disorder, and on the potential of the State to assert its control and capacity for exclusion over an increasingly broad range of the socially undesirable. Critics have pointed out that this revival of the notion of 'dangerousness' in the wake of the late modern State no longer being able to maintain and guarantee social cohesion, has produced a new and broadly based criminological 'other' which groups, at differing moments and combinations and with differing emphases: sex offenders; anti-capitalists and street protesters; drug users; the homeless; young offenders; 'problem' families; sections of the mentally ill population; and latterly, once more – the much demonised football hooligan.

The Labour government's obvious determination to pursue this narrow and disturbing agenda reflects, perhaps in part, the inability of academics and others to deliver a coherent and agreed position on the hooligan phenomenon and its seriousness, and thus a cogent and realistic (read 'low cost') social policy programme to combat it. This is also because changes in material circumstances alone do not usually solve hooliganism. The sorts of 'solutions' to hooliganism of the kind mobilised by the FA Premier League and its clubs over the past ten years, for example, may not be so appropriate – and perhaps not desirable – for smaller clubs. Support for the England national team also requires new ideas about 'doing' the English national identity abroad, as a means of challenging the established hooligan label.

But the government's current strategy also reflects a wider neglect: an unwillingness or inability to 'join up' a number of connected areas of concern about inequality, gender and identity construction in England today. Such an approach would take in not only the most obvious manifestations of football hooliganism and the limited internationally shared dimensions of the phenomenon, but also the following factors: the specific resonances of the tabloid press here on issues of national difference, 'race' and gender politics would need to be addressed; as would the inadequacy of facilities in public spaces here, especially those aimed at the large group of the urban low paid. The associated growing gap in England between private and public provision in a highly marketised, acquisitive and consumption-driven society would have to be accounted for. More broadly, the impulsive and often exploitative approach to the sex/emotions couplet among English 'lads', which is partly reflected in the success of a generation of sex/football/drinking glossy monthlies, as well as in the very high levels of 'unwanted' teenage pregnancy in the UK could not be ignored. The generally higher levels of personal crime, illicit drugs experimentation and aggressive binge drinking, especially among young males in England would be compared to the experience of other European Countries, and lessons learned. The poor educational and skills performance at lower levels, and the continued negative linking by many boys of 'book learning', and of most sorts of personal development, with the passive/feminine would be dealt with as part of an education strategy. Finally, there would need to be a serious study of the connected lurking uncertainties and anxieties apparent among many Englishmen about sexuality and the body which, in football contexts and elsewhere, routinely helps to produce exaggerated and macho bodily displays (tattoos, flab *and* muscles) and aggressive public performances including verbal and non-verbal abuse, usually centred around accusations against their rivals of homosexuality and other forms of sexual 'deviance'.

The realities of political life make it unlikely, I would suspect, that *any* government in this country would want or be able to connect these issues in the way I myself would want to and, moreover, it is unlikely that they would see making these connections as the beginning of a means of combating a problem such as the English variant of football hooliganism at its roots. But seeing the links, at least, would certainly take us forward. The alternative is that under this new, emerging penal policy, a range of demonised 'others' are lumped together and the legal rights of individuals begin, effectively, to be overridden by the assumed qualities of the feared sub-groups to which individuals are thought to belong. Football hooligans are merely the latest, high profile, example of this sort of focus it seems. They are unlikely, I would suggest, to be the last.

KEEPING WITH THE ENEMY

Dorothy Rowe

Football fans are so inconsistent. Supporters claim football as 'the beautiful game'; according to one bestselling T-shirt 'Football is life – the rest is just details.' It's a sport that brings out the best in people; a global language, uniting nations across the globe in their love of the same sport. Yet some of these fans, often without provocation, will fight each other, and many of those who at least manage to restrain their physical aggression sing vile songs about the opposing side and hurl offensive, racist, xenophobic and anti-semitic abuse at the players and fans of the other team. Anybody who's been at Old Trafford or Elland Road when Leeds play Manchester United; Highbury or White Hart Lane for Spurs versus Arsenal, an 'Old Firm' game or Wembley for England versus Germany or any other game with a history to it, can hardly fail to recognise the difference between good-natured banter and this kind of offensive behaviour. David Beckham has spoken of his distress caused by the abuse and curses which have been directed at his wife and child. Jim White, journalist and Manchester United supporter, described the years of insults he has received. 'I have been accused of being a glory hunter, a bandwagon jumper, a man who fails to understand the fundamental purpose of football support. I have had to listen as people accuse my team's players of everything from treachery to paedophilia. Someone once dismissed me of being incapable of applying intellectual rigour to any subject solely because I supported Manchester United. He wasn't joking.'

Fans talk of the admiration, love and loyalty they feel for their team, but when their team loses many of these fans don't commiserate with their team and praise their efforts. Instead they react with a cold detachment, heaping blame on their own side. In Euro 2000, at the game between Romania and England which England narrowly lost, the England team acquitted themselves well. I would have expected that England supporters who truly loved their team would have shown that love by recognising the brilliance and courage of their team. However, at the end of the match, the England supporters stood in chilly, disappointed, rejecting silence. Terri Paddock, the American wife of an Englishman living in London gave a transatlantic fan's view: 'I have been on hand to witness England's performance in international football competitions since their defeat by the Germans in the 1990 World

Cup. Over these years I have been amazed – and frankly disgusted – by the reaction of the press and so many of the so-called fans to the team's performance. When any international tournament comes round, the general approach seems to be: expect the English team to be the very worst and don't be satisfied unless they are the very best. This means that the manager and individual players can be freely criticised and taunted both on and off the field. They, for their part, are expected to absorb abuse uncomplainingly, overcome it and deliver winning results. When they don't, the knives are out again.'

Football hooliganism is greatly criticised but the ways in which the game itself has changed is hardly ever accounted for. There has been a major change in the way the sports which involve vast amounts of money are now played. When big business takes over a sport, profit and loss become more important than the game itself, and the idea that participating honourably, doing one's best, and being appreciated for doing one's best simply disappears. With commercialisation the era of the plucky amateur is over. Now, while some fans continue to support their local or national teams through the bad times as well as the good times, many players and supporters feel that they are entitled to express their anger, hatred, bitterness and resentment as violently as they feel capable of getting away with. These emotions originate in the way we are impelled to defend our sense of being a person. The group we choose to belong to and identify with is an essential part of how we experience ourselves as people, and the need to feel that our identity is coherent, valuable and strong can often lead us to behave in ungenerous, unpleasant and, eventually violent ways.

In discussions about football hooliganism various theories are put forward to explain this behaviour. These theories tend to fall into two groups, genetic theories and sociological theories. Genetic theories are based on some kind of physical mechanism which causes behaviour such as aggression. This mechanism used to be called an 'instinct', in the '50s it became a 'trait', and now it is seen as a 'gene', but, whatever it is the argument about identifying the mechanism as a cause is circular. In its simplest form it goes: Why is this person aggressive? Because he has an aggression gene. How do you know he's got an aggression gene? Because he is aggressive.

No gene for aggression has been discovered, nor is it likely to be. As the geneticist Steve Jones and the neuroscientist Susan Greenfield are always pointing out, genes cannot explain why people behave as they do. All genes do, says Susan Greenfield, is express a protein, and these proteins have complex and constantly changing interactions with the multitude of proteins present in our body. Both genes and proteins are affected by environmental events. Or as Steve Jones neatly put it to demonstrate that genes are always subject to their environment: 'The most important events in the human genetic future have been the invention of the bicycle and the 747.'

Sociological theories use a model of a human being as a puppet moved by strings controlled by certain features of society. Thus poverty is deemed to make people behave criminally, and aggression shown by parents is deemed to make children aggressive. If this were the case, all poor people would be criminals and all the children of aggressive parents would be aggressive, yet this is patently not so. Obviously, living in poverty or having aggressive parents will have an effect on each individual, but what has to be explained is why no two people ever demonstrate any effect in exactly the same way.

The explanation as to why this is so was given by the ancient Greek philosopher Epictetus, 'It is not things in themselves which trouble us but our opinions of things.' Neuroscience has now shown that Epictetus was right. When we learn from our experiences connections are set up between certain neurones in the brain. Since no two people ever have exactly the same experience, no two people have identical sets of neuronal connections in their brains. It seems that these neuronal connections are the neural parallel of the interpretations we create. Now Epictetus's statement can be expressed as: 'What determines our behaviour is not what happens to us but how we interpret what happens to us.'

We are in essence meaning-creating creatures. Every moment of our lives we are interpreting what is going on. The interpretations we choose can come from only one source – our past experience. As no two people ever have the same experience no two people ever interpret anything in exactly the same way.

We develop the ability to create meaning while we are still in the womb, and all the meanings we create from then on come together to form a structure which we know as our sense of being a person, what we call 'I', 'me', or 'myself'. Altogether, our meaning structure or our sense of being a person is made up of the theories we have constructed about who we are, what our past history was, what our future will be, and what the world we live in is. As these are theories, not snapshots of an absolute reality, we can only hope that our theories are as close to reality as we can possibly make them – but, like all theories, they are always in danger of being disproved. Each time one of our theories about who we are or what is going on is disproved we feel anxious, even terrified, and so we expend much energy in defending ourselves against being disproved as a person. In fact, every idea we hold and every decision we make has, at least in part, the aim of defending ourselves as a person.

The greatest threat to our sense of being a person comes from other people who will question and even destroy our beliefs. Yet at the same time we need other people to confirm our theories, to assure us that we are valuable and lovable, that our life will unfold as we expect it to unfold, and that the world is the way we see it. To get such confirmation we join and identify with those groups whom we expect will provide that confirmation. Most people get much of the confirmation they need from their family group, but when that fails or is inadequate we look to other groups to confirm our identity.

We all want to feel that our life has significance, but for most people the circumstances of their life do not readily create a sense of significance, and so they look to some organisation whose beliefs and practices endow an individual with significance. The Christian Church used to provide many ordinary people with the desired sense of significance, but with the waning of the influence of the Church many people looked elsewhere, including football, which for many is indeed a faith. Regarding football as being 'more important than life and death' is not a joke to those who believe it is that important. When we see our membership of a certain institution as giving our lives significance we then project on to that institution many of our fantasies about what we want our life to be. Usually we choose certain parts of that institution as the object of our projections. Just as the members of the Catholic and Orthodox churches each choose a patron saint who will look after their interests, so football fans choose a particular team as a patron saint who will provide them with the significance they desire. We are drawn to people who share our views, and so all those who share a particular team as their patron saint come together as a group with shared attitudes, rituals and songs.

Feeling that our life has significance makes us feel good about ourselves. How we feel about ourselves is central to every decision we make and determines whether or not we are happy. Nowadays the need to feel good about ourselves is burdened with the jargon term 'self-esteem' which is spoken of as a commodity. You can have, or you can lack, self-esteem in the same way as you can have, or not have, a car. Or you can have high or low self-esteem in the way your car can have a full or empty tank of petrol. The use of this jargon term prevents us from understanding just how complex our feelings about ourselves actually are. These feelings concern, firstly, how much we care about ourselves, in both the sense of loving and liking ourselves and in looking after ourselves; secondly, how much we see ourselves as being valuable, worthwhile and acceptable; and, thirdly, what measures we use in judging ourselves, and how harshly or benignly we do this.

There seems to be no behaviour however painful, self-harming, illogical, ill-considered, crazy, or criminal which we cannot use in order to try to feel good about ourselves. Some of us lead highly virtuous, unselfish lives, denying ourselves pleasure and relaxation in order to assure ourselves that we are good. Some of us try to manufacture feeling good about ourselves with the effects of drink or drugs. Others of us choose to identify with the only group which will accept us and our inadequacies, despite the fact that such a group is likely to be as inadequate as we are. To keep the acceptance we have gained we do whatever we can to fulfil the demands of that group, even if the group sees itself as pitted against a society which it wishes to destroy. Many otherwise timid men will riot and commit crimes in order to be accepted by their group, just as law-abiding men will kill to defend their family or their country, or in order to prove that they are not cowards. For many people, being rejected by the group with which they identify is the greatest of all possible fears.

Even if we don't have to go to extremes in order to feel good about ourselves it is still something of a battle to maintain our self-confidence in the face of a harsh world which cares nothing for us. Here our group can help us. The group we identify with is one which we regard as being the best and the greatest. If you identify with being English then England is the best and greatest of all nations. We can cheer ourselves with the thought, 'I mightn't be the best person in the world but I belong to the best group in the world.'

To maintain our belief that our group is the best in the world we need to see our group win any contest it enters. Thus, when our team loses we can feel diminished as a person and so find it impossible to give generous support to those who have failed to minister to our greatest need. However, many of us derive our sense of being valuable from our belief that we are weak but noble, and that we show our nobility in the courage with which we face the assaults and insults of the world. We can see our football team in the same way, and so give our unwavering allegiance to an embattled team. To desert our team would be to desert ourselves. Or as Tim Parks wrote in *The Guardian*, 'There are probably more soldiers who have changed sides this century than football fans.'

We define our group in terms of who is excluded from that group, and outsiders can easily be seen as enemies. When I was researching for my book *Friends and Enemies* I identified the advantages of having an enemy (see page 59 of this book). Not all of these advantages apply to every person who has an enemy, but all of these advantages produce short-term gain and long-term misery (for instance, you win a war and end up poorer than when you started), and each of these advantages can serve to confirm our theories about ourselves, our life and our world. The presence of an enemy serves to strengthen the bonds between members of a group. An enemy can assure you that, even if people around you ignore you, someone somewhere is thinking of you. We can project on to our enemies all those aspects of ourselves which we find unacceptable. Enemies are always described as being dirty – hence 'ethnic cleansing' – aggressive; enemies always start the conflict (even if we got our retaliation in first) and lack all the virtues, while we are always clean, unaggressive and entirely virtuous. We can act out our internal conflicts against the enemy instead of trying to understand them. Don't think about

THE ADVANTAGES OF HAVING AN ENEMY

1. We can project on to our enemies all those attributes we find unacceptable in ourselves.
2. The enemy binds our group together.
3. The anger and aggression which would tear our group apart we can turn on our enemy.
4. An enemy provides a simple explanation for why things happen. We do not have to grapple with the complexities and uncertainties of life.
5. An enemy can interest and excite us much more than our friends.
6. An enemy is a distraction from our own angers, fears and failures.
7. We can comfort ourselves with the knowledge that, no matter how bad we might be, we are better than our enemy.
8. Having an enemy can seem to be a sign of our strength and our importance in the world.
9. An enemy allows us to act out our internal conflicts without having to understand them.
10. An enemy allows us to feel special by belonging to a special group.
11. We can make sure our children will stay close to us by teaching them about the enemies which threaten us.
12. Condemning and criticizing our enemy in public can be very pleasurable.
13. Our enmity has a cosmic dimension: we are the embodiment of good and our enemy is the embodiment of evil.
14. We can enjoy the glory and nobility of martyrdom.
15. Having an enemy means that someone, somewhere is thinking of us. We are never forgotten or ignored.
16. In seeing our enemy as being uniformly bad we save ourselves the hard work of trying to understand people whose ways of seeing themselves and their world are different from our own.
17. In seeing our enemy as uniformly bad we save ourselves from the pain of pity.
18. We can profit from our enemy's misfortune and not feel guilty.
19. An enemy can provide the excuse to cling to a leader and not take responsibility for ourselves.
20. An enemy provides us with the pleasures of war.

(From Dorothy Rowe, *Friends and Enemies*, HarperCollins, London 2001) how much you hated your brother and wanted to kill him. Kill your enemy who happens to be just like your brother.

A very important part of feeling good about ourselves is feeling that we belong to a group of like-minded people who love and value us. The success of the internet comes from the fact that family and friends who will supply such a sense of belonging are often very scarce. Even if you can't always join your group of fellow football supporters to keep the faith or savour those often rare moments of celebration, you can look at your team's website, send an e-mail, join in a chat-room. In his account of football websites Paul Truman wrote, 'As an ex-brummy who still supports his home-town team of Aston Villa (no laughter at the back, please), a daily visit to the excellent www.heroesandvillains.net is a requirement.'

Studies which show the connection between the way a child is brought up and the way that child behaves as an adult take many decades to complete, but such work has been carried out since the 1960s by John and Elizabeth Newson at Nottingham University and by Murray Straus at the Family Research Laboratory at the University of New Hampshire, USA. Their studies of boys have shown a clear link between the infliction of corporal punishment in childhood and violent and anti-social behaviour in adult life. Not all children who receive corporal punishment grow up to be violent and anti-social, but violent and anti-social adults are very likely to have received regular corporal punishment in their childhood. As a clinical psychologist for many years in the NHS, part of my work was with men who resorted to violence either in their personal life or in their criminal activities. From what they and others told me of their childhoods it seemed that as children they did not enjoy confirmation of themselves by a loving, accepting family. They might have suffered from a brutal or neglectful father, they might have done badly at school, or, as middle-class boys, they might have felt unable to meet the onerous demands to conform as required by their social group. Lacking the confirmation of their worth which they needed from family and society they felt themselves excluded from society. Whenever we are excluded from a group we can try to survive this blow to our sense of identity by denigrating, even trying to destroy, the group which rejected us. When Andrew Frain and Jason Marriner were convicted of planning violence at a game it was revealed that, not only were the two men blatantly and extremely racist, they had even visited Auschwitz in order to insult the memorial and people there by giving a Nazi salute and trying to climb into an oven. These were individuals who didn't just hate the supporters of an opposing side and want to do serious damage to them; they were actively opposed to just about every foundation of a civilised society.

Football hooligans note: Do not call me as a psychologist for your defence in court even if you did have a horrible childhood. An explanation is not an excuse. We are not compelled by our childhood to behave in any particular way. Every interpretation is a choice, and we can always choose to behave differently.

Free will exists in the sense that, while we have little control over what happens to us, we always have a choice about how we interpret what happens to us. The disadvantage of this is that we have to take responsibility for the choices that we make, but the advantage is that in making our choice we are exercising our power, and feeling powerful strengthens our sense of being a person. Being seen to be powerful is, for many men, an essential part of masculinity. If society has not offered a man the chance to be seen as being powerful as a business tycoon, or a sporting champion, or a media celebrity, or a war hero – he can still demonstrate his power by being a thug. Beating up other people not only allows him the chance of releasing the anger and bitterness which has built up over the years of being disconfirmed and rejected, and of punishing the other person the way he punishes himself for his continual failure – but also, as his enemy collapses, he can experience the intense pleasure of having the power to act successfully and triumphantly upon the world.

Not all football fans use physical assaults as a way of confirming their existence, but they do all use the excitement a game can produce to help this confirmation. Only events which we see as significant have the power to excite us, and feeling excited about something assures us that our life has significance. For many people it is the feeling of excitement that assures them they are alive, and if events will not provide this excitement the person will do something in order to provoke a crisis which will create the necessary feeling of excitement. And some of these people will choose to start a fight.

Excitement, like hope, can exist only in a world where chance exists. A secure world where everything is already determined is a dull, hopeless world. Tim Parks told a story about an incident at a game in Verona in Italy.

> One Sunday at half-time, the guy beside me offers this word of wisdom: 'There are three things a man fears in life: the horns [meaning your wife has betrayed you], death and relegation.' He sighs: 'The first two are inevitable but with the third you've got a chance.'

When chance exists there is always the possibility that something will happen which will confirm that we are alive, we're strong, valuable and loved, and our world is the best there ever was. The behaviour of different football fans might appear to be puzzlingly diverse but the underlying meaning is the same – 'I matter. I'm important, I'm strong, and I can sing!'

INDECENT EXPOSURES, MEN, MASCULINITY AND VIOLENCE

Beatrix Campbell and Adam L. Dawson

We are two friends whose feelings about football come from opposite ends of the spectrum – one of us loves it while one of us hates it. Both of us agree that it is bigger than any other sport, and for a century it has been one of the most important features of this country's popular culture.

Despite our differences both of us are interested in football's effects and resonance in politics and popular culture, and in the particular problem of violence associated with the game.

One of us resists the description 'anorak', but admits to an encyclopaedic knowledge of football facts. When he was a boy he used to be able to name every FA Cup final winner and finalist since 1946, and most of the scores; he regularly attends matches at Old Trafford, following in the footsteps of father and grandfather, and several other relatives.

The other is anti-football: she would never choose to watch it, when she does she is surprised by how dull it seems, and resents the hegemony of it. She recoils from the roar and hysteria of the football crowd, and from fans' megalomania – their assumption that football is conversational currency at any time, in any place. But like most people she simultaneously knows nothing and something about football just by living in a community and culture saturated in it.

Together we are interested in the relationship between football and hooliganism. We both agree that a key factor to consider is the importance of identity and territory among football supporters – what is often described as 'tribalism' – and the way fans take their mass identity with them, putting it on parade in a place designated enemy territory, a phenomenon that the academic Robert Connell has described as football's 'irresistible occupation of space'.

One of us resists the idea of tribalism to describe football fans' local affiliations and their camaraderie; the other however does not feel that the term carries negative connotations, but on the contrary that it affirms a sense of belonging and shared experience. But whatever our differences we agree that when supporters arrive in another city for away matches, however benign their behaviour, it takes the form of joyful spatial domination, an appropriation of social space. Away fans, with their colours, songs, chants and styles, are always making a statement and staking a territorial claim: 'This is us! This is ours!'

We do not believe that the conventional wisdoms about class or criminality help us understand football culture. The dominant themes in public debates rely on alibis like: 'They're drunk! They're yobs! They're low-class scum! They're on drugs!' These snap judgements come from the 'common sense' of commentators who wilfully disconnect football violence from football culture – the men who do it from men in general; the values that sustain it from the scaffolding of mainstream masculinities. This became palpable in the aftermath of the England fans' riotous behaviour in Belgium during Euro 2000.

Euro 2000 was the detonator of these traditional discourses – finally xenophobia and the pleasurable aggression associated with it could no longer be ascribed to the media and politicians' usual suspects, the lumpen proletariat.

But sexism – and the ideologies that structure men as, if nothing else, 'not-women', formed in sexually-segregated spheres uncontaminated by the presence of the 'opposite' sex – is the unspoken term, the blankety-blank, in the formulations of official policy on football.

Our argument is that the debates about football violence have suffered from the same difficulties as debates about community and crime: the determination to disconnect the obvious and historic correlations between masculinity and crime. Our case is that football culture dramatises the construction of masculinity as an identity that is inscribed in the drama of both dominion and defeat. We explore these themes as we have done many times in our conversations with each other – starting from utterly different perspectives, trying to make sense of each other, to each other. We begin as we usually do, with the fan's standpoint. We start with the biography of a fan in a family with a long history of football fanship. We then consider the meaning of that narrative for the people who live with it, but who are excluded from it; and finally we look at the problem of football violence and the government's response to Euro 2000 in the context of radical interpretations of violence, crime and gender.

The Fan's Own Story

To understand the power of football to control one's emotions I believe you have to have experienced it for almost as long as you can remember, or at least since junior school. Even at the age of six, seven, or eight, rivalry between fans of different clubs becomes fairly intense. Growing up in Nottingham in the 1980s I was lucky enough to inherit from my Mancunian father support for Manchester United. However, it did not seem particularly lucky at the time, as my early years supporting United involved us never being as good as our fiercest rivals, Liverpool. Liverpool were a team that seemed to win the league every year, even if United did frequently beat them in one-off games. This was made worse by the large number of Liverpool supporters at school, particularly once we went to secondary.

Kids in schools in cities such as Manchester, Liverpool, Leeds, and Newcastle, will in a large majority support a local team. Nottingham was not like that in my experience. Of around twelve members of my first-year class that were heavily interested in football two of us supported United, four Forest, the rest Liverpool. The year was 1988 and although Knoxy (my fellow Red) and I tried to convince ourselves otherwise, United were miles behind Liverpool at the time. Their success meant our misery, particularly in the face of their fans' frequent taunts that United had not won the League since 1967, and that we would never win it again. This was certainly how it felt then, because as 11-year-olds we had never experienced United as the country's top team and it was hard to imagine any kind of Liverpool decline. When you are that age and interested in football it is perhaps more important emotionally than in later life, because each game becomes the be-all-and-end-all and breaktime supremacy depends on it. When you get older you look at the bigger picture and realise that however disappointing an individual result may be there will later be a chance to avenge it. But when you are eleven years old and time passes much more slowly, the next day's mocking at breaktime, in the event of a defeat, is all important.

The butterflies in the stomach before a big game involving United were comparable to the feeling you had when waiting outside the teacher's office having misbehaved, knowing that trouble awaits; intense nervousness, to be followed either by joy or despair. 1992 was the worst for Manchester United fans – we hadn't won the league for 25 years, longer than I'd been alive, and we were top of the league all season, then it fell apart in the last five or six games. That was the worst because it was finally our chance and we'd thrown it away. It felt like we were never going to do it! I remember the day, it was made even worse because the match that confirmed we weren't going to win it was a game at Anfield. I was depressed for the next couple of weeks at least – it was like when Labour lost the General Election in the same year; if we couldn't win then when would we win? We just weren't quite good enough.

Our obsession with football, and United in particular, also gave Knoxy and me the chance to travel on our own, and our first experience of a kind of independence. Until we were 13 or so trips to Old Trafford were resticted to three or four times a season when our dads took us. That was usually in the seats, but when we began to go on our own we wanted to stand in the famous Stretford End. We also discovered *Red Issue*, the most popular United fanzine which was full of abuse of Liverpool, Manchester City and Leeds, and much to our liking. As two lads who – although we'd lived there for most of our short lives – felt no affinity with Nottingham as a city (as for instance Geordies feel about Newcastle) I think being United supporters gave us as sense of identity, reinforced by the fact that both our fathers had stood on the same terraces 20-odd years before.

Each rivalry is individual – there is a particular reason why you hate the other team. It might be spurious, it might be historical, so you can't give an explanation for all rivalries in one sweeping statement. The most obvious one though is something usually to do with locality. When I was in Nottingham I used to hate Forest, but then I moved to Newcastle and didn't have a problem with Forest after that. Before I moved to Newcastle I didn't have a problem with Newcastle United, but when I moved there I wouldn't say I hated them – I wouldn't have given them the satisfaction – but I didn't like them. As far as I was concerned their fans talked bollocks and didn't know anything about football. It was as simple as that, a wind-up or a response to them insulting your team. Imagine you're in school; you're in the same class all day, six hours a day, including lunch and break, scoring points off people. When you spend all that time with people they're looking for your weak points. A lot of school is about that, people looking for other people's weak points and exploiting them and you then trying to hide your own weak points.

Standing on terraces at a football match is an experience not available to today's young supporters of Premier League and most First Division sides, but it was certainly a much more intense way of watching your team. For starters to ensure that you got in you had to start queuing at 12.30 in the morning at the latest, therefore getting into the ground around two hours before kick-off. This meant the singing gradually built up before the game as more people filled up the terrace. Supporting the team became a physical, as well as a mental experience. We were packed close together with thousands of strangers. A goal for us would result in being thrown three or four steps forward and perhaps losing your mate for a while. The constant singing and chanting, magnified by the low, sloped roof, left a ringing in your ears as well as a hoarseness in your throat. The whole experience reinforced the feeling we had for the club, and the sharp, coarse, blokey humour was ideal for two 14-year-old boys enjoying their first cigarettes and alcohol. At that age it is the only place where you see grown men swearing and cursing and telling filthy jokes – it's new and illicit, and you haven't even started properly boozing or clubbing yet. There's the sense that for everyone there is more to the experience than just watching the game.

There were women, but they'd either be with their boyfriends or very hard women who you do not want to fuck with.

The days approaching a big game against your biggest rivals (in our case Liverpool) are always more interesting when you are at school, or when you work with fans of the opposition. Liverpool and United Fans tend to hate each other in fairly equal proportions for various historic and geographical reasons. The cities of Manchester and Liverpool have traditionally been rivals due to their close proximity, and the United and Liverpool teams have tended to represent that rivalry as the most successful side in each city. There are rivalries between Man City and Everton, but not the same intense competition as the two red teams.

Despite the rivalry the two clubs have much in common. Both largely enjoy worldwide support because of legendary Scottish managers in the post-war period – Matt Busby and Bill Shankly. Both clubs have huge followings in Britain, Europe and the rest of the world as well as in their own cities. They are also the two most successful sides in the history of English football. In the 1980s Liverpool's success inspired intense jealousy in United fans, only for the situation to be reversed in the following decades. Therefore the rivalry is partly driven by the fact that both sets of supporters expect to be the most successful team in the land – but irrespective of whether or not they are, they can live off the glory of years past.

This is different from the kind of rivalry United have with Leeds. Leeds and Manchester United supporters will often refer to the other as 'scum'. Leeds fans refer to Reds as 'Munichs' (a reference to the 1958 air crash), while United fans calls Leeds fans 'sheep shaggers' (because of course everyone in Yorkshire shags sheep, didn't you know that?). Unlike the United-Liverpool rivalry, which is pretty much equal hatred on each side, Leeds hate United more than vice versa. United fans hate Leeds when they play them, but while Leeds see United as their number one rivals the opposite is not true. Most United fans would see Liverpool as their main rivals.

The rivalry between the two Manchester clubs is different again. City fans believe they are the original Manchester club, despite being formed after United, and that all United fans are glory hunters from Kent, China and all points East, West, North and South except Greater Manchester. This ignores the fact that even in the few years when City were more successful, United have always attracted much higher crowds, a huge proprotion of whom are locals. Indeed in 1974-5, when United were playing in Division Two while City were challenging at the top of Division One, City's average crowd was 33,000, while United's was 48,000. The reasons for this exceptional support are manifold. Some commentators attribute it to the aftermath of the Munich air crash and the club's subsequent recovery in the following ten years, climaxing in the winning of the European Cup in 1968, being the first English club to do so. However this ignores the fact that United had huge support even before Munich.

Rivalries don't always derive from issues of locality. Chelsea and Leeds fans have had a fierce loathing for each other for years, which probably started when they met in the 1970 FA Cup final. However local rivalries are usually the most intense, whether between two close cities (for example Newcastle versus Sunderland), or between two teams from the same city (Arsenal versus Spurs). In these situations the rivalry or hatred for other local teams usually overwhelms any sense of regional pride. For instance when Newcastle and Manchester United were competing for the League Championship in 1995–6 two mates of mine who were Sunderland fans became temporary Manchester United fans – for that season at least. An outside observer might have thought that they would prefer a local team, even if it was not their own, to prevail over a team from a different area. This would be to misread totally the mentality of local rivalries. Sunderland's own lack of success at the time meant that Newcastle's was all the harder to take. Hence my two Mackem friends relished the eventual Manchester United victory. Many supporters have a similar attitude to English teams in Europe. A Liverpool fan would be very unlikely to wish for Man Utd success in Europe and vice versa. Of course some people, especially sportswriters and football commentators, like *all* England teams to do well, but not most committed fans. We never like to see our closest and bitterest rivals succeed. Whatever the scenario, 'national interest' has little or nothing to do with it.

Wot About the Women?

The dynastic bonding in Adam's family around Manchester United did not, however, extend to the women. Conversations with Adam's mother and grandmother tell a quite different tale. His mother remembers boys at her junior school in hob-nailed boots and short trousers playing football at play-time, taking up the whole yard. She recalls:

> I remember them booting the ball at us girls, who were not allowed to play. Girls played all the other playground games, like 'British Bulldog'.
> But football was only for the boys. At home I hated Saturday nights as a young teenager, it was your only chance to stay up late but then *Match of the Day* would have to be on the TV. At grammar school my 'hippie-type' friends didn't like football – it was uncool. That suited me. Once I went with a youth club on a trip to Manchester, I was about 16. The trip included watching a match at Old Trafford. I remember Georgie Best playing. He was wonderful – I could see why people were so excited by him. I also remember watching the 1966 World Cup and enjoying it. I can see that the game in some circumstances can be exciting.
> While I was living in London in the '70s, I went to a Millwall versus Crystal Palace match with a woman friend. I couldn't believe it. Her behaviour was violent and aggressive. She was pushed around by the police, and then gave as good as she got. I was appalled by my friend's behaviour, and by the conditions at the stadium too. I thought if you paid to go to a cinema or the theatre you wouldn't be treated like this. The police were treating the fans like cattle.

My most recent experience of a live match was in Marseilles in the 1990s when we took our boys there for a treat. It was warm, sunny, safe and the atmosphere was enjoyable – it seemed completely different from an English football match.

When I was first married football didn't seem such an obsession with Adam's dad, although wherever we were on a Saturday afternoon at 4.40 he would need to find a television shop to watch the results. He played, but didn't seem to watch it so much on television. However, my in-laws' home in Manchester was different. Football dominated the weekend. On Saturday lunchtime the men would go to the pub, followed by the match, then home at 5.30 for more football talk. There would be a row about what the papers said about United. More of the same on Sunday. I thought it was horrible. The women would remain silent.

A few weeks after Adam was born I wasn't well and was in bed with him. I was very stressed out. Adam's grandad, uncle and dad came to the house after going to a big match involving United away in London. They seemed oblivious to us. They just had to watch the match again on the TV and talk, and talk, all about the game. It felt like nothing could interrupt that. It was as though when all of them were together they as individuals forgot whatever else might be important. The whole experience was too much for me. I think that's when I really became intolerant of football.

Adam's father's passion for football seems to have grown over the years and the bonding with his sons, which is very strong, seems to be inextricably connected to it. Thus to interrupt the football interrupts that relationship. I have felt excluded because the only way of being in it would be to engage with something that I now really dislike. So I can remember weekends when Adam and his brother were growing up, and the sound of the crowd on the TV, and the three of them holed up in the living room.

I think football is a powerful thing. It was non-negotiable in terms of us watching something else when there was a match on television. There were no arguments that could be brought to bear that would persuade the men not to watch a big match. I think this attitude is tolerated about football, when it would not be in other circumstances.

Adam's granny remembers that his grandad had been a football fan even before he moved to England from Dublin in 1940:

He used to play for his local team in Dublin, and when he settled in Manchester he began going to the games at Old Trafford. He regularly collected tokens from the football programme which meant he always managed to get Cup Final tickets. On the Saturday of a home game I would go to the shops before making him his lunch. At one o'clock he would start preparing himself, and then sneak off for a quick pint before the match.

Father and son would return at about five o'clock and then would argue about the match until dinnertime. Then later on they would watch *Match of the Day* – despite my protests. But I didn't resent the way they would take over on a Saturday. My feeling was I would rather they were watching and playing football than spending the day in the pub. However, I did put my foot down during the 1966 World Cup when they thought they would monopolise the telly every night. They were only allowed to control it on alternate days – though I suppose they went off to watch it elsewhere.

What seems remarkable about the biography of a fan is the intense emotionality, an exhausting sense of total excitement, anxiety, dread, and the possibility that pride is endlessly put at risk, threatened. It presents a picture of these little boys who seek an identity and find it in something so precarious and brittle, and so polarised between victory and humiliation.

It reveals how full of feeling it is to be a football fan. As a fan it is as if you put yourself in a place that promises security – attachment to a team, with all the colours and the camaraderie. It means fans can go to another city and know where they are going – even if they get lost they still know why they're there. This is a culture full of certainties, yet it is completely insecure. What fans seem to visit upon each other is not just comradeship but risk and humiliation, and hatred.

This account of football culture sounds horrible and frightening as well as at the same time suggesting a more pleasurable sense of community, being part of a witty and amusing congregation enjoying the artful display on the pitch. But even reminiscences about the terraces and the experiences of solidarity among strangers are also about discomfort and dangerousness. If we were to ask what is equivalent in the formation of women the reply would have to be: there isn't one.

Something that seems self-evident about rivalry – which, in British culture is lauded as character-building competitiveness – is that it actually supports a 'structure of feeling' that promotes the viciousness and violence that pervades football culture. Fans who are in all other respects non-violent, pleasant people, are unashamed bigots when it comes to 'enemy' teams. In another dimension wouldn't we call it a kind of racism, or sectarianism? It is an expression of phobic contempt. So the notion of rivalry which infuses the support of a club minimises what is actually bigotry, a kind of emotional hooliganism of which football supporters are proud. Football culture is unthinkable without it.

Classic texts on football hooliganism tend to appeal to the 'common sense' that correlates crime and violence with class or rather with the 'lower orders'. But what this literature and the 'common sense' assumptions that it reinforces erase is the gendered character of football in our society and the historical assignment, across cultures and continents, of violence unique to masculinity. The classic texts tend to promote the notion that football violence is exceptional and pathological, a product of a sub-cultural stratum that precisely does not share the values of the mainstream supporter.

Eric Dunning, John Williams and Patrick Murphy, authors of a defining series of books on football crowds and their culture through the 1980s and early '90s, claimed that there were complex connections and sources of hooliganism – including competetiveness itself, and club affiliations – but their focus was the class origin of 'hard core hooligans'. In *The Roots of Football Hooliganism* they proposed that the football crowd lost its middle-class and female components between the two world wars and by the '60s, although the majority of the crowd came from the 'respectable working-class' and included a 'sizeable lower-middle-class' component, the game was attracting the 'rougher working class'. In their book *Hooligans Abroad* the same authors offered the notion that violence is typical of poor communities, but challenged the view that this is an effect of deprivation and argued rather that violence is also instrumental in producing the poverty of deprived neighbourhoods. According to this view violence is tolerated among the poor. Lower-working-class communities 'tolerate a relatively high level of violence in social relations'.

This approach is problematic methodologically because it relies on arrest statistics to suggest that football hooligans are a separate class milieu from the world inhabited by apparently non-violent football supporters. For Williams, Dunning and Murphy: 'a common feature is that such fans have social standards that are in crucial ways different from those that predominate in society at large. Groups who engage most persistently in football hooligan fighting appear to come from the 'rough working class'. The authors only bring gender into their analysis – belatedly and briefly – by extending their focus on the 'rough working class' to macho manifestations of masculinity in 'rough' communities. 'Violent macho males', they suggest, rely on fighting as a source of status and excitement that is socially accepted. This argument relies on a belief – unconfirmed by empirical research – that it is solely within the working-class that violent behaviour by men is expected and endorsed: 'Lacking the softening female pressure' working-class men's violence is 'reinforced'. The supposedly 'strong emphasis on kinship and territory' in poor neighbourhoods encourages local turf wars that are 'the preserve of the lads'. All of this contributes to what *Hooligans Abroad* depicts as the 'production and reproduction of cultures which generate reward and support aggressive masculinity'.

So, insofar as Williams, Dunning and Murphy engage in a gender analysis it is only as an epiphenomenon of class. This, of course, erases manifestations of macho masculinity in other forms and in other classes. Football hooliganism is, therefore, sustained neither by football nor by masculine culture, but by macho behaviour located by these same three authors in their book *Football on Trial* 'at the bottom of the social scale'. There it is unmediated either by other 'respectable' masculinities or by women.

But it is the rabble versus the respectable that continues to animate the Home Office and others' approach both to football crowd control and to hooliganism. In its announcement of 'new proposals to tackle football hooliganism' in March 2001, based on the recommendations of a Working Group on Football Disorder set up by the government after Euro 2000, the Home Office urged a 'bigger role for "decent" fans'.

Like most post-war theories of crime, which search for evidence of family dysfunction and poverty as causes, these distinctions between 'rough' and 'respectable', and 'decent' and 'hooligan' fans, repeat an effort in ideology to polarise mainstream and marginalised masculinities. In the 1990s this approach was popularised in Britain by the promotion of right-wing populist texts on crime and community which proposed, more or less explicitly, the restoration of order by the rehabilitation of masculine privilege within the patriarchal family. The thesis – advocated by the British sociologists E.H. Halsey and Norman Dennis, and the broadsheet newspaper columnist Melanie Phillips and advanced by the American writer Charles Murray – is that communities are in crisis and crime is rising exponentially because there is an emerging lawless underclass spawned by fatherless families in which feral boys are bereft of fathers to patrol and police them. Francis Fukuyama, a former policy adviser to the US government, argued in an influential pamphlet *The End of Order* that the solution to young men's criminal tendencies lies in masculinity being disciplined and 'controlled by the institution of marriage'.

An older version of biological determinism within criminology represents some masculinities as inherently criminogenic. This still enjoys the endorsement of researchers who help frame Home Office legislative proposals. Michael Rutter, Henri Giller and Ann Hagell in their report 'Anti-Social Behaviour by Young People' for example, acknowledged that British statistics show a third of men will have a criminal record by the time they reach their thirties. But searching for causes takes Rutter and his colleagues not in the direction of masculine culture, rather to psycho-social factors in the 'hard core' offenders who constitute less than 10 per cent. These concern individual pathologies and family circumstances.

The Home Office research project 'Young People and Crime' reached different conclusions, arguing that family circumstances provide a 'weak' correlation, while peer-group cultures, including, crucially, gender, show a 'strong' correlation. This conclusion scarcely succeeds in challenging the Home Office orthodoxy, however.

In the 1990s new critiques have emerged that expose gender as the great 'unspoken' in criminology, until recently a discourse almost exclusively concerned with men, and yet emptied of masculinity as a category. There has been a paradigm shift which makes it possible to see crime not as a pathology, loss of control, chaos or identity crisis but as a way of asserting masculinity, or 'doing masculinity'. Feminist theorists have argued that gender is not so much biological as social, a creation of culture. Therefore, crime can be seen as a way of young – and old – men addressing the world. It is less about losing control than taking control. Crime and violence sanction modes of masculinity which may be deemed lawless, but which are also bequeathed by the cultural history of legitimate, law-abiding masculinities. But violent disorders are represented as contexts and cultures against which respectable masculinities define themselves.

The Australian academic Robert Connell shares this thesis that masculinity is neither biological nor inevitable, but that it is constructed. Gender, he argues, 'exists precisely to the extent that biology does not determine the social'. Since crime and violence are about dominion, they can be seen as contexts in which masculinity-as-domination is made. Masculinity according to Connell is: 'something that has to be made, and criminal behaviour is one of the ways of its making'. Connell supports a pro-feminist critique of traditional criminology and suggests that a great deal of violence and crime make sense 'only when it is seen as a resource for the making of gender, and in most cases that means it is a strategy of masculinity.'

Since these modes of masculinity are about power and authority, a law-and-order response may merely offer another opportunity for the performance of power in a challenging arena. Football hooliganism exemplifies the problem presented by Connell that the state's response can be: 'an incitement of masculine violence as much as its control or suppression'. Within this new criminology crime itself, its rewards and punishments, can be seen as a way of asserting spatial and physical control over other people and property. It is about dominion – it has a logic for boys and men who are structured in cultures of gendered domination and subordination, in what Connell describes as 'hegemonic masculinity'.

Hooliganism and violence are not effects of disordered psyches; on the contrary they are a logic of the quest for personal mastery. This argument does not rely on pessimistic and deterministic views of masculinity that assume it is all in the genes. Quite the contrary, it argues that football hooliganism has a rationale, it is worked for and planned, it is an achievement. The fact that other masculinities resist it, dread it, or just dislike it does not undermine this approach because violence – like the project of domination which it expresses – is about authority, losing it and gaining it, asserting it and submitting to it. That is why the criminal justice system has proved so ineffective in controlling crime and indeed football violence.

This helps explain why the spirit of hooliganism has survived the clubs' anti-racist vigilance, and the efforts of the game's administrators for 30 years to control the crowd and discipline the fans. Within the stadiums they have to some extent succeeded – to the extent that nowadays football violence tends to manifest itself away from the ground, any place where fans can find safe from police interference.

Fandom is flooded with the drama of dominion and of course the inevitability of defeat. The idiom of fandom is replete with annihilating contempt. Hooliganism is only one expression of that. Much of the language of 'support' is a kind of verbal violence that is echoed in the buzz and thrill of its physical manifestation. And both of these are well-established repertoires. More importantly they should be seen not so much as a scar on the face of the beautiful game, but as part of the equipment football yields to the project of making masculinity.

The presence of girls and women scarcely changes the culture or muffles the sexist excesses that are still shouted and sung. David Beckham, a 'new man' whose entire persona challenges the traditional profile of a 'man's man' – is routinely assailed by sexist abuse, usually targeted at his wife and regularly promoting the most abusive sexual scenarios as if to mock his – and assert the abusers' own – heterosexuality. The form of abuse exchanged between rival group of fans confirms that masculinity and its reputation are the eternal objects – 'the symbolic de-masculinization of the rival fans is another recurrent terrace theme,' comment Williams, Dunning and Murphy.

Our case is that England fans' behaviour in Belgium during Euro 2000 ignited new anxieties about the 'English disease' which has persisted despite the shaming history of England clubs sides' exclusion from the European arena in the 1980s, and despite the legislation implemented in 1991 to discipline football crowds and their culture. Not for the first time Euro 2000 unsettled the status of class in debates about football and violence. Despite this the then Home Secretary Jack Straw complained that there had been too little resort to his 'anti-social behaviour orders', part of the arsenal of criminal justice initiatives he introduced to clamp down on persistent young offenders causing grief to their communities. These were precisely the kind of people who were not among the England fans in Belgium. Hundreds of fans were involved in 36 hours of wild behaviour during the summer football festival. The Belgian police described the events as riots. Many fans, and commentators, too, denied that they were riots.

But in *The Independent* writer John Lichfield lamented the day he had spent with the 'foul-mouthed, racist, xenophobic, boorish, drinking, surprisingly middle-aged, mostly well-heeled expeditionary force we sent across the Channel'. He too rejected the term 'riot', but added that this made the phenomenon even worse than both the government and the fans' representatives were prepared to acknowledge: 'We are told that there is a hard-core of trouble-makers. It misses the point.' Of the 15,000 England fans abroad 'I would say ten per cent are outright trouble-makers (thugs); ten per cent respectable, law-abiding supporters (the fans); and a depressing eighty per cent are good-humoured, aggressive, drunken, racist, foul-mouthed boors (the slobs).' To tell them apart, he ventured, was almost impossible. 'All were dressed in shorts and baseball caps and bandanas, sports shoes and expensive watches. Most were in their late 30s or early 40s.'

In *The Times* correspondent Oliver Holt insisted that travelling abroad to England matches 'is like being on the march with a rampaging army as they lay waste to large tracts of other countries . . . the argument that it is only a small minority that cause the trouble has become an irrelevance'. Rogan Taylor, the Director of Liverpool University's Football Research Unit, noted that 'police spotters claim with unjustified amazement that the trouble seems to involve fairly normal men. The truth is that fighting – especially fighting foreigners – is a very English pastime. For a significant group of Englishmen fighting is fun.'

However, none of these commentators took the next step of investigating the characteristics and rationale behind violence and masculinity, sexism and football in the way that, for example, the links have been made between xenophobia, English imperialism and racism. The 1991 Football (Offences) Act banned 'chanting of an indecent or racialist nature'. The effect was significant in clearing out some of the routine racism that prevailed whenever black players ran on to the pitch. But it took a woman writer, Lucy Ward and one of the sponsors of women's football, the GMB, the massive general workers' trade union, to draw attention to the sexism that infuses football culture and is increasingly offensive to women in the crowd, women officials and players.

The Home Office – which resists joining up the obvious links between gender and violence – insisted that sexist abuse was covered by the notion of 'indecent' in the 1991 Act and in the 1986 Public Order Act.

One of the rare attempts to directly enlist police officers and professional footballers to take a stand against the sexist abuse of women and girls was the pioneering Zero Tolerance campaign launched in the early 1990s by the Women's Unit of Edinburgh Council. However, neither the Scottish Office nor the Home Office were prepared to take on and develop that initiative.

After Euro 2000 Home Secretary Jack Straw appointed Lord Bassam to bring together key groups with an interest in football violence to take part in a 'Working Group on Football Disorder'. But the representatives were drawn exclusively from the world of football. There was no engagement with other kinds of experience or expertise which might enlighten the debates about football violence, to elicit the connections with violence in general. It missed the opportunity to confront football culture with any insight coming from outside itself. That left the recommendations vulnerable to the historic difficulty created by the attempt, as Ian Taylor decades before put it, to treat football hooligans as if they 'are not really true supporters'. Insofar as non-violent supporters do not oppose the hooliganism it may be because they are animated by similar beliefs, hates and passions.

The Working Group's task was to contemplate football hooliganism and related disorder, to improve the image of the game and, finally, to exploit the potential of football as a vehicle for promoting social inclusion – which, given football's gendered history might be thought of as a contradiction in terms. The very citing of a 'social inclusion' ambition as a key aim repeated the belief that football violence is a practice of the 'lower orders'. None of the Working Group's recommendations confronted the status of hate as a way of having feelings among football fans, whether 'rough' or 'respectable'. Nor did they identify football's history in the making of masculinity. The Working Group did not learn from the connections between football violence and other forms of violence. It did not engage with football as a medium for dominance, or the way that its privileged currency in popular culture circulates not only in stadiums, but in the mass media (where it is given such huge space it dwarfs any other subject, sporting or otherwise), pubs and other public places, sitting rooms and schools.

Although the Working Group, creditably, addressed racism and xenophobia, from which, no doubt, 'decent' fans exempt themselves, it erased gender from its deliberations, and therefore avoided the sexism that runs through football, despite the growing presence of women in the crowd. The presence of women is mobilised as a kind of disclaimer: football may once have been, 'a kind of a bloke thing' but now women love it too! But, like the lover in the film of *Fever Pitch* these women are obliged to embrace the game's ethics rather than transform them.

Football violence cannot be disconnected from other contexts and forms of violence. Nor can football culture be disconnected from the gender system in which it has a unique status – much like militarism in an earlier era – in the making of masculinities. The problem is neither the practice of the game itself on the pitch, nor the violence associated with it, but football culture in general and its function as a strategy for making masculinities. To confine the problem of sexism in football to the law's definition of 'indecency' is to repeat the tendency to exempt sexism as a system and address only sexist extremism.

The burgeoning literature of football fandom illuminates some of the difficulties that football culture presents for progressive politics. If the 'irresistible occupation of space' describes football's status in the currency of popular culture, then the habit of dominion can be seen as something shared across all classes of spectator, with all its disparate consequences, from taxi talk to its command of the mass media; from affable abuse to violence. These phenomena are, of course, not the same but the point is that they are connected.

The relocation of football violence from stadiums to the streets and the pubs confirms that it is not solely a problem of policing or management; it is also a problem of spatial and sexual domination that is routinised in popular culture. Football naturalises the dynamics of defeat and dominion as the marque not just of the sport but of human society. Football violence should be treated not as a pathology, but as a pleasure.

BLACK, BROWN, BLUE AND WHITE ARMY

Vivek Chaudhary

Liverpool's Lime Street station on a wintry Saturday evening in 1983. A couple of hours after a football match it was a very hostile place. As one of the few brown faces who stood on the terraces in the 1980s following my beloved Tottenham Hotspur, police officers, particularly outside London, often posed as much danger as opposition fans.

Visting fans were often forced to walk the three miles from Goodison or Anfield to Lime Street station, where home fans would lie in wait in side alleys waiting to ambush the cockneys. Once at the station, fans were herded like sheep into one corner of Lime Street, while sharply dressed Scousers lurked outside.

Waiting for a train back to London after an away match at Goodison Park, I was singled out by two police officers who grabbed me by the collar and physically threw me out of Lime Street. There was no explanation from the officers; there had not even been any trouble at the station, but being singled out by fans and occasionally police was one of the perils of being a brown face in a sea of white at football in the 1980s. The problem was particularly acute in northern cities and I can recount a list of incidents not only from Liverpool, but also Manchester and Newcastle.

While white fans were also mistreated, your chances of being picked on increased if you happened to be black or brown. Thankfully, times have changed and the impact of the Macpherson Report has gone some way to improving police behaviour towards ethnic minorities. Back in the 1980s however, I justified the risks I took and the abuse I put up with as all being part of my way of showing my support for Tottenham Hotspur – neither reactionary police officers nor racist fans were going to keep me away from following my Spurs. They never did and they still haven't.

Back to that evening in Lime Street. The small group of designer-clad Evertonians who saw me being dumped out of the station wasted little time greeting me. Insults such as 'Paki twat, cockney bastard', and an altogether completely new racial category of 'Paki Yid' were accompanied by punches and kicks, resulting in several bruises, a bloody nose and one of my brown eyes turning black. The injuries, accompanied by a Tottenham away defeat made for a very miserable journey back to London after I eventually got back into Lime Street station (once the police had gone) to catch a train home.

I recall the incident of 18 years ago because it contained all the elements of what we have come to call 'football hooliganism': territorialism, regionalism, racism and violence combined with good old-fashioned football rivalry. Collectively, all these ingredients have formed a potent mix that has resulted in one of the most examined and analysed of modern-day phenomena. Accounts of modern culture have for the last two decades attempted to get to grips with football hooliganism. Politicians have spent the same amount of time split over how to deal with it, often wheeling out the hooligan to prove their points in law-and-order debates or using him (it usually is a him) as some sort of moral folk devil. This was particularly acute during the 1980s, when English clubs were banned from European competition because of crowd violence. Margaret Thatcher, who attempted to introduce the much hated football fans membership scheme, once declared in 1985: 'We have to try to get the game cleaned up from football hooligans at home and then perhaps we shall be able once again to go back overseas.' And a group of Tory MPs famously suggested a novel way of dealing with football hooligans: 'We have a lot to learn from the Middle East, and the Saudi Arabians in particular, where prisons are for punishment and not rehabilitation. We need merciless, eye-for-an-eye punishment retribution.' Former Labour leader Neil Kinnock described football hooligans as 'destructive in their attitude, like animals who go on the rampage at football grounds.'

Hooliganism, in Britain at least, is something that we have also come to celebrate. Books written by former hooligans sell incredibly well, often topping bestseller lists, and many former thugs are only too willing to give interviews to the media while the media in return is only too happy to give them the exposure. Perhaps it is the voyeur in us. Like gangsters, hooligans intrigue and repel us at the same time. We are fascinated by what makes them tick. Why would a group of grown men pay to travel around the world only to smash up bars and cause mayhem? Are they just morons? I believe that our fascination and revulsion with hooliganism tell us something about the state of our society, which many of us find difficult to accept.

Anybody who has regularly followed a football team home and away will soon come to know of the 'hard men' amongst the supporters and the reverence they are held in by a substantial number of fans; not just by those who cause trouble but ordinary fans too. I can think of half a dozen names and faces that I have come across over the years of following Spurs that were known as the hard men – ET, Hawkins, MacGregor – these names were as well known to me and many other fans as those of the players.

Walk into an average football pub and the talk is often of epic battles with clashes against an arch enemy going down in the club's unofficial history.

The talk in the run-up to local derbies is often about what is going to happen off the pitch rather than on it. I have often sat in the press box at England away matches where fellow journalists sometimes ask 'How did our boys get on?' or 'Have the boys been naughty again?' This is usually before the match has kicked off and the 'boys' referred to in these questions are certainly not the players on the pitch while the 'getting on' does not refer to the score or the team's perfomance. The inference from the questions is quite clear. They are our boys and a bit of bother is something that we have come to expect whenever England play and when we are up against Johnny Foreigner, then we should all stick together – on and off the pitch.

Violence and the other ingredients that go to make up football hooliganism have become part of the British game's culture for a significant number who follow it. This is not to say that we all support hooligans or think that the violence is a good thing but my point is that the spectre of hooliganism continues to loom over the game. Of course, it does not have to be that way.

How many times have we heard fans talk about a particular game followed by the statement: 'I bet there'll be loads of trouble at that match'? Britain is the only country in the world that has a press pack dedicated to reporting on hooligans, and despite the gentrification of the game and the advent of all-seater stadiums saturated with closed-circuit television cameras, hooliganism has never gone away.

One of the complaints I often hear from other football fans is that of the 'self-fulfilling prophecy': that violence is inevitable because large amounts of journalists follow the England fans expecting trouble and everything is blown out of proportion. While this argument is very popular with England fans in particular, often prompting attacks on the media, it is also extremely misleading and totally baseless. I have often been on trips following England or English club teams where there has been no violence and nothing to report – for example England's June 2001 visit to Greece, Manchester United in Barcelona for the Champions League final, Chelsea in Sweden for the UEFA Cup final. Believe me, those of us that report on hooliganism (dubbed 'the rotters' by the sports press) are avid football fans ourselves and receive no joy in reporting violence. When it happens we report it and when it doesn't we don't.

Football thrives on many of the ingredients that go into making up football hooliganism. Taken separately, they are an essential part of football. Imagine how dull the game would be if there was no rivalry between fans over their teams or the areas they came from. Rivalry is vital to football, particularly to the supporters, and without it the game would become stale and lose its edge. In crucial derby matches, players are often quoted as saying that winning is important because it means so much to the fans and a win in a derby match is often dedicated to the fans. Supporters in crucial derby matches will often say that the most important result of the season is beating their age-old rivals. Imagine a football world without the rivalry of, say, Tottenham and Arsenal, Liverpool and Everton or Manchester United and Manchester City. How dull a footballing world would it be?

The dividing line between rivalry and outright violence will sadly always remain a thin one. Such is the tribal nature of British football. We need the rivalry, our game thrives on it for its edginess, but what also makes it distinct is that it is rooted in some of the most established traditions of British society: class, religion and region. Generally, in countries where football is not rooted in such traditions there is little violence. Hooliganism in Sweden, Norway or even France is barely heard of.

But the crucial question facing those of us who care for the game is how can sentiments such as rivalry and territorialism be maintained without them degenerating into violence? How can we preserve the best traditions of the British game without descending into open warfare? Are we locked into such a situation that nothing can be done to tackle hooliganism? Is the current state of affairs so depressing that we will never be able to do anything about it, given that it has become such an integral part of our game's culture?

I firmly believe that there is hope. Fifteen years ago, football supporters would often argue that you would never be able to combat racism on the terraces (remember those sickening 'monkey' chants that used to be made against black players?) because that too was integral to the game. Visit a football ground nowadays, particularly in the Premier League or the First Division and while racism has not been totally eradicated it certainly is less common than it used to be. There have been occasions when, while sitting in my seat at White Hart Lane I have challenged racist comments being made by a small group of fans. I was supported by those who sat around me and thankfully the club stewards, who threatened to throw out the offending supporters. Certainly I am not alone. Fans in some grounds do feel more empowered these days to challenge racism and therein lies the crucial point; the role that the fans have to play is vital.

While the emergence of black players in teams across the four divisions has certainly been instrumental in combating racism, supporting the fans with organised campaigns and messages of condemnation of racism from players has also played an instrumental role. Engaging the fans in any campaign to combat hooliganism has to be the priority. It is they who watch and fund the game and experience has shown that they are the ultimate custodians of it. It will not be an easy process, but asking the fans what they want and how changes should be made is the first and most crucial step. Consultation groups with England fans around the country could kick-start the process while setting up a permanent fans–FA consultative forum would also be crucial.

Self-policing can be a potent weapon in the battle for change but it has to be supported by the FA and the players themselves who, sadly, have all too often remained quiet whenever English hooligans have brought shame to the national game. Stewards in grounds must also be made aware of how the law can be used to kick out disruptive fans, and individuals who challenge racist or anti-social behaviour must also be supported by club officials. The legislation is already there but sadly is not used enough within English football – at either the national or international levels.

Even in the darkest moments of English football (Sweden 1992, Marseilles 1998, Euro 2000), I cannot think of a single moment when the FA or the England team has apologised or condemned its own fans. Until now, the FA has had a myopic approach to hooliganism, trying to distance itself from it, almost believing that the fans have nothing to do with the team. Imagine how powerful a message it would have been if the England team had stated publicly in Marseilles, for example, that it was not willing to play for fans who were so hell-bent on causing problems. The FA has until now been scared to confront its fans and publicly criticise them, believing this could jeopardise its standing within the politics of world football. The situation thankfully is now changing with the FA's decision to scrap the England Members Club and replace it with the *englandfans* organisation which aims to be more inclusive while preventing those with football violence charges from joining.

There are, of course, no overnight, easy solutions. At times I am filled with complete despondency, not to mention fear when I see how England fans behave abroad and the trail of carnage they leave behind in their wake. Many supporters feel too intimidated to challenge them but the Scots were able to change their image from drunken hooligans to the 'Tartan Army' mainly through self-policing – so why can't the English? Given the right support from the FA and the England team itself, I'm sure that it would be possible.

Already, the FA and some supporters' groups are attempting to put the mechanisms in place so that change can come about. A new trend I have witnessed recently is that of England fans arriving two or three days before a match and staying for a few days after it, taking in a country's cultural sites and mixing with the locals. These are not the fans who are interested in getting drunk and smashing bars but they are the fans who could save England's reputation and they can often be seen trudging around a city playing host to the England team, guidebooks in hands. Believe me, that has not been a very common sight when it comes to England fans. Ultimately, these people just might be the fans who can lead the way in self-policing. They may be few in number at the moment but the potential for growth is there. The FA has to tap into this audience by making the association between cultural tourism and football much closer. Fanzines could provide information on other activities available to football fans watching their team abroad, while the FA too could publicise widely what else is available for fans to enjoy on their trips abroad. Perhaps the organised away trips abroad could also offer three-or four-day options as well as those which customarily involve arriving on the morning of the match and leaving again immediately afterwards.

The FA has to be instrumental in attempting to break the link between international football and violence and it has to initiate the cultural change. The message has to come from the top that if you want to travel then causing trouble is not part and parcel of that. Of course, the message may fall on deaf ears but at least some sort of signal will be sent out which is an improvement on doing nothing.

Covering England matches can sometimes feel like war reporting rather than sports news reporting and one of the key phrases that we have come to use recently during the reportage of hooliganism is that it is 'not just an English disease'. Certainly, when it comes to an England away match or a match on the continent involving an English club side there is no shortage of willing locals only too keen to come and test themselves against the island visitors and dent their tough reputation. But a new aspect of the hooliganism in some European countries is the political and social frustration it is born out of. For anyone who was in Brussels during Euro 2000 or in Marseilles during the World Cup in France 1998, it was plain to see that the violence may have been sparked off by England fans but was finished by angry, frustrated youths mainly from immigrant North African communities. Indeed, after a point the violence had nothing to do with football hooliganism and was more about locals venting their anger against the police and the local authority for years of being treated badly.

During the violence of Euro 2000 I wrote a report from the Turkish and North African areas of Brussels, the home of many of the youths involved in clashes with England fans. There is no doubt that the trouble had its roots in English racism but in confronting these people the English hooligans had unleashed an enemy that they were unable to handle. As I wrote in *The Guardian*: 'English hooligans have at last come across a formidable foe that is fuelled on something more potent than watered-down lager and a cheap sense of nationalism.'

It was the same in Marseilles during France '98 and indeed, at one stage, most of the English troublemakers had retreated to their hotels leaving locals of North African origin to battle it out with the police. For many North African and Turkish communities across Europe, English football fans have become public enemy number one and they are quite aware of their racism. Frustrated by poverty, racism within their own country, and having been generally treated like second-class citizens, fighting the English is not only a way of defending their communities and honour but it soon explodes into overall anger against the authorities of their country. In Marseilles and in

Brussels last year, the violence that was initally started by England fans soon became a way of settling personal scores between locals and the police, with the English becoming bit-part players.

The majority of England fans are probably unaware of the racial politics of mainland Europe but there are certainly many far-right-wing elements amongst them who choose actively to threaten these communities with violence, almost as if they are an extension of Asian communities back home. Such incidents have led to the birth of a new type of hooliganism, one that is particular to European cities and has its roots in something far more potent than loyalty to team or regionalism. I refer to the incidents in Brussels and Marseilles because those who rush to defend the English game continually point out that it is not just English football fans who become involved in trouble. I would suggest you cannot compare the two categories of hooliganism because they are born out of completely different circumstances. The English march on beer bellies; their non-white European counterparts march on frustration and anger.

So what does the future hold? Will there ever come a day when England football fans will be able to celebrate like the Scots who follow their national team and use the game to bring the world football family together rather than tear it apart? They are proud of their nationality, fierce in their rivalry but friendly in their manner. Will there ever come a day when black, white and brown alike will be able to celebrate the England team and be proud to stand around the flag, celebrating what is already a multi-racial team? When will the fans in the stands begin to mirror the players on the park?

There are those who claim that the time may never come, that English football is so rooted in the traditions of this country that racism and violence will always be part of it. That is defeatist. That would be giving our game away to those who do not care for it or cherish it. If I believed this was the only outcome then I would not have dedicated a life to following Tottenham Hotspur and ended up at Lime Street station on that fateful day. England, my England? Not yet perhaps, but from those who run the game to those who watch and play it, the belief and the commitment to eradicate the disease that has plagued the game for so many years has to be there. Call me a dreamer, but isn't that what being a football fan is all about?

THE USUAL SUSPECTS:
STADIA, MEDIA AND XENOPHOBIA

ALL GONE QUIET OVER HERE

Simon Inglis

Forgive me for yawning but really, hooliganism? Like the miners' strike, the poll tax and all those braying stockbrokers in red braces we endured during the 1980s, hasn't football hooliganism had its day in this country? Without wishing to appear complacent, I've been going to football more or less every week since 1967 and cannot recall witnessing a single serious outbreak of fighting, off the pitch that is, either in or around a British football stadium since, I don't know when. Does seeing a lippy geezer being thrown out of the main stand at Northampton Town a few years back count? No, I thought not.

So have I just been unusually fortunate in my choice of games and the routes I've taken in travelling to them? Maybe, for only this morning I read a full-page article in *The Guardian* on the resurgence of hooliganism in Europe. A poll in *The Observer* on 18 March 2001 meanwhile, shows that of all the factors that make respondents feel embarrassed to be British, 33 per cent chose hooligans and lager louts (three times as many as those who opted for the next category, litter and dirty streets).

I have also only just discovered the existence of websites so full of threats and counter-threats between e-male antagonists across Britain that maybe I have, after all, been living in a fool's paradise. (Hooligan chat-rooms – there's a lovely oxymoron to rival that favourite of 1980s football, police intelligence.) One particularly nasty exchange on the web referred to a match I went to only last weekend with my ten-year-old nephew. We saw and heard nothing untoward, yet now discover that the 'deasant firm' (sic) attached to my team, Aston Villa, inflicted 'a slapping on a bunch of sad paki loving twats, aka Leicester fans' (sick) at a railway station not 400 yards from where we were parked. Goodness! So the boys still like fighting, at home as well as abroad.

England fans on the rampage in Belgium we all know about. So what? If news reports are to be believed the French, the Dutch, the Italians, the Germans, the Turks, they're all at it. Whereas domestically, I had honestly thought from my own experiences that hooliganism had become just yesterday's news.

Take the Taylor Report. Have you read it recently? Though barely a dozen years old it reads like the script from a black-and-white 1950s Central Office of Information film. That bit about making sure wire-cutters are on hand next to the perimeter fences. Wire cutters! Perimeter fences! It's all coming back to me now. Policemen with hate in their eyes. National Front thugs hurling bananas at black players. Maggie Thatcher and her Identity Card crusade. Deary me. What were we like, eh? I met a twenty-two-year-old Tottenham fan the other day who had never once stood on a terrace at a football match. Twenty-two!

Perhaps that explains why, now, as we contemplate the end of history and emerge, blinking and confused, into a world of post-political mundanery – a world in which we can all become quiz-show or lottery millionaires and yet still be poorer than one of our footballing heroes – hooliganism as a phenomenon still manages to possess a sort of risqué attraction to scholars, rather as gunslingers in the wild west or bandits in mountain country once did to film makers. But then sooner or later most cultural phenomena get dusted down for a second term, be they flares, kipper ties, prominent cleavages and even Ken Livingstone. Maybe it really is the turn of hooliganism to make a comeback.

Phoning round a few trusty folk in the stadium business fails to convince me that this is the case. Whatever else is 'going down' at railway stations or in pub car parks, none of the stadium architects I call seem overly pre-occupied by the issue. One explains that it is not that he no longer considers the effects of hooliganism. Rather, he designs for the safety and comfort of all spectators, rather than for the containment of a few. He then trots out the old adage. When we caged fans in like animals, they behaved like animals. Now that we treat them like reasonably decent human beings . . . you know the rest.

A Premier League stadium manager tells me that damage to his facilities has been negligible over the last five years. He recalls a toilet block being wrecked in 1995. A year later a mirror was broken. Since then, apart from a few broken seats, he struggles to come up with any further examples. One of his colleagues in the First Division also has to think hard to remember any serious damage done to his ground. He mentions one damaged urinal and a bit of graffiti – in the women's loos, of all places – but otherwise, he says, sorry, it's been all quiet on the hooligan front.

Surely, I felt, a ground safety inspector (who, in his previous job as a policeman, was regularly drenched with saliva at First Division grounds in the 1970s) would have a few decent tales. But nor can he oblige. Insisting that he's not wearing rose-tinted spectacles, he says the situation today is 'way, way improved'. It's not that hooliganism doesn't exist, he emphasises. It's just that policing methods are now based on prevention rather than brute force, while the redesign of grounds – their 'socio-spatial transformation' as sociologists would have it – has allowed the trouble-makers fewer places to hide.

Of course Lord Justice Taylor's all-seater rule has proved a major factor in that process, but no one should fool themselves. In itself it was no panacea. Instead, there was a deep-seated malaise in football far more dangerous than hooliganism or terracing. 'Complacency', wrote Mao Tse Tung – he of the pre-Beckham Chinese Red Army, 'is the enemy of study'. Lord Justice Taylor called it the enemy of safety.

From 1990 to 1996 I was a member of the Football Licensing Authority, the agency established by government to, *inter alia*, make all you buggers sit down, or at least sit down in between the spells when you stand in front of your seats. The complacency we found at many, though not all, football clubs during the early 1990s, the sheer neglect of spectators' interests, would have been breathtaking had it not been so predictable. We found safety certificates gathering dust at the bottom of filing cabinets. We found fire exit doors locked during matches – this less than six years after the Bradford fire. We found terraces that did not meet basic standards first recommended in 1973. We found a stand roof partially propped up with a car-jack.

This may seem unrelated, but in fact it has everything to do with hooliganism, or at least its containment. For in common with any 'public assembly facility' – to borrow another phrase from academia – be it an arena, cinema, dance hall or fun fair, if the management of a football stadium (which is quite different from the management of a football club) is poor, then you can be fairly certain that troublemakers will seek to take an advantage.

Strong management, on the other hand, employs staff who say things like 'We don't want your sort here', or 'Oy! You! You're banned.' Precious few football clubs ever did that before the 1990s, so by the time they realised, or rather, acknowledged, that hooligans had colonised whole sections of their property it was too late. They could do only what any weak manager does in the absence of a contingency plan or a crowd management policy. They cried 'Help!' and then dialed 999. The introduction of 'police control rooms' into grounds from the 1970s onwards was an abject admission of failure. It was the desperate act of weak administrators. For a start, Old Bill was never trained to represent the interests of the leisure and entertainment industries. Old Bill was taught that where there is disorder, and where no one else seems to be taking responsibility, Old Bill will step in. No one should blame the police for this, even if they did somewhat lose the plot during the 1980s (and not only at football matches). Had you sat down with the directors of a typical football club circa 1990 and asked them what was their policy towards 'customer care', you would have almost certainly have been met by a prolonged and embarrassed silence. Only 5 of the 92 League clubs even had a safety officer, and some of those were part-timers.

Now, a decade later every club has one, not to mention a statement of intent, a stewards' training manual and maybe even a customers' charter and an annual survey of supporters' attitudes. Except in Scotland, the 'police control room' has become virtually obsolete with civilians ruling the roost in most stadiums, and the police on hand only as and when needed. Under the gaze of myriad CCTV cameras and whole battalions of stewards – 14,000 employed by the 92 clubs as of late 2000 – you are probably safer from assault inside a modern stadium than you are inside a hospital or an inner-city comprehensive school.

I well remember the delight with which the first, post-Taylor generation of safety officers and their counterparts in the police played with their new toys – their cameras, computers, walkie-talkie radios and all – in the early 1990s. I saw a pair of unsuspecting teenagers caught on CCTV rolling a joint in the shadows of a sparsely-occupied terrace. At one ground jovial police officers went out on to the terraces, handing out to specific troublemakers photographs of themselves captured a few minutes earlier from CCTV cameras and then printed out in the club's spanking new control room. The message was clear. We know who you are, what you look like and where are you are. And here's a free piccy to prove it, compliments of the local constabulary.

Nowadays we take such methods for granted. We're all under surveillance, on the streets or via our modems. Will it be long before our DNA will be read as we pass through the turnstiles? But in the early 1990s the all-seeing eyes of the spotters and cameras inside football grounds made us all gasp; a few with horror, most with relief. If the police couldn't beat the thugs, went our reasoning, technology could.

Making the thugs sit down after the Hillsborough disaster made it even easier. Anyone stupid enough to incite violence from a seated area nowadays is as identifiable as a tomato plonked onto a plate of peanuts. Nor need officers wade in en masse as they used to on the terraces and therefore risk exacerbating unrest even further. Look carefully and you'll often see that the troublemaker is no longer in his seat after half-time. On the concourse he'll have felt a discreet tap on the shoulder, and that is the end of his match day experience. Strong and sensible stadium management always get its man, and always makes sure it's the right man. True, mean-spirited gauleiters often go too far. Not all stewards are properly trained, or motivated enough to cope when push comes to shove. That is the way of the world. Innocent fans will always suffer from insensitive crowd management, whatever the conditions, all-seated or all-standing. But it's the 'software', as it were, that controls the strategy – the club's safety team, the police, the stewards – not the 'hardware'; the barriers, seats or terraces. The man with his finger on the button remains more important than the button itself.

Which is why, in my view, the most significant factor in the containment of hooliganism in British football grounds over the last decade has not been the all-seater rule but a wholesale change in attitude among those at the operating level; the realisation that on the one hand 'safety' and on the other 'security' – or law and order – are two quite separate issues that must be kept in perfect balance. At Hillsborough in April 1989 that balance was jettisoned with fatal consequences. Even then, with 95 fans dead (plus one more who would die later) and the whole football industry in shock, it took some months, years even, before the message sank in. That is why so many clubs' redevelopment plans drawn up in the immediate post-Taylor period turned out to be so woefully inadequate. In effect their stands were planned as mere terraces with seats bolted on.

Removing perimeter fences per se was certainly never going to be enough. There had to be a lowering of mental barriers too. On both sides of the divide, fans and clubs had no choice but to enter a new era of trust. Quite literally at some grounds, where virtually all barriers were removed at pitch level, this required fans not to cross a specified line if this new relationship was to succeed. And on the whole, the vast majority of fans responded favourably to that compact.

Growing in confidence as the 1990s wore on and the fear of violence receded, stadium operators were then able to concentrate on providing a higher standard of amenity. It was in this phase that the real socio-spatial transformation of our viewing environment began in earnest. One view of this transformation has it that the move towards seated accommodation had precious little to do with the eradication of hooliganism and more to do with the marginalising of 'terrace culture'. I sympathise with this argument, but see the opposite view as equally valid. Professional football has always been a business, and as such has to attract all the paying customers it can accommodate. Modernising grounds was therefore not about alienating one set of supporters, but about attracting a whole new set (as well as luring back the millions who had drifted away from football in the early 1980s). By installing seats and, at the same time, effectively removing the fear of hooliganism, grounds became actually more inclusive, and not only to women and children. (A similar process has also been taking place in the licensed trade, where 'theme-pubs' and 'gastro-pubs' now vie with each other for family and female-friendly business. Have you ever been to an O'Neill's or a Harvester?)

But I accept that what has also changed, quite radically, is how we, as fans, now interact with our clubs as a result of the physical reconstruction of our spectator accommodation. On the terraces there was virtually no interaction. Apart from paying at the turnstile and buying a programme or a pie, we had no other meaningful contact with representatives of the club. Seats have changed all that, in the most obvious, and the most subtle, of ways. The simple plastic tip-up seat might seem innocent enough on its own, as a manufactured object. But with its controlled area of personal space, with its individual number and its own, specific ticket, the seat has become the football industry's single most important tool in its drive to turn us from anonymous terrace fodder into 'customers'. Quite literally, clubs have our number now; our credit card number, our house number and postcode, and with smart cards soon to replace season tickets, it will not be long before they know what we like to eat at half-time and what kind of merchandise we buy. The terrace, on the other hand, though nominally part of a private estate, was regarded by most of its users as a public space. You paid cash to enter, but once inside, you were part of a free-form gathering. As long as consensus prevailed – in the form of self-policing and mutual respect – there was seldom any need for concern. But if greedy operators allowed in too many people, or allowed in the wrong sort of people – both the consequences of inadequate management – then trouble was always likely. In those circumstances, both safety and security would be compromised.

For the sake of argument, let's call that old-style of crowd management the 'analogue' way. In the 'digital' age, every spectator has a ticket, a number and a place, and, just as importantly, an obvious route to that place. Every ground, and every section of every ground, has a strict capacity limit, with computerised monitoring of turnstiles to ensure that no unnecessary queues develop. Safety in such conditions thus becomes a matter of design and planning, rather than of hope and a prayer. Security, similarly, becomes a matter of management policy and surveillance.

Now if the safety management structure at a stadium is sound and robust, the chances are that other branches of the club's operation will also be pretty sharp. Well-run clubs tend to appoint hard-working and talented management teams. So if the stadium is modern, well designed and well managed, so too, I warrant, will be the club shop, the marketing department and the catering department. You seldom have one without the other. Indeed you cannot have one without the other.

In short, no honest evaluation of the modernisation process can be reduced to single issue rhetoric. It is not a matter of safety or a return of the terraces, of commercialism or lower ticket pricing, of vocal young working class males or parents and children. To pick off one issue or interest group at the expense of another, or to pit one against the other to suit one's own particular gripe is to miss the point entirely. Football is and always has been a business. That nowadays business is better than ever, at the gate and in the corporate lounges, only confirms what many of us continually argued during the dark days of the 1980s; that only when the interests of all ordinary, law-abiding fans were brought to the fore could football's fortunes as a whole be improved.

I therefore ask this question. If we, who stuck loyally to football when it was unfashionable and uncomfortable, loved the game so much – as I suppose we must all have done – should we be so surprised that others, the johnny-come-latelies and the so-called prawn-sandwich brigade, should start to love it too, in its reinvented, satellite-era state?

We should also remind ourselves that the spatial transformation of our stadiums began some years before the Hillsborough disaster. The ratio of seats to standing places rose steadily during the period 1960–90. Executive boxes started to appear not in the mid '90s but in the mid '60s. Also in the period came the advent of segregation barriers. Installed usually on police orders to keep rival fans apart, these barriers directly penalised law-abiding fans by reducing their once-treasured mobility within the ground. (Who remembers changing ends at half-time?) If older fans are to be believed, all had been high-spirited bonhomie on the terraces up until then; reds and blues whisked together in a jolly mix of purple passion, City and United or whoever mingling like comrades in arms.

After segregation became the norm, it would seem, football fans – though apparently not followers of rugby or cricket – lost the ability, or the will to police themselves. No longer could we, as a named and shamed social group, be trusted to spend 90 peaceable minutes in each other's company.

And now? Now, it would seem, we are united only by our relative passivity. Safe, secure, and relatively silent. Though followers of different teams, we have become consumers of the same brand – football as family entertainment, fit for the sponsors and for the viewers back home. Only in one respect do we share a common trait with our pre-1960s counterparts. They did not sing much at football matches either, by all accounts.

Naturally there are aspects of the bygone, pre-Taylor world whose passing many of us mourn. We all know what they are: the sense of risk, the constant fear and uncertainty that spiced our Saturday afternoons spent watching football. After hours of waiting, would the turnstiles close before we reached the front of the queue? Once in, would we be able to gain a decent view? Would we be able to get to the toilets? Would we regret eating that half-heated, soggy meat pie? Would a crowd surge separate us from our shoes and send us hurtling into the midst of strangers? During the worst days of hooliganism we might on occasions wonder if matches would even make it to the final whistle before a pitch invasion halted play.

Innocence, then, was no protection. As a teenager I was twice evicted from grounds after random police swoops, and often found myself being chased through town centres or railway stations. In common with most of my contemporaries in the 1960s and '70s I got thumped, hit by coins, splattered with spit or urine, and had scarves and hats nicked on a regular basis. That's just how it was, week after week after week. We all have our own tales and memories.

But if I sound a tad nostalgic, be sure that I would never confuse aggro with atmosphere. Hooliganism grew and then thrived within our major football grounds not because it was an essential ingredient in the mix, but because, like an untreated virus, it spread with impunity. The writer J.B. Priestley famously wrote of football fans in his 1928 book *Good Companions* that by passing through that turnstile, we seek to escape from the 'clanking machinery of this lesser life, from work, wages, rent, dole, sick pay, insurance-cards, nagging wives, ailing children, bad bosses, idle workmen'. To that mostly admirable list let us add 'hooligans'.

Not, as I repeat, that I've actually seen any for a while. Not for a long while. In fact I'm still struggling to think when. Or have I just been looking in the wrong direction? Perhaps I'll see some next Saturday afternoon. I promise to keep my eyes open. But I also promise never to denigrate or devalue the advances we have made in British football stadiums. If the price of excluding the thugs is a higher-priced burger and a plastic seat, then I for one am prepared to make that sacrifice.

Violence in the stadium? Been there and seen that. Now, let's move on.

WE ARE LEEDS!

John Sugden

There is a black economy that currently thrives in the shadow of professional football. The independent travel business is central to this because many of the activities that are associated with football's black economy – ticket touting, peddling fake replica (snide) kits, tobacco smuggling, and the like – can be discovered taking place within its embrace. In addition, and of particular importance for this chapter, the independent travel business attracts as customers categories of supporters who, either by choice or prohibition, are not catered for by official travel clubs.

Travel Free is run by Tommy, or 'Fat Tommy', as he is routinely known in the close-knit world of Manchester's grafters (black marketeers, touts, and general shady dealers) because of his ample girth. His is a world where *Only Fools and Horses* meets *Miami Vice*. I first came across Fat Tommy in Marseilles in 1998. I spotted him and his gang working the tables in the Irish pub on the quayside of the city's Old Port. He was co-ordinating a major ticket touting operation around the World Cup. I managed to infiltrate Tommy's gang for a couple of days, watching them make small fortunes out of France '98's chaotic ticket distribution system. This gave me a glimpse into one aspect of football's underground, black economy and I was determined to follow it up once I had the time.

I managed to track Fat Tommy down about 18 months later, by which time he had graduated seamlessly into the independent travel business. He was the right man, in the right place, at the right time. Tommy's career in football started out on Old Trafford's Stretford End, where he rubbed shoulders and joined in with the top hooligans in United's elite fighting crew, the Red Army. In the 1980s Manchester earned its reputation as Mad-chester, a name that reflected the city's frontier image as a northern boom-bust city during the Thatcher years. Extravagance and affluence rubbed up against depression and poverty and in the cracks survivalist creativity flourished, feeding a divergent, entrepreneurial culture. Mad-chester became a national leader in popular culture. It produced the biggest rock-and-roll bands, the best nightclub scene, and the most vibrant and pernicious drug culture. It rivalled Brighton as the gay capital of Britain and challenged London and Liverpool as a centre for armed robbery, gang warfare, and murder. And of course, it had Manchester United, the nation's number one football club.

This was the culture of hedonism and consumption towards which a generation of unemployed grafters from north Manchester's run-down council estates were drawn like wasps to an open jam pot. There were T-shirts to be knocked up and knocked out at rock concerts; raves and acid-house parties to organise; and there were drugs to be bought and sold. There was also football with its unprecedented wealth. Some, like Fat Tommy, saw football's black economy as an alternative to the highly profitable but exceedingly dangerous and violent Manchester drug scene.

Tommy started with the tickets racket. He realised that because of United's enhanced status and its massive nation-wide and global following it was getting more and more difficult to get tickets for games, both home and away. If you moved in the right circles, though, there were always ways and means of getting your hands on tickets, and gradually Tommy squeezed his way into Old Trafford's touting network. Simultaneously the merchandise side of football was taking off. When Manchester United opened their chain of replica kit, souvenir, and memorabilia stores, Fat Tommy and gangs of other Manchester grafters likewise went into business making and selling fake gear. At first the counterfeit merchandise was cheap and its poor quality reflected this. But it was not long before the grafters began to source their materials from the same Far East sweatshops used by the official retailers. Soon their snide replicas were virtually indistinguishable in style and quality from the real thing, and were selling at less than half the price. According to Fat Tommy, for the impoverished mothers of fanatical kids from Manchester's run-down estates, he and his ilk were viewed like Robin Hoods while the club itself, as it churned out yet another away kit at forty pounds-plus a shirt, were regarded as 'robbing bastards'.

The end of the post-Heysel ban on English clubs participating in European competitions extended English Clubs' official commercial reach and presented the Manchester grafters with new opportunities in the football black market. In the 1990s Manchester United's, (and Glasgow Rangers') successful commercial model was readily adopted by the rest of British football and flourished across Europe. The arrival of satellite, cable, and digital TV not only provided a direct injection of a substantial volume of cash into the game, but it also projected English football's brand image throughout Europe and beyond, enabling the Clubs to extend their official commercial reach. This also encouraged a pan-European expansion of the Manchester grafters' black market empire as they followed high profile English teams' sporadic forays into UEFA's knockout competitions and pre-season European tours, flogging swag and dealing tickets.

Then came the makeover of the European Cup competitions and their rebirth as the Champions League and an extended UEFA Cup. It meant that in any given year, at least six, and potentially more, British clubs would participate in a pre-programmed series of games abroad. The rationale for the expanded format of UEFA's blue ribbon competitions was clearly a business one. The increasingly greedy appetites of Europe's biggest clubs, with their threats of breakaway super-leagues, drove UEFA's pan-European strategy. Their new initiatives appeared heaven-sent for the football black market. For Fat Tommy and a few other far-sighted grafters it opened possibilities for generating more regular income around a semi-legitimate enterprise with fewer risks and higher margins.

Grafting tickets and flogging swag is hard work, high risk, unpredictable and, for the most part, illegal. The innovative European competitions gave Fat Tommy a new structure within which to deploy all of his hard-come-by street wise skills, catering for the travel needs of a new generation of migrant fans. Most clubs have official ticket allocation and travel schemes, either run by themselves or as sub-contracted commercial ventures. Many choose to travel independently because official one- or two-day trips are not long or flexible enough to permit the kind of sight-seeing mini-break doubled up around football. There are also tens of thousands of fans who are ardent supporters of their teams but are sworn enemies of their club as a commercial entity. They choose to turn their backs on official schemes of any kind. Some others have no choice but to make alternative arrangements because, for a wide range of legitimate reasons – work commitments at weekends, working away from home, playing Saturday football – they can't fulfil club requirements for access to allocated tickets and package deals. Then there are those supporters who are banned from taking part in officially approved travel schemes because of their records of hooliganism and related convictions. Fat Tommy's Travel Free caters for all of these groups, but his core customers are the Lads.

Fat Tommy's is a remarkable business concept. Getting started, he used his old hooligan and touting connections to corner and cater for a market of regular customers who will always travel abroad with their teams, not simply for the football, but more importantly for the thrills and spills of being abroad with like-minded groups of likely lads who want little or nothing to do with official packages. Fat Tommy refers to these punters as 'the Lads'. He means more than the neutral, common usage of the term 'lads' as a generic descriptor of those young, male and macho. The Lads for Tommy are the hard core, thirtysomething, hooligan-hedonists who are the unofficial ringleaders of football's die-hard supporters. Subsequently, he expanded his market reach, and by leafleting outside grounds and advertising in local newspapers, Travel Free now caters for quite a diverse group of clients. But he still views the Lads as the keystone to his whole operation.

In the past these groups of fans had to go it alone, getting hold of tickets, finding transport and booking accommodation. This is where Fat Tommy and the independent travel business come in. Beyond the reach of UEFA, the English FA and individual clubs, Fat Tommy has put together quite an operation. He books flights and hotels, and acquires tickets for targeted matches abroad. For the bigger games, against clubs like Barcelona or AC Milan, Fat Tommy charters his own planes. Travel Free rarely, if ever, gets an allocation of tickets from the clubs themselves who generally disapprove of the independent travel business. Tommy likes to posture as a businessman, but he's still an experienced and knowledgeable tout who skilfully works the local underground ticket economy in places like Madrid and Milan to garner enough briefs (tout slang for tickets) for his clients. So long as you don't mind who you're sitting next to, Tommy will get you in – making a nonsense of UEFA's policy on fan segregation. In Brussels, Fat Tommy managed to get a small number of Leeds Lads into the pre-match VIP hospitality lounge for the Anderlecht match and a few even watched the game sitting amongst the players' wives!

Fat Tommy started business with those he knew best, the Manchester United Mob, but when Leeds qualified for Europe he went to Elland Road to make contact with the Leeds Lads and offer them cheap deals. At first Leeds were reluctant to travel with Fat Tommy because of his reputation as hard core Manchester United. It is usual for anybody who does not support Manchester United to profess a hatred for them. Leeds' enmity, however, is in a league of its own. The Leeds fans routinely refer to Manchester United and its supporters as 'scum' and profane songs and chants about them, including irreverent references to the 1958 Munich air disaster, are regularly aired at Elland Road. Some supporters even go so far as to have 'Munich 58' tattooed on parts of their bodies. But Travel Free's prices are hard to beat and a handful of Leeds Lads took a chance and went with Fat Tommy to Prague when their team played Sparta. They came back mightily impressed after a cheap and cheerful, hassle-free trip during which they had been put up in the Renaissance, the Czechoslovakian capital's top hotel. Since then, whenever Leeds play in Europe, Travel Free takes hundreds, sometimes thousands of Leeds Lads over. 'Aye,' laughs Tommy, 'but because they know we're Man U, even though they travel with us and enjoy themselves, they still call us Scum Airways.'

Tommy explains how he chartered an aircraft and took a planeload of Leeds fans to Istanbul for the ill-fated Galatasaray game in 1999. Kevin Speight and Christopher Loftus, the two Leeds fans who were stabbed to death before the game, were Fat Tommy's customers. Jimmy, Fat Tommy's right-hand man at the time, was the courier for the trip. He was in the bar with the victims when the trouble started.

'The lads weren't causing any trouble,' he recalls. 'Just having a few beers and a bit of a laugh. Then the Turks came. Some of them were tapping on the windows with those long kebab knives, challenging us to come outside.'

When they did eventually leave the bar, Galatasaray fans attacked them. According to Jimmy, the Turkish police did nothing to protect them. On the contrary, they set about the Leeds fans even as two lay bleeding to death on the pavement. Most of the Leeds fans were blissfully unaware of what had happened. Jimmy had the harrowing task of ringing around the hotels the next morning to let all the people on the Travel Free package (most of whom were close friends of Speight and Loftus) know what had happened. Tommy and Jimmy went to the funerals in Leeds and, some time later, Travel Free organised and gifted holidays for some of the grieving relatives.

The following season, 2000–01, Leeds played in the pre-qualifying round of the Champions League. They were drawn in a two-legged contest with the German team, Munich 1860. Fat Tommy was doing a trip to the away leg in Munich for some of the hard-core Leeds Lads and Jimmy was going to chaperone this trip, just like he had done for the visits to Prague and Istanbul.

Travel Free would take about 150 for this trip and as soon as the draw was made Fat Tommy bought up Lufthansa's cheap seats from Stansted to Munich. The flight left at noon by which time the Lads were well beered up and into the swing of things. At Munich Airport there were rigorous checks by nervous police and immigration officers who looked bemused and certainly not amused as a group of tipsy Leeds fans marched defiantly into the airport whistling the theme from *The Great Escape* – not the Germans' favoured Christmas day viewing. The local police worked from lists of known hooligans supplied by the British authorities. In the wake of the disorder around Euro 2000 Jack Straw, the then British Home Secretary, had pushed a Bill though Parliament that increased the use of banning and exclusion orders on fans deemed to be persistently unruly, but he had hitherto been unsuccessful in having this ban extended to prevent these individuals from travelling abroad. However the German authorities had agreed not to let the listed fans into their country. Several of Fat Tommy's customers were collared and repatriated before they got through customs and many others were given a good grilling.

Andy, from Travel Free, was in arrivals with his impromptu 'Welcome' sign, hand-scrawled on a piece of cardboard, out of place among the glossy corporate logos and professional VIP meeting-boards – including the ones from Leeds' Official Travel Club. We boarded an awaiting coach and headed into the city. Andy spent most of the half-hour journey like a harassed schoolteacher, trying to stop some of the Leeds Lads from smoking at the back of the bus.

As we were checking in at the hotel the police arrived with three Leeds Lads who had come in on the earlier morning flight. They were ordered to their rooms to retrieve their belongings before being taken into custody. They had been part of a group who had made straight for Munich's

Hofbrauhaus. The 500-year-old beerkeller is famous for good beer, oom-pah-pah music, and lederhosen. It is also infamous as the venue for the 1923 Munich Putsch, where Adolf Hitler first surfaced and publicly proclaimed his political ambitions. The Hofbrauhaus is a massive, cavernous place of stone columns and arches, with rows and rows of trestle tables and bench seats around which buxom serving girls buzz, clutching improbable numbers of huge, two-litre steins, brimming over with frothy Bavarian beer, waiting on up to 1,300 drinkers.

The Hofbrauhaus is a lager lout's paradise, which, with its associations with Hitler, is even more attractive for those – like some of the Leeds Lads – with far-right sympathies. Travel Free had included suggestions of visits to the Hofbrauhaus, and to the notorious former SS-run extermination camp, Dachau, on the tour itinerary. A few had wanted to go to Hitler's Bavarian mountain eyrie, but it was a little too far away to squeeze in before the match. Some of the Leeds Lads went to Dachau and most downed a few litres in the Hofbrauhaus. Some, no doubt, made these visits out of genuine historical curiosity, but others, equally without doubt, made the pilgrimage because they were pro-Nazi. One of Tommy's customers had obviously come kitted out for the full tour. He was blue eyed and shaven headed. Each day he sported a fresh military issue drill shirt (black Tuesday, blue Wednesday, and khaki Thursday) and combat trousers topped off with a military-style canvas cap.

Public, Nazi-type displays are constitutionally outlawed in Germany – even in ultra-conservative Bavaria. When the Leeds Lads' advanced guard began giving the straight right-arm salute and chanting 'Sieg heil' in the Hofbrauhaus, other tourists looked shocked and bewildered while the local drinkers looked away. Suddenly the police swooped, making 13 arrests on the spot. Another three culprits, identified from the beerkeller's security video, were spotted in the crowd at the match the following evening and were arrested by a police snatch squad at half time. They faced a maximum custodial sentence of up to three years in prison or a fine of up to a year's earnings. In the end after a few weeks languishing in a German prison they were deported back to England without having to face trial.

Months later, in Spain for the Madrid game, I met one of those who had been arrested in the Hofbrauhaus. Appropriately dressed in a beer-stained Fatty Arbuckle T-shirt the thirtysomething computer programmer for Leeds City Council talked openly about his ordeal. He claimed that he just happened to be standing in the beerkeller when the German police swooped; another innocent bystander.

'Aye, I were in t' Munich gaol for two weeks. Put me in t' cell with seven Turks! I've never been in prison before. Weren't too bad. At least now I'll be able to tell people I've been in prison!' He had earned his campaign medals and was proud to show them off.

For the Munich 1860 trip, I was rooming with Andy and once everybody was billeted we headed into the town centre to see what the Lads were up to. A group of about 20 of them had gathered around tables in the stylish, open-air courtyard restaurant at the old town hall. This was the team whose two mates, Speight and Loftus, had been murdered in Istanbul the night before the Galatasaray match. This was their first trip away with Leeds since. One of the murdered men's brothers had been in Istanbul that night and he was on this trip. They had just been on their own pilgrimage to the Hofbrauhaus, led by Benny, the team's main fixer.

Andy explained how the Leeds Lads are really a group of loosely connected gangs. Fat Tommy deals with the various ringleaders, like Kevin and Benny, when he's setting up different packages. The ringleaders then co-ordinate the gang's arrangements. This time, because he's brought a big crew out with him, Fat Tommy has given Benny a free trip. Casually well dressed, with a mop of thick, black hair and olive complexion, Benny's in his mid-thirties. He owns and operates his own business with a turnover in excess of £1 million per year. He's followed and fought for Leeds, home and away, as long as he can remember. Benny's profile is not untypical of many of Fat Tommy's regular customers: thirtysomething, married (or with steady partners) with children, self-employed, and not short of a bob or two.

As the figurines on the ornate town hall clock dance to the tune of the passing hour the rest of the establishment's respectable, bourgeois, clientele look on aghast as the Leeds Lads knock back gallons of lager and get louder and louder. They aren't being intentionally objectionable. In their own world they are 'just having a laugh'. But just having a laugh can be deeply offensive to those not sharing the joke, particularly in sensitive cross-cultural settings. Grim-faced waiters wearing black waistcoats and ankle-length aprons, hover around the Lads' tables. A stein falls to the floor, shattering on the ancient cobbles. Sensing the unease of the waiters and the immanence of a call for the police, Andy suggests to Benny that he takes his Lads to a nearby Irish bar where this kind of behaviour might be more acceptable.

If you want to find the headquarters of English fans in any foreign city whether it be followers of the international team or the country's big club sides, make for the Irish bars. For the Leeds versus Anderlecht match the Leeds Lads set up shop in O'Reilly's, on Boulevard Anspachlaan, opposite the Bourse in central Brussels. This is the same place that England fans occupied during the early stages of Euro 2000 before it was invaded and closed down by Belgian robo cops after a series of increasingly violent confrontations. Likewise, when Manchester United played PSV, it was to Eindhoven's two Irish pubs that the Reds' fans flocked. 'No surrender to the IRA', may be a favourite chant in the stands, but the open-plan layout, non-continental ambience, English-speaking bar staff, English papers and TV coverage and, of course, familiar beer, make the network of ex-pat Irish bars ideal for the Lads' European tour.

Andy's good at spotting potential trouble and steering his charges to places where they are less likely to fall foul of the authorities. He also knows when to take himself out of the firing line when trouble kicks off. In Madrid, on the day of the Leeds–Real game, I stood with him in Calle de Espoza, a narrow street in the centre of the City, outside an Irish pub that had been taken over by Leeds fans who had spilled onto the street to drink their lager in the warm, early spring sunshine. The Lads were having a laugh: bottles got smashed, cars were held up and passers by were heckled and jostled.

Moments before the inevitable arrival of the riot police Andy tugs my shirt and we make off down a side street and take refuge in a small tapas bar. As the wailing of police sirens competes with the café's juke box, a group of Leeds Lads bursts in, seeking sanctuary themselves from the riot police. The atmosphere in the place turns menacing as the 'We are Leeds' mantra rings out. The proprietor tries to quieten his new customers, but to no avail. One of the lads whips off his shirt and points proudly to his fat belly which has 'Munich 58' tattooed around his hairy navel. Time we left.

Back in Munich, once they have had a skinful of Pils, the Lads are in full Saturday night mode. What happens next? They look for a curry house of course. Lads from Leeds, Doncaster and Bradford – the home of the British love affair with Indian food – demanding a curry in Munich is a bizarre and complex expression of ethnocentrism. A dozen or so drunken, white males stumble into an Indian restaurant, abusing the Asian staff, ordering lager and demanding the hottest food on the menu. A large potted plant balanced on a table near the entrance crashes to the floor as the Lads make their entrance. Only Andy's diplomacy and Benny's wallet prevent the proprietor from calling the police.

And after a curry, for some it's off to the 'brass house' (brothel). Some of the Lads have sniffed out a seedy Munich nightclub that is also a brothel. One tries to negotiate a deal with a working girl, but once he hands over his money no sexual favours are forthcoming. He gets into a fight with the Madame who holds him in a headlock and tries to wrestle him out of the door. His friends intervene and she punches one of them before being decked herself by one of the Leeds Lads. The Lads flee out of the club and are hotly pursued by a gang of irate Germans in a black Mercedes. They have a narrow escape, but it was a good laugh and they are able to entertain the rest of the gang with tales of their adventures in the bar the next day.

Going to sex shows and using prostitutes is a standard feature of the Lads' itinerary. Most continental European cities have red light districts that are more accessible than their UK equivalents. Also, there seems to be less inhibition about taking advantage of such services when abroad. Some cities are better than others. When Manchester United played PSV for instance,

Amsterdam rather than Eindhoven was the favoured overnight spot for the Lads who wanted to do a bit of window shopping as well as visit the City's coffee shops. Although Manchester United failed to reach the last stages of the Champion's League, some of the Reds' Lads consoled themselves by going on their team's end-of-season, goodwill tour to Bangkok. With its cheap beer and good food, the unofficial global capital of the sex industry is the Lads' paradise. Bangkok is also the main source for high-quality fake designer clothing, especially snide, replica football gear. For some it's a case of 'been there, done that and paid for the trip with a suitcase full of fake Man Utd kits'.

In Munich the next day is match day. The game doesn't kick off until eight in the evening. In the morning Andy has to go to the airport to meet more punters coming in on planes from Stansted and Manchester (via Paris). Both flights are scheduled to arrive at the same time but at different concourses. I volunteer to be Andy's assistant and pick up the group off the Manchester/Paris connection while he waits for the larger party from Stansted. The day before, Lads who had come via Paris, unlike the arrivals direct from Stansted, had sailed through immigration without any bother. Today is different. The authorities have spotted this loophole and as anybody who looks remotely like a football fan approaches the sliding door exit into the arrivals hall, they are intercepted by two undercover policemen – long hair, blue jeans, casual shirts – and carted off to a side room for searching and interrogation. One of my group who has 'football hooligan' written all over him – shaved head, beer-belly, away kit, shades – never makes it through and is taken away for further questioning, only to be released later as a case of mistaken identity. In defence of the German police, it is hard to tell one shaven-headed, beer-bellied English football fan from another. As well as being a sign of tribal affiliation, in times of increased high-tech surveillance a high level of uniformity is an obvious form of camouflage and a protection from individual culpability.

By about 3 p.m., once everyone is safely checked in, Andy and I head off into town to see what the Lads have been getting up to. Andy's put them on to the Schiller Bar, a rough-and-ready joint open 24 hours a day and a favoured haunt for taxi drivers, small time crooks, grafters and hookers. The bar's extensive French doors open onto the street where many of the Lads are gathered around tables with their shirts off, allowing the hot Bavarian sun to redden their ample bellies, faces and shaven heads. Andy's arrival sparks a chorus of 'Stand up if you hate the scum, stand up if you hate the scum', sung to the tune of the Village People's 'Go West'. They all get to their feet to ridicule his associations with Manchester United. Andy shrugs and heads into Schiller's dark interior. The walls are plastered with fading photographs of boxers, footballers and minor show-business celebrities, mostly in the company of the Schiller's proprietor. More Lads prop up the bar and sit around tables drinking strong German lager.

HOOLIGAN WARS

A well-made-up woman in her late thirties sits at the bar talking to a lone and very weary looking black waitress. She might be a working girl; she might not. One of the Lads, determined to find out, approaches her and gallantly asks, 'Ere luv, where can you get a fuck in this town?' She gives him a tired smile but otherwise ignores his oafish overtures. The red light district in Munich is Kunst (in English 'Arts') Park. When Andy explains this to the Lad in question, he roars with laughter and shouts over to his mates, 'Ere lads, if you want to get a jump in this town you've gotta go to cunts park!'

As one of the main gathering points for the Leeds Lads, it is not long before the police, accompanied by the media pack, turn up at the Schiller. A blue-and-white mini bus full of riot police sits outside while television camera crews and newsmen patrol around the edges hoping for a bust-up and good copy for the evening news – a depressingly familiar scene wherever English fans gather abroad. But nothing is going to happen today. The Munich 1860 fans have stayed away, as have the local Turkish population. With no one else to goad it is time to pick on Andy again with another chorus of 'Stand up if you hate the scum'.

Then the first black man I have seen in the company of the Lads enters the bar with another thickset man who looks like one of the undercover cops from the airport. They stroll around the bar, looking at the various groups of Leeds Lads. The man I am talking with breaks off his conversation, waves to the black visitor.

'Hi Stan, how's it going?' he calls.

'He's brave, who is he?' I ask Jimmy.

'Oh, that's just Black Stan,' he replies, 'He's Leeds' undercover police liaison officer. A bit of a joke really, all the Lads know who he is, but he seems to get on all right.'

The match itself is a cagey affair which Leeds manage to shade thanks to a second-half Alan Smith goal that takes them through to the main Champions' League competition. The ageing but still mightily impressive Olympic Stadium is about three-quarters full but few, if any, 1860 supporters have come to fight. After the game back at the Irish bar Benny and his Lads arrive in ones and twos. None of them are wearing any Leeds colours – too easy to be identified by the enemy – but they wear a uniform of sorts: dark designer leisure shirts, windbreakers and expensively anonymous baseball caps.

It turns out that there has been a bit of a skirmish outside a bar near the ground and it has caused dissent in the ranks. It seems that the Lads were badly outnumbered and the more seasoned campaigners decided to leg it. At least one newer recruit stood his ground against the 1860 charge and has been bottled for his trouble. He managed to escape and miraculously, apart from a bad headache and ringing in his ears, has managed to make his way back relatively unscathed. He berates the rest of the gang for being chicken and for a moment it looks like they will start fighting among themselves. Benny calms things down and the Lads spend what is left of the night talking about the fight that never was and embellishing their roles in it.

In the months to come the pattern of the Munich trip repeats itself in Milan, Brussels, and Madrid as, against all predictions, Leeds go all the way to the semi-finals, where they are finally overcome by a classy Valencia. For this trip Fat Tommy takes 650. Not for them the classic splendour of Southern Spain's most historic city, instead they are off to 'relax by the pool in the sun and spend the evening in the rocking bars of Benidorm', as the sales pitch on Free Travel's leaflet puts it. This will be all washed down with English beer and fish and chips in one of the Costa Blanca's tackiest ex-pat, package holiday resorts. This is a town that's well used to Englishmen behaving badly even without the added spice of a football match.

Which of course is the point of it all. Football notwithstanding, these campaigns are tailor made for men – mostly middle-aged – behaving badly. A season in Europe gives them frequent opportunities to travel to relatively exotic cities like Prague, Rome, Amsterdam, Munich and Madrid. The same can be said for elements of England's travelling support. They may from time to time be under the eyes of the police and media, but they're away from home, out of sight of partners, bosses and the other institutional checks and balances. Heavy drinking, soft (usually) drug taking, sex (usually paid for), the rituals and myths associated with fighting and, occasionally, fighting itself, are the mainstays of the Lads' European adventures.

In short, for many independent travellers these trips are enhanced Lads' Saturday nights out. They are experiences where social barriers collapse, identities are masked and/or exchanged and, (almost) anything goes. This sense of being on the edge of control is often accelerated through drink and/or drugs. While this can help to make the party happen by lowering inhibitions and heightening emotions, it can also help events to spin wildly out of control. The Lads do not come to the carnival as neutrals. They come armed with hang-ups about their masculinity and their national identity. They come possessed by ideologies that are racist, sexist, ethnocentric and xenophobic. On a Saturday night in virtually every town and city in England a Lads' night out can easily turn very nasty, as the student Sarfraz Najeib discovered to his cost. Whether Bowyer and Woodgate were involved in the alleged assault is immaterial. The point is that assaults such as this are frequent occurrences and are celebrated elements of the Lads' culture. That Bowyer and Woodgate might have been involved is enough to elevate, rather than diminish, their status with the Leeds Lads.

The space and freedom for adventure, particularly of the Lads' variety can come at a price. If this Laddish Saturday night fever is dangerous at home it is potentially fatal when taken and exaggerated on tour abroad. There can be little doubt that the Leeds Lads in Istanbul did not directly provoke the violence that was meted out to them, but by transporting the ethos of a Saturday night in Leeds to Istanbul, the Lads put themselves at extreme risk. Indirectly their aggressive nationalistic, racist and macho-sexist behaviour would have provoked an aggressive response in a country likewise noted for its intense national pride and male bravado, as well as strongly conservative sexual mores.

The Lads may define their public displays of drunken camaraderie as 'just having a laugh', but they cannot control how this is interpreted in other cultural settings, particularly one as 'otherworldly' as Turkey. The Lads may express contempt for foreign police, but without their protection (as was the case in Istanbul) they are very vulnerable to the kind of attacks that led to the deaths of Christopher Loftus and Kevin Speight. In these circumstances, once trouble starts retribution is brutal and indiscriminate. In no way does this excuse the Turks' deadly reaction, but it does help to explain it.

Although not formally structured as such, the Leeds Lads are at the centre of a loosely connected travelling subculture that both helps to create and revels in the club's growing reputation, both on and off the field, as the new hard men of Europe. The hard-core Lads are the ringleaders who plan the trips and mastermind the trouble. They are surrounded by an inner circle of foot-soldier Lads who are always up for a scrap and are happy to be led into battle. Then there is an outer circle of supporters who do not travel bent on trouble but still like to be on the fringes and share in the aggressive 'having a laugh' antics of the hard core and their foot soldiers. When trouble starts, given its usually indiscriminate nature, particularly when the police move in, these camp followers (or lads with a small 'l') are as likely as anybody to get a hiding and get arrested. Then there are the large numbers of peripheral supporters who want little or nothing to do with the central activities of the Lads' brigade, but who, whether they like it or not, by doing things like shaving their heads, taking their shirts off, flaunting them and baring bloated bellies, taking part in assertive and aggressive chanting, are guilty of providing succour and cover for the serial trouble makers. Of course there are many other kinds of Leeds fans who travel abroad who are not in any way connected with the gratuitous, macho, and ethnocentric displays and rituals described here, but they tend to get lost in the crowd. After the Madrid match for instance, a headline in *El País*, declared, '3,200 hooligans de visita en Madrid'. The Lads had made their mark.

In this regard, it is appropriate to question the judgement of the club itself and its decision to allow the players to shave their heads before the Valencia game. This was claimed as an expression of solidarity with Lee Bowyer who was handed an eleventh-hour suspension by UEFA preventing him from playing in what turned out to be Leeds' last Champions League game. Given that this happened against the backdrop of the controversial GBH trial and that over the years (the shorn Beckham interlude not withstanding) the skinhead has come to represent white, male aggression in British culture, regardless of players, intentions, this can be read by some as a reinforcement if not an endorsement of the 'backs to the wall, up and at em', xenophobic values of the Lads.

For Leeds, the 2000–01 campaign was approached as a once in a lifetime experience, both for the club and its fans. Most of the 150 who boarded Travel Free's wagon for Munich back in August 2000 were determined to stay on until the wheels fell off, whatever the cost, and many of the 1,000 or more others who boarded en route felt the same way. Tommy may be 'Red until he dies', but as a businessman he realises that it is in his best interests for Leeds to stay in the competition for as long as possible. So Fat Tommy's laughing all the way to the bank, and why not? He is a proud product of the Thatcherite '80s, a self-made man who makes loads of money providing a service for customers who came of age during the same era. That some of them cannot or will not behave themselves among foreigners is hardly his fault or his problem.

FAR OUT WITH THE FAR RIGHT

Nick Lowles

Amsterdam, June 2000. The European Championships have just kicked off with Holland taking three points against the Czech Republic. Amsterdam is alive with colour. Dutch and Czech fans dance into the night, while England fans are arriving in numbers for the game the following night with Portugal. It's a hot summer's evening and the mood is jovial. Most of the English have congregated in the red-light district running along the canals in the centre of the city. A small group of jubilant Dutch fans, adorned in orange hats, costumes and face paints, wander on the opposite side of a canal to a similar-sized group of English fans drinking outside a bar, surrounded by women plying their trade from shop windows, the white-and-red neon lights reflecting on the water. The English are also wearing uniforms but nothing so bright as the Dutch. Their uniforms are smart, expensive designer clothes – Stone Island jumpers, Hackett T-shirts and Burberry caps. The Dutch stop and face the English crowd keen to enjoy the festival of football. The two groups begin exchanging football chants. The Dutch, as all self-respecting football fans do in Europe, sing in English – a sign of the affectionate respect English football is held in abroad. The respect, however, is not reciprocated.

The cheerful banter does not last as this English crowd becomes more vocal and vitriolic. To them, there is no such thing as a festival of football. This is simply two sets of rival fans preparing for battle. As in any such conflict, there can be only one winner. The English singing becomes louder and the songs are about anything but football. They sing about their love of their country and their hatred of others. The chants attracts others and before long the English contingent has swelled to over a hundred. The Dutch continue singing on the other side of the canal but their songs are drowned out by the choruses of 'Rule Britannia' and 'God Save the Queen'. Before long, the Dutch stop singing and begin watching nervously.

The police arrive but keep their distance. Their presence, however reserved, acts as a catalyst for louder and more offensive songs. 'If it wasn't for the English you'd be Krauts', the English sing. Even the prostitutes stop work to watch the unfolding spectacle. As the police begin to close off the surrounding area, the English crowd has grown to 200.

The noise is getting louder. The police numbers are growing. The English believe they are just having a bit of fun, representing their country abroad, while the police and most onlookers are getting increasingly worried. 'I'd rather be a Paki than a Turk,' the group sing, with memories fresh of the killing of two Leeds United fans in Istanbul only two months before. As the crowd get ever more boisterous, an England fan lobs a bottle at a passing boat. A few more quickly follow. A cart is overturned and rolled into the canal. The police are unwilling to move in for fear of people falling into the canal, and are hoping the singers will eventually tire, but 30 minutes later there is no sign of that. By now the songs are about Ireland. 'No Surrender to the IRA' rings out, to much applause.

The police policy seems to be working. A local immigrant gets kicked and women are jeered at, but there is no widespread trouble. When police eventually move in most in the crowd grudgingly disperse. The Dutch, who are still watching from the other side of the canal, begin to drift away, shaking their heads at the spectacle they've just witnessed.

'Why are they like that?' one Dutchman asks me, puzzled.

'Fuck off you cunt', interrupts an Englishman menacingly.

Across the water, a few stragglers remain, defiant until the end, refusing to move on for anyone. A fat man in his thirties steps forward and throws out his right hand repeatedly in a nazi salute. Another drops his trousers and pulls a moony. 'I'd rather be a Paki than a Turk,' they sing again.

These scenes have been all too familiar across Europe over the past 20 years. On this occasion there was no serious trouble but this was only because of firm but low-key policing and an absence of someone to fight. While only a minority of English fans get involved in violence, it is always enough to hit the headlines and earn the condemnation of our European partners.

It is commonly thought that fuelling this violent, racist and obnoxious behaviour are small groups of well-organised hooligans, many of whom are members of fascist groups. Fascist organisations began targeting football in the 1979–80 season as part of a concerted effort to – in the words of Derek Holland, a leading National Front organiser – 'win the hearts and minds of young people'. The National Front, Britain's leading fascist party in the 1970s, was on the decline. Having once attracted thousands of votes in London (100,000 votes in 1977), Leicester (33,000 votes in 1976) and Bradford (9 per cent of the vote in 1977) – and with a membership of 17,500, the party was contracting dramatically. In 1979, the National Front stood 359 parliamentary candidates but achieved a derisory 1.7 per cent of the vote. The poor results, coupled with the election of Margaret Thatcher who had attracted much of Britain's racist vote when she claimed to understand the fears of those who felt 'swamped' by an immigrant culture, gave added impetus to those within the party who argued for elections to be ignored, and instead for placing an emphasis on street politics.

The National Front were joined on the terraces by the British Movement, a hardline nazi group formed in 1968 which had already abandoned the electoral process. The British Movement was smaller than the National Front but its membership contained a high concentration of young men, particularly in London, many of whom were already involved in football violence. The increasing activity of racist hooligans coincided with the skinhead revival between 1976 and 1980, which, this time, was closely associated with racist politics. Chelsea, West Ham, Charlton, Arsenal and Millwall all had significant groups of skinhead supporters linked to the British Movement.

In 1981 the youth wing of the National Front launched *Bulldog*, a magazine aimed at attracting young people through music and sport. One page was always dedicated to football, with reports of racist chanting and violence. Of particular interest to some fans was *Bulldog*'s 'League of Louts', a table charting racism within the game. Leeds United, West Ham, Chelsea and Newcastle fans would regularly battle to be labelled the most racist in Britain. The National Front would boast of its violence and racism within the grounds and before long the League of Louts would provide an incentive for its units around the country.

Bulldog provided the fans, particularly right-wing hooligans, with their own football competition to rival events on and off the pitch. In the mid-1980s, one of the leaders of the Leeds Service Crew, the hooligan gang attached to Leeds United, wrote an angry letter to *Bulldog*: 'Isn't it about time that those who organise the Racist League should play the White man? I am talking about putting the true Whites of Leeds United Service Crew on top where they rightfully belong.' He went on to express his irritation at the London bias of the editors. He ended the letter by writing, 'We have a lot of respect for *Bulldog*.'

Certain grounds became known for racism among large sections of the fans. Leeds, Chelsea and Newcastle were among the worst of the big teams. Leeds had been a centre for strong National Front support for many years and this moved into the football stadium in the 1970s. It was common for visiting black players to be met by the racist chanting of thousands of Leeds fans. In 1988 Micky Brown, a YTS trainee, played at Elland Road with Shrewsbury Town. It was one of his first outings with the senior side. He was treated to a level of racist abuse which he was later to admit that he had never experienced anywhere else in the country. Shrewsbury Town had their own share of racists (with the 'Nigger, nigger, lick my boot' chant) but this was nothing when compared to the thousands who jeered Brown at Leeds. A year before, Luther Blissett, the Watford and England player, told the *Daily Mirror*, 'Normally the abuse is from the terraces, but at one Leeds game whole groups in the stand were doing nazi salutes and shouting "Sieg heil".' The racism became so bad at Leeds that, in the same season, Crystal Palace player Andy Gray publicly urged Coventry to beat Leeds in the FA Cup semi-final after being subjected to abuse himself during a league game. He told reporters:

> I hope Coventry stuff them in the Cup. They are thugs and their racist abuse is aimed at coloured guys like me . . . Elland Road is the worst ground of the lot. I've played here twice. The first time was my debut and I was taken off – and I was glad to come off. I wasn't in the team for this season's match – and I wasn't unhappy.

The National Front was quick to exploit the racism of the Leeds crowd. Paper sales outside the ground before matches sometimes attracted over 30 sellers and dozens of papers were bought. There were also Leeds United National Front badges on sale. Racist abuse was encouraged by NF publications, as was the throwing of bananas at black players.

Another ground that saw considerable fascist activity during the 1980s was Stamford Bridge, the home of Chelsea. Like Leeds, the club has attracted considerable right wing support. More racist papers were sold here than at any other ground in the country, with as many as 200 being sold by the NF, and later the BNP, in pubs around the ground before a game. Racism really hit the headlines in the mid-1980s when the home crowd booed Paul Cannonville, Chelsea's first black player. Even Leeds fans never stooped to this depth when black players were brought into the team.

In Chelsea, like Leeds, support for racists groups such as the NF, BNP and Combat 18 – a hardline Nazi street gang formed in 1992 – was particularly strong amongst the hooligans, which, in the case of Chelsea, took the form of the Headhunters. Many of the early Headhunters, such as Stuart Glass, originated from Hounslow, West London, where the NF had long had a strong base. Glass had stood for the NF in a local council election in 1978 while most others simply provided muscle for fascist events. The annual NF Remembrance Sunday demonstration, down Whitehall to the Cenotaph, attracted dozens of Headhunters on several occasions. While they were joined by hooligans from West Ham, Crystal Palace and Millwall, it was always the Chelsea contingent that was biggest. In 1988, the Chelsea hooligans led an attack on the anti-apartheid protestors outside the South African Embassy in Trafalgar Square. The link between the Headhunters and fascist groups continued well into the 1990s. In 1992, as many as 20 Chelsea Headhunters joined a group of Nazis in protecting a rally addressed by the holocaust denier David Irving. These included Stuart Glass, Andy Frain, Mark Alloway and Ian Cockburn, all convicted Headhunter hooligans. In September 1995 over 50 Headhunter hooligans joined a similar number of Combat 18 supporters in attacking anti-Nazi protestors outside a by-election count in Hounslow where Glass's younger brother, Warren, was standing for the BNP. It took the police over 30 minutes to restore order but not before the victorious Labour candidate was struck on the head with a brick.

The racism amongst sections of both sets of fans coincided with the declining fortunes of both clubs during the '80s. Down in the lower half of the old Second Division, many fans found the hooligan culture a compelling alternative route to stardom. Travelling to the towns of Grimsby, Shrewsbury, Bournemouth and Scarborough in the thousands, fans of former giants such as Leeds, Chelsea and Wolves hit the headlines for their violent behaviour far more regularly than the teams they supported. The racism that accompanied the hooliganism, sometimes stoked up by the minority of political diehards, was another element of this compensatory behaviour. Many Leeds fans revelled in the notoriety of their hooliganism and the threatening atmosphere of Elland Road, with Nazi salutes and racist songs. The politics and imagery of Nazi groups provided hooligans and some fans with an identity that would instil fear into their opponents.

Ken, a long-time follower of the Chelsea Headhunters and the NF says:

> It's natural to rebel. If you have nothing and are from a working-class estate, you say, what's wrong with this? I am white, I am working class. I haven't got a job, and it's your way of rebelling back. Rather than just taking it, you hit back. The right wing is the most shocking thing because it's constantly put to us through the television, the press, everything, that the worst thing to ever happen is the Nazis. So the biggest way to rebel is to be seen to endorse it.

Ken was once part of a Nazi group who used an England away game to visit a concentration camp in Germany. They posed for pictures and made insulting gestures to other tourists. They even sent abusive postcards back to people in Britain.

> We did it because it was a laugh. No one really believed that the Holocaust never happened but we knew that to say so would infuriate people. Going to the camps was just the final straw. There was nothing more insulting than that. It was all just being provocative – it was us sticking two fingers up at a society we didn't like.

Other clubs also experienced racism amongst its fans. The Lancashire clubs of Rochdale, Burnley and Blackburn were intermittently targeted by NF and BNP paper sellers, while hooligans from Portsmouth, a club that also has a long history of racism, ran amok through an Asian area of Derby before a match in the town. Aston Villa and Birmingham City both attracted the attention of the NF during the 1980s, while in the North East, Newcastle and Sunderland attracted BNP leafleters.

However, despite the activity of fascist groups at football grounds around the country, there is little evidence to show that many people were recruited into political activity. This is particularly so with the hooligans, who, generally, proved too ill-disciplined and independent for groups such as the NF. The chance for a physical confrontation with their political opponents was an attraction for racist hooligans, but few seemed interested in undertaking the more mundane tasks such as leafleting, attending meetings and electioneering. As a result, recruitment amongst the hooligan fraternity was never systematic or widespread. One or two would become involved but they always represented the minority of the group. Even among the hooligans of Leeds and Chelsea who openly aligned themselves with racist groups, few actually joined any organisation or took part in party activity. Despite agreeing with the political agenda of the racist groups, the bulk of hooligans only turned up when there was a chance of a fight.

The late '80s saw a reduction in fascist activity in football. The declining political fortunes of the NF were compounded by splits within its leadership that ripped the organisation apart between 1986 and '89. Football was less of a priority as the party turned to the environment, anti-Americanism and nuclear disarmament. The majority of NF-supporting hooligans drifted away from the party after the leadership travelled to Libya in search of funding from Colonel Gadaffi. The NF saw itself as a component of an anti-American and anti-Zionist (read Israel) bloc that consisted of the Iranian regime under the Ayatollah Khomeini, Gadaffi and the American black separatist leader, Louis Farrakhan. Joining forces with black and Arab leaders was too much for the crude racists of the hooligan gangs.

There were other factors contributing to this decline. A clampdown on organised hooliganism saw police operations rise against supporters of several clubs, including the main NF-linked gangs. While few of the early morning raids actually resulted in convictions, a layer of hooligan leaders was removed, albeit temporarily, from activity. The move against hooliganism coincided with changes within football culture itself which was to prove important in reducing the ability of fascists to promote racism within grounds. Ordinary fans were no longer willing to accept the racist and hooligan activity that had become associated with football. Leeds, Newcastle and Sunderland all experienced anti-fascist campaigns organised by supporters themselves to drive the racists out. More generally, the fanzine culture helped introduce a positive response amongst the general fan base and this helped marginalise those inciting racism. The changing climate was mirrored within hooliganism itself when, in 1989, violence seemed to be on the wane. The emergence of the rave scene led many hooligans away from the grounds, either to attend the raves, or as was sometimes the case, to organise the events and the distribution of the drugs. Equally important was the increasing number of black players within the English game. Even at grounds with a bedrock of racist support such as Leeds, where racists once revelled in the absence of any black players in a team wearing an all-white strip, the bulk of fans became less inclined to abuse other black players when Chris White and Chris Fairclough became successful members of their Championship-winning side. Sporadic racist chanting continued but it was on a smaller scale than before.

The rapid decline of racism within the larger stadiums, particularly at Leeds and Chelsea, reflected the softer nature of the fascist influence among these supporters. While a diehard section would remain racist and align themselves to fascist groups, these people became an ever-dwindling minority.

The fascists continued to appear occasionally at football grounds but their presence was increasingly ignored. Those who were present were there as hooligans not as political activists. Even sympathetic hooligans began to keep their distance. During a period where designer clothes had become the hooligan fashion, being associated with the NF or the newly emerging BNP was decidedly uncool. 'When I grew up in football,' a Shrewsbury Town hooligan said, 'I always thought of the BNP and NF being like a bunch of blokes in anoraks and grey suits. They looked like a bunch of train spotters to us. We didn't take them seriously, they were a joke.'

While racist abuse remained an issue at several clubs around the country, it did not take place on the scale it once did. The same went for politicised hooliganism, at least on a domestic level. With the exception of a few gangs, racist politics is far from the minds of most hooligans. This partly reflects attitudes within wider society and the increase in black players in the game, but it is also indicative of the rising number of black hooligans. Even at Chelsea, whose hooligans are most associated with racist politics, there have been several prominent black hooligans. There are now very few hooligan gangs without at least one black face, while some like Birmingham, Leicester, Manchester United and Huddersfield have larger numbers. Unsurprisingly, many black hooligans do not take kindly to the overtly racist views of their fellow hooligans. In 1998, the Nazi group Combat 18 was making inroads into the hooligan supporters of Cardiff City's Soul Crew. A meeting held in the city that summer attracted 35 local people almost all of whom were hooligans. Others in the Soul Crew, particularly the black hooligans from the dock area of the city, were less impressed and several Combat 18 supporters were told in no uncertain terms to keep their political views away from football. The equilibrium was restored; racist and black hooligans continue to fight alongside one another.

Sheffield and Birmingham are the only two cities where their hooligans have been divided by race, with the gangs of Aston Villa and Sheffield Wednesday both being 'white only'. The hooligans of Aston Villa have a long association with racist groups, with as many as 15 of its followers regularly attending Combat 18 events in the West Midlands during the mid-1990s.

The removal of any black hooligans from Sheffield Wednesday is a more recent development and emerged after a struggle for the leadership of the group. Unlike Villa, the Wednesday gang has no public link to the BNP or Combat 18, though its leader is closely connected to the Headhunters of Chelsea and is a strong Loyalist. The 'white only' nature of these mobs has given an extra dimension to local rivalries; both Birmingham City and Sheffield United have a number of black hooligans in their ranks. The few other politicised gangs include Oldham, Swansea, Sunderland, Reading, Charlton and Everton. All are white-only gangs and leading members of each have links with Nazi groups such as Combat 18. Yet these are the exceptions rather than the norm. While there are many other all-white gangs, none has any real connection to racist organisations. There are active Nazis within hooligan gangs but they are isolated individuals in larger groups which often include black hooligans. This is certainly the case at West Ham, Oxford and Wolves.

A further factor undermining the ability of fascist groups to exploit and utilise football hooligans in the domestic scene are club rivalries, which on many occasions have proved to be severe obstacles in building bigger groups along racial lines. While committed fascists would put aside club hostilities for a political cause, the bulk of hooligans would not. In September 1993, following the BNP council by-election victory in Tower Hamlets, East London, Combat 18 sought to recruit in the local pubs of Millwall. According to one Combat 18 leader at the time, Steve Sargent, they failed largely because they were perceived as being 'a Chelsea mob'. The 657 Crew from Portsmouth have a history of racism but any attempts to bring them in to a larger right-wing network has consistently failed because of their fierce and violent rivalry with Chelsea. On more than one occasion England away matches provided the venue for violent clashes between the two gangs. Wider regional splits have also hampered the right. The politics might have been the same but the racist hooligans of Leeds would never contemplate travelling to London to join up with their Chelsea counterparts. Likewise right-wing hooligans from Lancashire and Yorkshire would rarely cross the Pennines for anything other than hostile intent.

Even when race does become an issue among hooligans, fascist groups do not automatically benefit. The events in Oldham, following the attack on an elderly pensioner by a gang of young Asians illustrate this clearly. Fascist groups quickly seized on the attack, which was the latest incident in rising racial tensions in the Lancashire town. The leader of the BNP immediately announced his intention to contest the local seat in the 2001 general election, while the NF applied for a march in the town. Even C18 had an influence on locals, having several supporters amongst the Fine Young Casuals, Oldham's hooligan gang. Dozens of hooligans wrote in to football websites expressing their disgust. 'It's about time England fans started to support England and not just the soccer team,' wrote Terry Allen on one website. 'I'm sick to the back teeth of fucking jam rakis [Pakis] thinking they own the place, no-go white areas my arse, it's our fucking country,' added a Man City fan under the heading 'Fucking paki bastards'. Like several other hooligans, including some from Halifax, Burnley and Bolton, he wanted to know the details of the NF march.

The weekend after the attack saw Stoke playing at Oldham. Before the game, 400 of its hooligans marched through a predominantly Asian area smashing windows and chanting racist abuse. After the game, this group was met by a similar number of local Asian youths who had mobbed up for a confrontation. The local papers saw the hand of fascist groups behind the trouble. 'FOOTBALL RACE RIOT THUGS ARE NF MEMBERS' read the headline in the *Manchester Evening News*. 'Yobs who sparked a race riot in Oldham on Saturday claimed to be members of the National Front,' the article continued. 'An investigation has now been launched into allegations that members of the extremist nationalist group infiltrated Stoke City fans.'

In truth, the NF had no involvement in the actions of the Stoke hooligans, and likewise, few of those expressing outrage at events in Oldham on hooligan websites openly identified themselves with the NF or the BNP. For every hooligan who supported the fascists, there were two or three who supported their activities in the town without agreeing to their political programme. 'I don't believe in the NF policies but I do believe in having your own views and not being afraid to show them,' wrote one Portsmouth fan. 'I must say that I'm not a racist but the time is here for young, white, English lads to stand up and be counted,' added a Burnley hooligan. 'I'm not a racist but you are spot on,' replied one Leeds hooligan, in response to an open question about whether anti-racists had condemned the attack on the pensioner.

A week later, hooligans were again back on the streets of Oldham, with the Fine Young Casuals being joined by hooligans from Huddersfield, Stockport, Stoke and Chelsea. Over the next few weeks, hooligans from Shrewsbury, Manchester United, West Ham and Everton travelled to the Lancashire town. While it is undoubtedly true that many hooligans identified with the racist cause, others turned up principally because of their connections to the Oldham hooligan group, who are themselves one of the most right-wing gangs in the country. Despite the promises that hundreds of hooligans would descend on the town, numbers coming in from outside were often relatively small and there was no sign that those coming in from other gangs took racial violence back home again. That said, hooligans rather than the racist political groups of the BNP or NF perpetrated the trouble in the town.

Apart from racism, the fascists have concentrated on Loyalism, where its perceived links to the paramilitary groups has earned them the respect and support of hooligans who would otherwise ignore their racist message. For the hooligans, support for the Union, and therefore the Loyalists, derives from their own strong English nationalism. Most see the IRA as 'killing our boys' and so worthy of hatred. Hatred towards the IRA, and the Irish generally, has become a cornerstone of English hooligan identity, with 'no surrender' chants often dominating the England end at away games.

For many hooligans, joining Nazi-organised demonstrations against the IRA and other Republican groups is the nearest they get to supporting the Loyalist cause. It was a process begun in the mid-'80s when the NF organised annual protests against the Bloody Sunday march in January and the Troops Out march every August. Dozens of hooligans, led by Chelsea ones, would turn out in hope of a clash. In Manchester, the NF counter-demonstrations to the Manchester Martyrs march would attract smaller numbers of northern hooligans. Generally, it would be Nazi hooligans bringing out one or two of their friends but occasionally larger numbers would turn out. It was not uncommon for 30–40 Chelsea Headhunters to appear on NF-organised anti-Ireland protests in London.

The anti-Irish sentiments of the hooligans grew in the early '90s, largely as a result of the intensification of the IRA's mainland bombing campaign and the emergence of Combat 18 in 1992 – which was set up with the tacit support of the London brigade of the Ulster Defence Association. In January 1993, over 400 hooligans from over 20 different firms came out onto the streets of London in an attempt to disrupt a march commemorating the Bloody Sunday shootings. Rivalries were put aside as hooligans answered the Combat 18 and UDA call, with Chelsea, Arsenal, Tottenham, Brentford, West Ham, Oxford, Reading, Portsmouth, Wolves, Aston Villa, and Sheffield Wednesday all represented on the day. Two months later, and only four days after the IRA placed a bomb in a shopping centre in Warrington, over 300 hooligans, again led by Chelsea and Combat 18, ran amok through Kilburn following England's World Cup qualifier with Holland.

Since the mid-'90s hooliganism has become increasingly associated with the national team. Following England has become more important for hooligans, especially those who follow the clubs who are unlikely ever to play in Europe. Operating with relative anonymity, hooligans can get involved in trouble knowing that at worst they will get arrested and deported back home. With trouble likely everywhere England play, almost everyone wants to go and the numbers travelling are sometimes quite phenomenal. While hooligans continue to represent only a minority of English travelling support, it is a sizeable minority that is unrivalled by hooligans anywhere in Europe.

Most English hooligans adopt an aggressive nationalism when travelling abroad. They glorify everything about England and ridicule everything different about other countries and ethnic groups. English racism comes into its own here. It is within this context that it is widely believed that fascist groups have exerted most influence over English hooligans and fans. The derogatory songs sung about the Turkish people during Euro 2000, and about the Irish before them, have heavy racial overtones. The violence of recent English forays into Europe have increasingly been targeted against the local black and North African communities as opposed to rival hooligan gangs.

The fierce nationalism and racism of far-right groups is sometimes adopted by hooligans who back home would not have any truck with fascist politics. Nazi salutes and racist chanting are much more commonly witnessed abroad than in the domestic game. There, England is white and nationalist – just the image conjured up by the fascist groups. When two mixed-race QPR hooligans asked a leading Chelsea face if they could tag along for a friendly in Germany, they were told emphatically, 'Sorry, but England abroad is white.' Away in Poland for the Euro 2000 qualifier, a black hooligan from Huddersfield was attacked by Villa hooligans because of his colour. On their way to the Warsaw match, Shrewsbury hooligans stopping off in Berlin attacked and stabbed three black people, one of whom lost an eye as a result of this unprovoked assault

Some English hooligans abroad try to explain their violence through a political justification. This was certainly the case in Dublin, when, in February 1995, English hooligans stopped a friendly international with the Republic of Ireland. It was not only the media who immediately blamed Combat 18 and other nazi groups. Many of the hooligans did as well. A 20-year-old hooligan from Newcastle returning to Britain told a journalist:

> It was all political. They started singing some IRA songs. I mean, we didn't go there to fight, but if there was a chance of it, we were going to go straight in. You've got to show some pride in your team. It's fucking pride. I know two blokes who are in Combat 18 because they believe in the English, no black in the Union Jack and all that. I mean, I'm really there for the football, but I do agree with them.

He was backed up by a 21-year-old hooligan from Peterborough. 'England once owned three quarters of the world didn't it? It's fucking pride. I mean the niggers and the Pakis own a lot of businesses.' Asked why he got involved in the fighting, he replied, 'I hate the Irish.' Several others in the pub also expressed their support for fascist groups. 'I mean, I love the BNP,' said a hooligan from the north of England, who like the others, wished to remain anonymous.

Of course, Combat 18 and the BNP had nothing to do with the violence. Combat 18 was primarily a London-based group and only two of its supporters travelled to the match. However, the initial keenness for some hooligans to identify with these groups illustrate the strong symbolism that Nazi groups have among a section of the hooligan crowd. Its unrepentant nationalism and violent xenophobia fits neatly into the mindset of many hooligans who, when abroad with England, believe that their country has been cheated out of what is rightly theirs.

Paul, a hooligan from the West Midlands, says:

> They're confusing pride in their heritage with fascism.' They think because they're proud to be English that means that they've got to be fascists as well. So there's a lot of misconception that goes on. A lot of people, well, a lot of the boys, they're like normal people – it's when they get together, it's like the sheep brigade, they all sort of follow on, and if the one who's shouting loudest is the fascist, then they're going to shout with him.

In 1993, Combat 18 were creating a stir on the hooligan scene. Paul adds:

> They've started to get a bit more of a following due to the fact that they look more like a football firm because they dress well, they're keen for an off, they never run. They always seem to be doing the right thing, the same things as any other football hooligans would do. So obviously now they've got far more notoriety which does give them an impact – it means that people are starting to take them seriously.

Paul travelled regularly with England and often came across Combat 18 discussing their politics. It was at a time when Chelsea were dominant on the English hooligan scene, which only added to the Combat 18 image.

> You're sat talking with a bunch of lads, and it's all like 'Yeah, we hate blacks' and 'I do'. A lot of it – it's the fear factor as well that starts its off, because these lads are so well known for being game for it, you don't want to look like pussying out in front of them. It's keeping face, a lot of it. And you end up sitting down and listening, and they start shoving propaganda at you.

However, while Combat 18 gained a reputation, there was little actual recruitment. They were, after all, more of a football gang than a political party. It is certainly true that they became widely known on the hooligan scene in the mid-'90s, but few recruits were made directly through football. That is not to say that some hooligans were not keen to associate themselves with the nazis. Paul says: 'In Shrewsbury some Combat 18 graffiti began to appear and some of the younger lads talked excitedly about the gang. Combat 18 were thought of as hard and uncompromising and people wanted to be part of it.'

While the fascists might exploit the nationalism of some English supporters abroad, the sad truth is that many young men who follow the national team do not need the involvement or direction of racist groups to express their own bigotry and xenophobia. Time and again they have proved themselves more than capable of performing this role alone. Unpleasant as the truth may be, the events of English hooliganism abroad say more about the nation we are than the mischievous manipulation of a few. The violence combines the drink–and–fight culture that is still so strong in English society with a nationalism that is both aggressive and xenophobic. The social life of the majority of young people is based around the pub, where drinking to excess is still a regular occurrence and regarded as normal behaviour. Being ill from drink is regarded as an occupational hazard and generally laughed off with some amusement later. Abroad, many English fans do very little else than lounge around all day drinking in the sun. It is little wonder that most trouble in recent years has occurred in the late afternoon or early evening by which time many supporters are both inebriated and bored.

Fighting occupies a similar position in British society to that of drinking. From the school playground to football hooliganism, fighting is an integral part of our society. Every year English hospitals have to deal with over 10,000 serious facial injuries resulting from glass and bottle wounds. One in three young men have a criminal conviction by the age of 21.

Fascists exploit this aggressive nationalism but their involvement is restricted. The xenophobic nationalism of the English hooligans is not necessarily simple racism. It is not a question of a different colour of skin – though that helps to differentiate in given circumstances – but it is about nationhood.

Publicly, the BNP disowns the activities of football hooligans but privately it relies on these people to provide muscle and recruits. The party's chief steward, who is responsible for security, is Warren Bennett, a convicted Hearts and Scotland hooligan. Also in the Scottish BNP are hooligans from Rangers, Ayr, Hibs and Dundee. In Wales, a BNP meeting in April 2001 saw three–quarters of its audience coming from the ranks of the Swansea hooligans. The BNP's local chairman in Swansea is Andrew Toose, the leader of the Swansea Jacks hooligan group. Even in Oldham, where the BNP publicly denounced the white youths involved in the trouble there, party leader Nick Griffin personally sought to recruit the local hooligans for an election canvassing session. The crossover between hooligans and the BNP should be of no surprise. The anti-social, tribal and nationalist behaviour of many hooligans fits neatly into the profile of BNP members.

However the systematic and widespread recruitment of football hooligans into the BNP, NF or Combat 18 has not taken place. It is a mistake often made by press and politicians, to blame football violence and racist chanting on these fascist groups. Some mistake the nationalist and racist actions of hooligans for the work of fascists, while others deliberately play up these links because it suits their political agenda. It is far easier to dismiss the violent actions of football fans on a small clandestine group which virtually everyone in society can despise than answer the far more difficult question of why so many young men in England enjoy terrorising others in foreign countries. Fascist groups have influenced some football fans and hooligans, with their aggressive nationalism and racism proving an attractive identity, but their support, with Oldham aside, is soft and often over-stated. Football mirrors society and so any general increase in racism, like that of the late '70s eventually leads to race becoming more of an issue in football. However, there is no orchestrated political conspiracy behind football violence; it's just the English being English.

TEARS, TANTRUMS AND TATTOOS: FRAMING THE HOOLIGAN

Emma Poulton

> As ever, stereotypes were scrupulously obeyed: tattoos crawled across bare
> torsos and heads were shaven. Ragged shorts were worn in deference to the
> heat of the day, as well as plastic bowler hats, imprinted with the name of
> their newspaper of choice. Thus attired, they set themselves to serious swilling
> and chanting: *'Ing-er-lund, Ing-er-lund, Ing-er-lund'*, interspersed with bovine
> choruses of *'Two World Wars and one World Cup, doo-dah, doo-dah!'* A sweatier,
> steamier, smellier bunch of patriots you never did see; at least, not since
> England's previous game.
> *Mail on Sunday*, 18 June 2000.

Not all football fans are shaven-headed, beer-bellied, tattooed, drunk-and-
disorderly young males. In fact not even many of the so-called 'football
hooligans' conform to this description either. Yet this is the popular image of
supporters, who are frequently presumed to be potential troublemakers –
especially by hostile host police forces. This is due in the main to media
representation, which continually perpetuates the convenient, but simplistic,
stereotype that it itself helped to construct. Hysterical headlines, emotive
language, evocative imagery (usually borrowed from the 'battlefield') and
graphic photographs, all help to frame the football fan-cum-hooligan as a
member of a homogeneous group of 'drunken, tattooed, crop-headed oafs'
(*Sunday Mirror*, 18 June 2000).

The defining pictures that have helped to confirm these identikit images
in recent times are the 'Pig of Marseilles', alias James Shayler, during France
'98, and the 'Made in Stockton', 'Pussy Hunter' (according to his much-
photographed tattooed torso) Lee Owens, who became the 'face', and
paunch, of the 'English Disease' during Euro 2000. The other enduring
image of Euro 2000 was the apparently dyslexic fan, who displayed a 'crude
tattoo of a Union Jack-patterned map of his native land labelled, "GREAT
BRIT*IAN*"!' (*The Sun*, 19 June 2000).

Challenging these images are the revelations that fans, and 'hooligans', are
just as likely to be well-dressed, middle-aged professionals – many with a full

head of hair, no pot-belly, and none of the apparently obligatory tattoos. Reporters and columnists often struggle in their apparent quest to construct a neat typology of the modern football fan. This was compounded when some of those deported after the mass round-ups in Belgium during Euro 2000 were revealed to be barristers and engineers, leading to the apparent bemusement of the Home Office and the Football Unit of the National Criminal Intelligence Service (NCIS) – since 'Most of those arrested in Charleroi could not have been barred from travelling because they were not known to the football violence experts' (*Daily Telegraph*, 19 June 2000). The then Home Secretary, Jack Straw, commenting after the deportations, observed that: 'England was suffering a "cultural" problem which had seen the appeal of drunken thuggery apparently extending beyond the hardcore hooligans to attract people who otherwise led respectable law-abiding lives' (*The Guardian*, 19 June 2000). Of course, the indiscriminate nature of the Belgian policy of 'administrative detention' – which did not actually require an offence to have been committed for an 'arrest' to take place – may have meant that those with 'respectable' professional careers, as well as the butchers, bakers and candlestick-makers, could well have been innocent parties and not 'hooligans' at all. This was certainly the claim of many of those arrested and deported without charge.

The media coverage of football-related violence is highly complex, thanks to its contradictory nature. The media often ignores the frequency and scale of domestic football-related disorder, which occurs on a weekly basis, because much is organised violence that takes place away from the stadia and CCTV. However, on other occasions, especially when English clubs and the national team play abroad, the press, in particular, amplifies the problem, sometimes blowing incidents out of all proportion. While newspaper editors and broadcasters may claim it is their duty to report violent incidents, and to bring them to the public's attention, the media do not simply and passively reflect events or current affairs. Through selective editorial practices and other processes in the codes of production, the media play an active role in relation to a social issue like football hooliganism.

Through mass communication, the media serve as primary definers of what constitutes 'hooliganism'. Yet the media does not always pay attention to detail and the actual specifics of an incident or, indeed, *all* of the facts. There is often a failure to distinguish between whether the incident was pre-planned or spontaneous or if it involved relatively small groups or large crowds. The timing and location of the violence – for example, to or from matches, or long after the game has finished – can be overlooked, as can whether it involved aggressive verbal abuse, threatening physical injury, or widespread damage and casualties. Contributing factors, such as provocation by local hooligans or mistreatment by the police, which can lead to a defensive reaction of siege-mentality, can also be disregarded.

The failure to distinguish between sections of England's support frequently results in the misrepresentation of the vast majority. As soon as trouble breaks out, almost all distinctions between the violent, xenophobic minority and non-violent majority is lost in the media coverage that emphasises the behaviour of the former. Consequently, the majority loses all sense of identity, voice and presence.

This is compounded by the press tendency to characterise hooligans as 'mindless' and 'sub-human'. A typical example of this is *The Mirror* (20 June 2000) front-page banner headline during Euro 2000: 'GRUNT GRUNT GRUNT'. The tabloid explained how, 'That's Neanderthal for: just behave, you mindless, pathetic excuses for Englishmen', before apologising to 'our normal, civilised readers but this REALLY is the only language these idiots understand'. Similarly, after the violent outbreaks during France '98, *The Mirror* (16 June 1998) called for government action with the challenge: 'Tough on crime, Prime Minister? These moronic, loathsome yobs are humiliating our country and they're making you look weak.' Likewise, *The Sun* (18 May 2000) branded those involved in the confrontations before the 2000 UEFA Cup final between Arsenal and Galatasaray as: 'SAVAGES!' Broadsheet writers too, sometimes employ this kind of language. For example, on the same day, the *Daily Telegraph* (18 May 2000) headlined with: 'Barbarians Bring Hate into the Football Arena'.

Descriptions and labels like these lead to the simplistic suggestion that hooliganism occurs either as a result of a collective spasm of irrationality, or the recourse to carnal animal instincts – neither of which are satisfactory explanations for the causes of football-related violence. Media analyst Gary Whannel has claimed in the academic journal, *Media, Culture and Society* that the frequent use of this stereotyped characterisation of hooligans had led to them becoming a new 'folk devil' in society:

> The football hooligan begets the football hooliganism problem. The establishment of a new folk devil leads to the development of a moral panic . . . Future incidents then appear within the framework of this moral panic as evidence of a trend, which is increasingly newsworthy in its own right.

In the run-up to a major competition, predictions about the likelihood of disorder occurring are always high on the media's agenda. Before Euro '96, France '98 and Euro 2000, there was extensive media interest in police preparation for hosting the respective tournaments centring on measures for preventing, and also dealing with, outbreaks of unrest. This was manifest in countless newspaper stories and television documentaries, which more often than not exaggerated the potential problems with alarmist prophecies, rather than playing down any prospect of public disorder.

The hype, and subsequent hysteria, usually begins with coverage of the police's carefully stage-managed pre-tournament dawn raids on 'suspected hooligans' and 'exclusive' exposés of hooligan firms that will run riot. For example, prior to Euro '96, *The Times* (5 June 1996) revealed how: 'Police raided homes in Manchester, London and Essex early yesterday to arrest suspected football hooligans before the European Championship. Weapons, including a sword, and match tickets for England fixtures were seized.' Days before Euro 2000 kicked off, the *Sunday Mirror* (4 June 2000) warned , under the strapline: 'Euro 2000: Countdown to Another Nightmare' how: 'An Army of 1,000 football yobs is heading for the Euro 2000 tournament hell-bent on bloodshed'. *The Sun* (8 June 2000) went as far as reporting on the eve of Euro 2000 how 'Belgian police last night admitted they have set up separate mortuaries for English and German fans as they fear trouble when the countries clash in Charleroi.' Meanwhile in the broadsheets, the pre-match build-up was not dissimilar:

> An *Observer* investigation reveals that Charleroi is set to be turned into a battlefield with visiting thugs, local Turks and Neo-Nazi troublemakers based in the town staging bloody confrontations. The authorities privately admit mayhem is almost guaranteed because huge numbers of mainly ticket-less fans will crowd into Charleroi's narrow streets. (*The Observer*, 4 June 2000)

If and when violence does occur, the media's predictions are proven to be true and consequently become self-fulfilling prophecies, with incidents often reported in a 'told-you-so' tone. This sense of inevitability characterised the remarks of Jeff Edwards, Chief Crime Correspondent for *The Mirror* (16 June 1998), after the 'Fighting on the Beaches' in Marseilles: 'The rampage by the pond life who call themselves England fans was as certain as night follows day.' According to one of his broadsheet counterparts, the violence during Euro 2000 was 'as depressing as it was predictable' (*The Observer*, 18 June 2000).

Reporters regularly stoke the feelings of shame and disgust by affirming that the English are synonymous with hooliganism. During France '98, for example, *The Mirror* (16 June 1998) lamented how: 'Anglais has become a byword for unspeakable thuggery, a byword for hooliganism.' What the English media tend to overlook too often, however, is that football-related violence blights countless other countries: Italy, Spain, Germany, Holland, Turkey, the Balkans, Brazil, Argentina, Colombia and China all have frequently reported serious outbreaks. Indeed, football violence occurs, to varying degrees and in different forms, in almost every country in which the game is played. In this sense, hooliganism is a global social problem. However, football violence, and the English 'hooligan' in particular, are convenient mediated scapegoats for the broader ills of society and indeed can divert attention away from deeper problems that may actually be contributing to the situation. The apparent source of the hooligans' anti-social, problematic behaviour is commonly viewed by the press to be the hooligans themselves and their 'natural' mindlessness and savagery. An editorial piece in *The Mirror* (20 June 2000) offered some strong opinions after the events of Charleroi and Brussels:

> Words, words, words. That's always been our weapon against these drunken, violent, mindless creeps who ruin it for everyone. It's not just a football problem. These are the same idiots who wreak havoc in every town in Britain every weekend and smash up Spain on their holidays. Britain has the most drug-ravaged, alcoholic, criminal, abusive, and utterly obnoxious collections of young males of any European country. And this is their big chance to show everyone just how moronic they can be.

Blame the 'mindless', 'lunatic', 'moronic', 'sub-human' football hooligan, and the deeper social roots and more enduring causal factors behind the phenomenon can be overlooked. In doing so, the conservative 'law and order' ideology, whereby the hooligans are cast as villains who must be controlled for the good of the game, and the nation, is preserved.

The *Mirror* editorial above demonstrates the tendency to take the blame away from football, denying the perpetrators of violence the title of football 'fan' or 'supporter'. Headlines like 'YOB TRAITORS' (*The Sun*, 19 June 2000) are commonplace once the violence breaks out. The *Sun* editorial continued: 'These morons have NOTHING to do with football. They have NOTHING to do with the fun the rest of us have . . . Each one of them is a traitor – not a hero. They are not patriotic; they are enemies of the state.' The day before, the *Sunday Mirror* (18 June 2000) lamented, 'Thanks to the actions of a band of thugs who call themselves football fans, shame, rather than glory, was heaped on England.' Former Labour Party deputy leader, Roy Hattersley, writing for *The Guardian* (20 June 2000) chastised the troublemakers, contending that, 'half the thugs whose pictures appeared in the weekend papers could not repeat the offside rule to save their lives.' However, the notion that those who participate in violence are not knowledgeable about football, or that they do not care passionately about their club and country, is misguided and simplistic. In fact, quite the opposite is usually true, despite editorials like the following:

> The spectacle of baying English hooligans, rampaging yesterday through the streets of Brussels and Charleroi, is a source of national shame. They have inspired disgust and fear among their Belgian hosts; sullied the efforts of the England team; and spoiled the enjoyment of many genuine football fans. The England-Germany game, it seems, was a magnet for hordes of English thugs – partly because they wished, in some warped way, to re-enact the antagonisms of the Second World War. As the hooligans wrapped themselves

in the flag of St. George, chanting their racist and abusive slogans, some undoubtedly believed themselves to be modern standard-bearers of patriotism. How wrong they were, and are. (*Sunday Telegraph*, 18 June 2000)

While the hooligan element may represent what many perceive as the more noxious side of 'Ingerland' – one which is bellicose, aggressive and xenophobic in character – one cannot dispute that most are football fans, or that they may well believe themselves to be patriotic standard-bearers.

Sport is one of few arenas in contemporary society in which national identity can be displayed and asserted. As it is, the prevailing national identity of the English in recent years has been broadly characterised by a Little-Englander mentality. Such ideas are not unique to sections of England football fans; many politicians and those within sections of the media share these views and indeed have helped to construct and reinforce them. The mentality is manifested in an aggressive assertion and defence of 'us', underpinned by a post-imperial hang-over that seeks solace from self-aggrandising notions of the nation's former status, together with a hostility to anyone perceived to be a threat. These traits are itemised by Paul Hayward, Chief Sports Correspondent for the *Daily Telegraph*. He noted:

> For the record, in case it helps anyone understand, the songs sung by thousands of England supporters in the Stade Communal on Saturday night were: 'Rule Britannia', 'God Save the Queen', 'No Surrender to the IRA', the theme tunes to *The Dambusters* and *The Great Escape*, and 'Cheer Up Craig Brown', which is aimed at Scotland's coach and team. Some medley, this. Some tableau of English nationalism. (*Daily Telegraph*, 19 June 2000)

Again, it is not credible simply to deny that those who sing such songs about military conquest (some of whom may also partake in violence) are zealously patriotic and proud of their nation and national team.

Yet there is a common tendency within the media rhetoric for a distinction to be made between 'patriots' and 'nationalists', in order to express disapproval for the hooligan element's behaviour and sentiments. 'Nationalism', with its negative associations with xenophobia, is frequently seen as being something adhered to by 'them', the hooligans, while the 'civilised', genuine football fans merely demonstrate 'patriotism'. However, usually such distinctions are for convenience only. What one calls 'nationalism' is simply the 'patriotism' of others, and what one calls 'patriotism' is one's own brand of 'nationalism'. Too often these details are overlooked in the sound-bite hysteria, as the media seek to point the accusing finger and apportion blame.

The coverage usually focuses on 'hooliganism' being framed as a direct indictment of the country, with those involved branded: 'A Disgrace to

England' (*The Sun*, 15 June 1998). The next day, with Tunisia defeated, *The Sun* (16 June 1998) headlined with 'Heroes and Villains of English Football'. Its front page showed both Alan Shearer, 'who led us to our first World Cup win', and David Shayler, 'the thug . . . who led the riot that shamed us all'. Similarly, when England beat Germany during Euro 2000, the *Mail on Sunday* (18 June 2000) heralded the 'Night of Glory' juxtaposed to the 'Day of Shame', following the 'sickening behaviour of England supporters in the streets of Charleroi'. Such indignant reaction is found in the broadsheet press too. After England's win, *The Observer* (18 June 2000) headlined: 'England's Glory Night Marred by Fans' Riot'.

These headlines also illustrate how press treatment can often excite the issue further by fanning public indignation, which can in turn increase pressure on the footballing authorities, police, and politicians, for a review of the problem and for 'suitable' legislation. This certainly seemed to be the case during Euro 2000. While the public has a right to be informed about incidents like those that occurred in Brussels and Charleroi, this needs to be done in a considered and reflective manner, which does not amplify the situation. Otherwise a media-generated frenzy can develop whereby the impact of a relatively minor incident is framed in such a way to appear much more than it actually was.

UEFA's threat to disqualify England from the competition after the assorted incidents in Belgium prompted a mixed response, although there was wide-scale denouncement of the public disorder. All of the radio and television broadcasters led their news programmes with stories of the violent outbreaks in Brussels and Charleroi and UEFA's threat of expulsion. A number of issues were raised during the bulletins. George Aligiah's opening lines for the BBC's *Nine O'clock News* on 18 June 2000 announced: 'UEFA says the government should have stopped the hooligans travelling. But England fans say the Belgian policing was over-zealous and over-the-top.' However, while acknowledging claims about the Belgian police, the selective footage and sound-bites seemed to imply the English fans' complaints were more about sour grapes.

In this connection, Steven Howard, a football writer for *The Sun* (19 June 2000), declared: 'WE'RE THE LEPERS OF FOOTBALL.' His newspaper's front page warned: 'OUT If There's Any More Aggro!' Tabloids and broadsheets alike delivered similarly stark warnings. For example, the *Daily Telegraph* (19 June 2000) announced 'Once More and England Are Out', while *The Guardian*'s front-page (19 June 2000) declared: 'England Told: More Rioting and You're Out'. Inside the broadsheet, in a rather ill chosen manner, Hugo Young was advocating that 'the best course is a retreat from battle.'

Some journalists and columnists do attempt to offer analysis on the causes of hooliganism, although this is often part of the rebuking of the hooligans.

This helps to contribute to the popular definition of the 'problem'. Again, this was evident in the coverage of Euro 2000. Dr Theodore Dalrymple was employed by the *Sunday Telegraph* (18 June 2000) to expound on 'the nature of English popular culture, which encourages and even glorifies such conduct'. Dalrymple claimed that 'much of what passes for social life in England is actually a low-intensity riot', which, he said, was characterised by 'the smell of stale alcohol and drying blood'. This, he contested, was due to the 'plain fact that the English can no longer associate in any numbers without there developing an atmosphere of menace'. To illustrate his premise, Dalrymple suggested a trip to Ibiza, 'where scores of thousands of young English take their holidays, and what you see is a chronic international football match, with people vomiting in the street, insulting foreigners, screaming and shouting abuse and vulgarities'. This, he contends, is a microcosm of 'a Saturday night walk through any English provincial town and much of London'. However, what these observations fail to do is to go beyond the scathing censure of English youths and their behaviour. He does not offer any explanation as to *why* 'scores of thousands of young English' should behave in the ways so graphically outlined.

In *The Observer* (18 June 2000) Charlie Whelan was concise and more insightful as he noted: 'all the ingredients for high drama were there: water cannon, riot police, huge amounts of alcohol, thousands of journalists and the intense rivalry of German and English fans.' Whelan's observation at least keeps the issue in perspective. Media commentators frequently exaggerate and sensationalise the nature of the problem, often framing it as a phenomenon undermining the very fabric of society, by taking football violence out of its full social context. Sports are cultural practices. There is therefore a need to understand the values that underpin a particular sport. Football is a sport that emphasises a very competitive, very aggressive, and very masculine style of play, especially in England. It is therefore unsurprising that there should be connections between the values that underpin the game of football and the values that underpin football-related violence.

Further to this, whenever there is a large gathering of people in one place, there is a high probability that some may eventually abandon their self-control and behave in a disorderly, sometimes aggressive or violent, way. It is therefore hardly surprising that whenever a large number of men – especially men divided by passionate support for rival clubs or countries – congregate in the intense context of a football match, displays of aggressive masculinity and, consequently, fighting, are a likely outcome. Such activities are part and parcel of the quest for excitement, or, as the participants describe it, the 'buzz'.

A *Guardian* editorial, instead of offering any answers, raised a series of questions as it considered calls for remodifying the 1999 Football Offences and Disorder Act. The editorial warned:

We should be very careful of revamping the 'sus' laws – which is what those arguing for pre-emptive banning of non-offenders seems to want. Those are tough law-and-order questions. In the aftermath of this tainted competition, others, deeper, more troubling, will have to be pressed: about the atavism of our tabloid press, the deformations of English nationalism and the brute incapacity of young English men to drink in a civilised fashion. (*The Guardian*, 20 June 2000)

One of the questions above concerned what was described as the 'atavism of our tabloid press'. This is a common accusation levied at the tabloids. For example, Hugo Young's piece on the opposite page to this *Guardian*'s editorial reinforced these charges. Young wrote:

… Not many of the football sots and oafs may read much history. It doesn't take prime place in the national curriculum. But they get their crucial bits from the tabloids they read, modern annals that are prime accessories in football's degradation of England. Derision of foreigners and hatred of their projects is a tabloid stock in trade. Smarming piously about morons and cretinous yobbos, *The Sun* yesterday extended Britain's apologies to 'the Belgians and the Germans, to the Dutch and the Portuguese', expecting the world to forget the years of bile and gallons of ink about the Huns and the Frogs it has poured into unresisting minds of the same simpletons and cretins brought up to suppose that Brits can do no wrong. (*The Guardian*, 20 June 2000)

Hugo Young rightly highlights the tabloid writers' tendency towards triumphalist incitements of history and the frequent scorning or mocking of all things foreign. Just days previously the *Daily Star* (17 June 2000) was encouraging the England team to 'GIVE IT SOME WELLINGTON', having reported how Kevin Keegan had 'moved his troops to Waterloo – the Belgian town that was the scene of one of England's greatest-ever victories'.

Young's argument also raises several other contentious issues. Firstly, the verbal reduction of all football supporters to the level of 'simpletons and cretins' is again in evidence. Secondly, Young implies that the 'football sots and oafs' are all tabloid, particularly, *Sun* readers. This of course is a huge assumption, as is his claim that the 'tabloids' bile' has been 'poured into unresisting minds'. To suppose readers of tabloid newspapers to be completely gullible and impressionable is a crass misunderstanding of the dynamics of media consumption. Readerships are not duped into believing, unquestioningly, their newspapers' rhetoric; nor are they impelled to act or behave in a way determined or encouraged by the newspaper. Media texts, whether in the form of press reports, television programmes, or radio programmes, can be resisted, misunderstood, reinterpreted and recycled by their audiences. Grand assumptions about the effects of the media on consumers are misleading since it invests the media with too much power. This denies readers and audiences the capacity for rejecting media content.

Roy Hattersley, writing for *The Guardian* (20 June 2000), made similar observations to Young, although these were milder in comparison and less presumptuous. Hattersley also highlighted the apparent hypocrisy and, by implication, irresponsibility, of tabloid reporting, as he considered the outbreaks of civil unrest during Euro 2000. His contention was that: 'Most football thugs are the sort of men who, regretting that we no longer rule the world, want us to control the penalty area – and fight them on the terraces as we were once ready to fight them on the beaches.' He argued:

> That pathetic tendency has been grossly encouraged by the tabloid treatment of international football – typified by Saturday morning's 'witty' headline which described the German team as 'krap'. Yesterday's *Mirror* included a massively indignant editorial which demanded 'Crack Down on Mindless Thugs *Now*.' Its lofty tone was in profound contrast to a column written for that day's paper by Tony Parsons: 'Yes, do mention the war . . . they had it coming'. Mr Parsons reminded his readers of 'boys in their teens who died at Anzio'. He called the Germans 'Huns'. The *Mirror* editor is explicit that 'at half past seven' he decided 'in light of the news that the column was inappropriate'. But it appears on the *Mirror*'s web-site. And it raises a question to which we have yet to hear the answer. If UEFA had not threatened to expel Britain [or rather, England] from the tournament and the story of 'jagged black shrapnel' had been regarded as 'appropriate', how much responsibility would the *Mirror* have taken for the next night's riots?

In the build-up to England's Euro 2000 game against Germany, and the violence in Charleroi, the press coverage gradually appeared to stoke Anglo-German antagonism. The match was framed as the one we *had* to win. The *Daily Star* (17 June 2000) recruited the comedian, Stan Boardman, who 'cheekily dressed as a German squaddie to send support to our lads, saying "Get out there and beat the old Fokkers."' Meanwhile *The Mirror* was warning: 'HANS OFF OUR PAGES', explaining how: 'They're [the Germans] famous for nicking all the holiday sunbeds, but yesterday they [the German tabloid *Bild*) were caught stealing *The Mirror*'s headlines.' *The Mirror* (15 June 2000) then offered the Germans five other spoof headlines, including 'FEAR THE WURST! BSE Found in German Sausages' and 'ACHTUNG! (No, OK, We Won't Go There Again.).' The latter was clearly designed to recall the newspaper's controversial Euro '96 front page: a bizarre act given that it had earned the paper so much criticism.

Only the day before, *The Mirror*'s editorial (14 June 2000) claimed that 'cheeky banter is part and parcel of football culture', but that the 'vile abuse screeched at David Beckham' could not be classified as such, condemning it as 'pathetic, outrageous and utterly deplorable'. Having made such a distinction, you wonder where the *Mirror* editor draws the line between 'cheeky banter' and the unacceptable. The intention here is not to be a killjoy or to advocate taking the rich humour and rivalry out of football. This is, indeed, a valuable part of the game. But there is something very clumsy and contradictory occurring when a newspaper evokes memories of a front page that was resoundingly lambasted and features an exultant list of '100 things that just don't matter today because we've beaten Germany!' (*The Mirror*, 19 June 2000) alongside an editorial calling for a 'Crack Down On Mindless Thugs *Now*'. This is further exacerbated when the previous page contains an article by a *Mirror* reporter boasting how he 'went into the lion's den to watch game with Germans'. The reporter went on to explain how: 'Having made a new will and spoken to my mother for what may have been the last time, I entered the Weaponsmith's Arms [an ironically named pub in the circumstances] to watch THE football game. Wearing an England shirt. Rooting for England. In Berlin.'

The vast majority of readers are well enough equipped to take what the press may intend as just for 'fun' in the way apparently intended. However, this is not to dismiss completely the media's capacity to over-hype matches through the public exhortation for 'our lads', that in turn can generate a highly charged mood of over-expectancy. This expectation is often too great, and the temperature often flamed too high through the tabloids' frequent charge, borrowed from Lord Nelson, that 'England Expects'. Occasionally, when the 'bubble' bursts following defeat, violence can be an outcome. The media, having contributed to the intensified atmosphere, are then quick to condemn others for the consequences. The unrest after England's exit from Euro '96 is an example of this. Unassuming hope, rather than such high expectation, would be more appropriate given our track record during the last 35 years or so.

The press is also guilty of sometimes displaying flagrant xenophobia in their gung-ho, nationalistic rhetoric prior to a game. The malign clichés that underpin the cultural denigration and antagonistic lampooning of the customs, traits and symbols of opposing nations often goes well beyond a 'joke' or 'cheeky banter'. It is therefore perhaps little wonder that some fans show a lack of respect to the cultural practices and sensitivities of host nations when in some corner of a foreign field. Sometimes, of course, this lack of respect may be unintentional, or, of course, misread. Yet Italian journalist, Giancarlo Galavatti, has remarked: 'People go to Rome to see the sights, not semi-naked Englishmen building mountains out of beer cans. It may not be a crime but it is still offensive.' (*The Sun*, 20 June 2000). What may be considered − or at least tolerated − as normal, high-spirited, 'laddish' behaviour in this country, such as heavy drinking, singing and chanting, may be deemed to be anti-social, aggressive posturing that is deeply offensive in some cultures and societies.

It is perhaps not surprising that fans are often suspicious of the media, seeing them as only interested in muck raking and trouble making, leading to a commonly negative perception of England's support. The sense of victimisation has sometimes resulted in acts of aggression and frustration towards media personnel. The *Sunday People* (18 June 2000) revealed how one of its own reporters was 'injured as he got caught up in the riots' during Euro 2000. Similarly, the *Sunday Mirror* (18 June 2000) confirmed that 'TV crews were attacked', while the *Daily Telegraph* (19 June 2000) reported how eye-witnesses had claimed 'some England fans roamed the square looking for opportunities to attack photographers and television cameras'.

Supporters' suspicions of the media are fuelled by reports like the following. Stating, yet again, that it was a 'foregone conclusion that there will be trouble in Eindhoven and Charleroi, and other points along the route', involving England supporters, the *Daily Telegraph* (12 June 2000) reported: 'In preparation, journalists and camera crew covering Euro 2000 for *Channel 4 News* were sent on a pre-tournament riot training course normally under-taken by those heading for a war zone.' The course was to include 'having 40 would-be hooligans throwing bottles at them and learning how to observe the general mayhem while trying to keep their heads down'. Similarly, the *Sunday People* (18 June 2000) told how 'ITV newsmen were issued with gas masks before the England–Germany clash because of fears that they could be caught up in rioting between rival fans.' This helps to confirm the idea that the media are 'looking for trouble'. There was also a handful of reports during Euro 2000, as fans have claimed before, that police 'tipped off journalists and TV crews' before they moved in to round up England supporters (*The Observer*, 18 June 2000).

The idea that the media sometimes attempt to instigate trouble, together with arrests apparently put on for the cameras, has been compounded by the press playing an active role in identifying 'hooligans' caught on film. During France '98, *The Mirror* (16 June 1998) featured mug-shots of 16 of the 'usual (tattooed) suspects', urging readers to 'name and shame' them by phoning a special hotline. Similar measures have been employed in the tabloids before and since. Prior to Euro '96, the *News of the World* launched its 'Shop a Yob' campaign, with the message: 'Only with your help can we stamp out this horror.' Consequently, it is perhaps understandable why many fans are seen attempting to cover their faces as news teams film their arrival and departure at away matches. In many cases, they may well be actually protecting their innocence, rather than hiding their guilt, as many news hounds would have us believe.

This is not to disregard or disguise that a hooligan element does follow England, especially away, and that there are outbreaks of violence. On the contrary, while David Mellor has been an unlikely vocal defender of fans on occasions, especially for their treatment by police forces abroad, sometimes his opinionated comments can similarly represent an embarrassingly one-sided view. Not all foreign police are guilty of prejudice and mistreatment, nor are all fans innocent. Once again, there is a need for *balance* in the media coverage. We seldom hear about the exemplary behaviour of the vast majority, or indeed about the constructive attempts to change the negative image of England fans. Rare exceptions are usually hidden away, to allow the 'tales of terror' to talk centre-stage.

For example, the *Daily Telegraph* (19 June 2000), after leading its first five pages with reports and comment on UEFA's threat to expel England, at least featured an article by a female member of the England Members Club, albeit on the third page of the sports supplement, who had 'seen little trouble, and had caused none' Another positive representation of England fans was that offered by Channel 4 during Euro 2000. Their documentary, *England, Our England* (23 June 2000) opened with footage of the infamous water cannon dispersing chair-throwing offenders in the square of Charleroi. Yet the narrative framed a refreshingly alternative picture of followers of the England national team:

> This is how the world may well remember England's 2000 campaign: hooligans fighting pitched battles in Belgium, their every move recorded for posterity by the media. But there is another side to the story: tens of thousands of England fans went to Belgium, not to disgrace their country, but to try to restore its reputation. This is the story of what Euro 2000 was for the *majority* of England fans.

The programme followed a mixed group of fans on their travels through the Low Countries in support of England. As a rule, however, it is generally a case of too little, too late.

The defence of English supporters is also infrequent. The media rarely defend the vast majority of completely innocent fans, who follow club and/or country home and abroad at great expense, wanting nothing more than to support their team and experience a foreign city, only to be picked on by locals or punished simply for being there, whether through heavy-handed policing, or deporting, purely on the grounds of being English. Only occasionally do newspapers include reports that contextualise or qualify a violent incident, but these tend to appear, if at all, several pages into the newspaper, after the graphic headlines and vivid images implicating English supporters. For example, the *News of the World* (18 June 2000) quoted an England fan who claimed,

> It was the Belgian police who were the thugs. I was having a quiet drink in a bar with a mate when it all blew up. Suddenly the place was full of police

wielding batons and spraying gas. The next thing I knew, I was in a cell with 40 other blokes. I was innocent and so were loads of others.'

Yet this account was featured in a tiny sideline on the fifth page of the newspaper. The *Daily Telegraph*'s Henry Winter wrote a reflective piece on England supporters, in which he considered the contrasting manifestations of patriotism among followers of the England team. He observed:

> The importance of being English is something keenly felt by the supporters. Few opportunities exist for them to express their Englishness so they gather ever more keenly around the banner of St George. Such pride is understandable yet, as a role of dishonour from Rotterdam to Marseilles indicates, the patriotism has a dark side and some are simply there for a fight. The sirens will wail in the Low Countries this summer. They always do, wherever England play abroad, whatever the authorities might try to do. Yet for every laughing England fan climbing into an oven at Auschwitz clutching a can of lager – as I have witnessed – another 20 are exploring the country, enjoying the experience of another culture and harming no one. But the far-from-small minority spoil it for the rest. (*Daily Telegraph*, 10 June 2000)

Or, we might add, the minority is *allowed* to spoil it, with news values being what they are. It makes for much better copy to concentrate on the ignorant individual in the Auschwitz oven, rather than follow a group of more respectful sightseers or a whole bar full of England and Germany fans having a good time together.

The FSA expressed their reservations about the coverage of Euro 2000. Its report on the tournament included a whole section on the media coverage. It found that:

- The media cannot be blamed for outbreaks of violence by England fans abroad. But the hype about the possibility of violence and the number of journalists, in particular television crews, certainly contributed to the ten-minute incident in Charleroi, and to the perception of it in England. Many people arrived in Charleroi for the Romania game tense and apprehensive, having heard exaggerated reports, and were surprised to find themselves welcomed by bar and café owners into a pleasant party atmosphere . . . The continual coverage of a few small incidents and the intensity of the media coverage of fans in general was unhelpful to say the least.

- The documentaries on hooliganism, in particular the *Panorama* programme, gave only a partial version of events. *Panorama* had an opportunity to address the issue of aggression and provocation from local youths in Brussels, but did not take it.

- We were glad to see, however, that the media did highlight the racist chanting and commented on the different styles of policing in the two host countries. Some days after the Germany game, some stories did start to emerge of innocent people being caught up in the mass deportations from Belgium. As the hysteria gradually died down slightly, more objectivity crept into the radio and TV coverage. Whilst maintaining a steady condemnation of the violent anti-social attitudes of a section of England's followers, questions were asked about the tactics and attitude of the Belgian police.

The BBC's *Panorama* 'Special', entitled 'England's Shame', was hastily commissioned and screened immediately after the Romania match (20 June 2000). It exposed 'known hooligans' who had defied banning orders to travel, unhindered, to Belgium and Holland. While the reporter, Gavin Hewitt, stressed that it was not the majority, but a 'significant minority' that formed the 'racist hard-core' of England's away support, little attention, credit, or indeed sympathy, was given to the former. There was only passing acknowledgement that some innocent fans *may* have been caught up in the use of tear gas, indiscriminate mass detentions and subsequent deportations by the Belgian police. Instead, emphasis was placed on the 'assertive, threatening nationalism' of England followers, with undercover cameras showing this element 'in action'. Footage was shown of apparently large gatherings of English supporters singing: 'No Surrender to the IRA', 'I'd rather be a Paki than a Turk', and 'If it wasn't for the English, you'd be Krauts', aimed at local Dutch and Belgians. Hewitt observed: 'When England travels away a significant minority uses the occasion to assert their national identity, an identity rooted in the last war, of an island nation undefeated and superior to others, a culture which is male and exclusive of other ethnic minorities.'

In a report for ITV (*Tonight with Trevor MacDonald*, 22 June 2000), Mark Austin was shown being accosted by a group of England supporters, one of whom protested: 'You lot have stereotyped all the England lot, so they've just arrested everybody coz we're all supposed to be thugs. And that's what it's all about. You wouldn't know a football hooligan if you'd seen one.' Another fan added: 'You show one minute of violence out of 24 hours. We've been here four days and we've not had one minute of trouble.' Viewers were not treated to Austin's response to these accusations. However, his agenda was evident throughout his report on 'England's Disgrace', which he claimed had been 'utterly predictable'. There was little analysis and no consideration given to the possibility of any provocation faced by England supporters by either other nationalities or the police. Austin's main concern was the outbreaks of violence in the main square of Charleroi, and how these scenes were 'pictures to shame Britain [or more precisely, England], as the whole drama was captured by the TV cameras'. These pictures, he said, made 'depressing viewing'. Depressing, indeed, especially for the forgotten majority of innocent England fans.

Yet this is the kind of tarnished image that England supporters typically have to put up with due to the ways in which they are framed by the media. Even positive moves towards improving the image of England fans can be negated by media spin. For example, a recent FA survey of EMC members on their views regarding restructuring the EMC and, in so doing, enhancing England fans' image, attracted some disproportionately negative media attention. Rather than extolling the virtues of the overwhelming majority who had responded positively to a series of questions about being an EMC member, the press focused on the 4 per cent who had supposedly given unsatisfactory answers. The *Daily Mail* (5 April 2001) declared: 'England's official supporters club includes more than 1,000 thugs bent on violence at foreign games, the FA has admitted. Of the 32,000-strong England Members Club, 1,300 do not believe they should behave well when following the national team.' The actual wording of the original questions was disregarded, as were the more significant and encouraging statistics. *The Guardian* (5 April 2001) took a similar line, leading with the negative findings by emphasising the 4 per cent and headlining with: 'ENGLAND SOCCER HOOLIGANS PROFILED'. The many positive results generated by the questionnaire were tucked away at the close of the article. This short paragraph, in a somewhat dismissive tone, told how: 'Of the other fans [in actual fact the vast majority] who answered the questions, 86 per cent agreed strongly or agreed that the EMC were ambassadors while 91 per cent said that membership brought with it the responsibility to behave well.' The angle of these reports is indicative of the media's apparent agenda when it comes to coverage of football fans. Yet again, this was a missed opportunity to promote the vast majority who want actively to improve the image of England supporters.

The media continually put all England fans in the frame for the hooligan element's misdemeanours. Yet the media could play a much more positive role. If the reporting of England matches involved the promotion of a more tempered, rather than tempestuous atmosphere, it might help to play down ideas about avenging the opposition and settling scores from on, or off, the field of play. This requires a shift of emphasis away from arrogantly high levels of expectation, recourse to martial history lessons, and talk of impending doom and gloom forecasting the likelihood of trouble involving English supporters. More considered, more measured, and, at times, more sensitive reporting, is called for. This involves the respectful treatment of opposing nations, their players, and their fans – but also our own.

We need to move away from representing all football fans as a homogeneous group. Dismissing all England supporters as 'that bunch of cretins in *News of the World* plastic bowler hats', which Richard Williams' claims characterises our 'rotten fan culture' (*The Guardian*, 9 October 2000), is not helpful. Nor, however, is simply blaming the media for supposedly inciting the behaviour of a small section of England supporters through their pre-match hype. The social roots and longer-term causes of the prevailing aggressively masculine and xenophobic national identity of their 'Ingerland' go much deeper than that. The media, as well as politicians and the police, would be wise to acknowledge this.

Once again, this demands a balanced approach to the treatment of supporters, rather than framing them all as 'hooligans'. This involves a degree of reflexivity and circumspection. First, the 'hooligan' is not some bestial 'other'; he represents a particular side of 'Ingerland' that cannot be ignored. That said, the hooligan element should not be allowed to dominate the media coverage of England supporters in the way they currently do, so over-shadowing the non-violent majority. Second, despite what broadsheet columnists may claim, this majority of fans are not tabloid-led imbeciles; although some may harbour Little-Englander views, since these underpin the prevailing national identity of the English. While these ideas may sometimes be expressed through certain songs and chants, this does not necessarily lead to the violence, or neo-Nazism, of the self-proclaimed 'hard-core hooligans'. Many of those who join in renditions of 'No Surrender', for example, may not have paid much attention to the full meaning and implications of the song's lyrics. The same may be true in relation to the humming, with the accompanying actions, of 'The Dambusters March'.

The problem lies in the latent denial of those forming the middle ground of England's support: passionate patriots who follow the national team (or their club) over land and sea, with no inclination towards aggression, racism, or violence. Yet it is these fans that get forgotten amidst the prevailing news values of the media. If more attempts were made to give due attention to these supporters, we would have a much more comprehensive, and more truthful, picture of English fan culture. By featuring and embracing story-lines about these supporters, which are just as authentic, just as real, the media could present a broader range of representations of what it means to be a fan of England. Perhaps then, the non-violent majority could begin to reverse their image that has been tarnished by portrayals of the 'hooligans'.

THE ENGLISH DISEASE?
NATIONAL IDENTITY AND FAN CULTURES

A DIFFERENT KIND OF CARNIVAL

Richard Giulianotti

Football violence has been popularly conceived of, at home and abroad, as the 'English disease'. A reasonable reflection of this diagnosis is the manner in which the word 'hooligan' has passed from English into all major languages, with football considered to be the prime place for its social application. However, since the late 1980s at least, there has been a rising public awareness of violence involving fans from outside England. In part, this focus helped to legitimise England's rehabilitation within world football following the Heysel disaster in 1985. English commentators suggest that whilst they haven't solved their hooligan 'problem', they know now it's not unique to them.

A useful starting point is to consider precisely what is meant by the term 'football hooligan'. A key defining factor must be the *subcultural identity* of specific supporter groups. Many hooligans across the world define themselves as such through actions as well as words. Within the group, there will be a shared commitment to engaging in competitive violence, principally with other hooligan groups; in the most intense club rivalries, non-hooligan rivals may be considered as legitimate targets. Accordingly, from this definition, we should exclude those apparent incidents of violence that are relatively isolated. Ironically, these would include many incidents that UK in-ground surveillance treats as priorities for eradication, such as throwing missiles onto the pitch, racial abuse of players or the vandalism of stadium facilities – offences that are often committed by lone individuals.

In most nations, there are distinctive and 'militant' forms of football fan subcultures, but there are significant differences in the degree to which they label themselves as 'hooligans' or engage in 'hooligan' practices. In this instance, therefore, we can certainly include those 'firms' or 'mobs' that follow clubs in the UK, and which seek to fight with their rival peers. These groups have equivalent counterparts throughout northern Europe, notably in Germany, Holland, Belgium and parts of France and Sweden. In more southern parts of Europe, as well as in South America, the picture is somewhat complicated by more traditional supporter subcultures that follow clubs. In Italy, Spain, Portugal and the Balkans, the *Ultras* are militant spectator groups, but their violent proclivities vary substantially, between clubs and between individuals within the same supporter community. A similar point may be made as regards the *Barras Bravas* in South America, notably in Argentina, Uruguay and Peru. Unlike, for example, the post-1970s soccer casuals of the UK, these supporter identities are not essentially concerned with defeating or humiliating their subcultural peers through intimidation or violence. Such objectives may certainly be shared by specific sections of *Ultras* or *Barras Bravas* whom we may therefore categorize as 'hooligan'. However, the unifying goal of the *Ultras* or *barras bravas* is to offer strongly expressive and colourful support for their clubs. Hence, we should avoid the clichéd statements of many UK sports journalists who, when venturing abroad, consider that *Ultras* and *Barras Bravas* groups are uniformly hooligan.

If hooliganism is so defined, then the first point to be made is that the modern phenomenon did not really originate in England. While a case might be found for the *Barras Bravas* in South America, most obviously we need only look north to Scotland for evidence of long-standing violent subcultures rooted in strong senses of rivalry. It has been claimed by the Scottish Football Association's former chairman, Ernie Walker (and with no great relish) that Scotland probably gave the world what we now take to be hooliganism, through the violent 'sectarianism' between Rangers and Celtic fans. Of course, underpinning the strong fan rivalries here were the deeper religio-ethnic divisions between the clubs, notably the Unionist and anti-Catholic roots of Rangers and their fan culture, in contrast to the minority, Irish-Catholic roots of Celtic. The 'Brake Clubs' (informal, travelling bands of supporters) that had followed the rival teams since before the Great War were certainly involved in violent clashes, but perhaps the most notorious incidents grew up out of the mythology surrounding the violent razor gangs which were deeply embedded within the supporter cultures. Most notoriously, there were the 'Brigton Billy Boys' that followed Rangers through the inter-war years and which continue to be celebrated in song at Ibrox through lyrics such as 'We're up to our eyes in Fenian blood, surrender or you'll die.'

English political and media concern with football hooligan subcultures did not really germinate until the late 1950s and early '60s. This paralleled broader unease toward the perceived deviance and delinquency of 'teenagers' and their associated youth styles (consider, for example, the moral panics about teddy boys, mods and rockers, etc). Thus, the older notoriety of Scottish supporter groups was accorded a greater subcultural status among the emerging hooligan groups in England. Curiously, that respect mirrored English awareness of Scotland's long-term contribution to the development of football in the south (through players, coaches, managers, officials and tactical innovations). It was also in line with the hospitable welcome that

Glasgow's more notorious criminal fraternity (such as Jimmy Boyle) received from equivalent London groups during business-and-pleasure trips to the South. Meanwhile, these Anglo-Scot relations were overlain with a mythology of masculine hardness surrounding the Scots. Such a view was strongly evidenced through the publicised disgust of conservative England during the 1970s at the antics of the Tartan Army on the biennial descent upon Wembley, Trafalgar Square, Soho, the London Underground and other capital landmarks.

Any examination of the relationship between British hooliganism and its European counterparts needs to look beyond the sphere of violence and to consider instead the broader realms of Britain's football terrace culture with additional reference to other trends within the national youth cultures. In the post-war period, since the early 1960s, continental youth styles and tastes have been heavily influenced by developments in the UK to a degree that perhaps outstrips the influence from the United States. This process is certainly demonstrated by the continuing cross-generation popularity of music groups such as the Beatles and Rolling Stones. Other subcultural styles to be exported to the continent have included mod, punk and skinhead identities; and latterly acid house, techno and garage (though these also demonstrate hybrid, UK-American trends). Within football, therefore, it was understandable that young European supporters would look to the UK for subcultural influences from the 1960s onwards. For fans growing up in Europe in the '70s and '80s, English football in particular possessed a certain mediated aura that went beyond the clubs' successes on the pitch. Football crowds played a crucial part in this regard. Unlike the Olympic stadia of many European cities, where the pitch is encircled by an athletics track, the rectangular and intimate architecture of British football grounds allowed fans to be close to play and enabled them to create a noisy atmosphere across the unseated terraces through chants and colourful displays. During the 1960s and 1970s, the emerging *Ultras* supporter groups throughout Italy borrowed heavily from English terrace culture, which was then more display orientated, through *Kop* songs plus flags, banners, scarves and other colourful paraphernalia. Many *Ultras* groups continue to tap heavily into the products of British popular culture, notably those of the 1960s and 1970s. In Genoa, for example, one section of the Sampdoria *Ultras* has called itself 'mods' while a section of the rival Genoa Ultras is more heavily into the 'skin' style. But it is apparent that this was not just a passive following of British styles and trends. Instead, on the continent, these British subcultures underwent what we may term a process of 'cultural creolisation', whereby a local society takes on board a more global or popular cultural practice, but adapts that practice to fit local conditions or needs. The Italian *Ultras* thus came to receive, but also to reshape, the expressive terrace culture of the UK, taking it off in directions of intense choreography and organised spectacle that were not explored by spectators back in the UK. First, Italian spectator displays became increasingly spectacular and competitive, as rival *Ultra* groups sought to trump each other in pre-match choreography and thus energise their players. Smoke-bombs, firecrackers, stand-sized banners and the continuing composition of new terrace choruses were all important to the *Ultras'* participant football atmosphere. Second, such spectacles required co-ordination and this was provided by the formal institutional structure of the *Ultras*, as reflected in their leadership elections, membership lists, group headquarters and other features of a rational-bureaucratic model of association. Third, *Ultras* groups established complex lineages of friendship and rivalry between supporters of different clubs. Thus, for example, in the mid-1990s, Sampdoria *Ultras* were linked to a lineage that included Parma and Verona fans, and thus stood in opposition to city rivals Genoa and their lineage that included fan groups such as those backing Pisa and Bologna. Inevitably, these lineages are not completely symmetrical and they are also prone to being amended by driving out some groups or including new ones. Meanwhile, at individual clubs, one often finds several *Ultras* groups that are distinct historically and culturally from one another, as reflected in their establishing separate organisations and locations within the home stadium. Nevertheless, this all points to variants of formal association and social exchange within and between supporter subcultures to a degree that one does not encounter in the UK. Fourth, the *Ultras* were formed within the context of acute political and civil conflicts, notably in the complex relations between the Italian state and paramilitary terrorists operating from the extreme left and right. *Ultras* groups borrowed stylistically and to some extent politically from these revolutionary movements, according themselves combative names, dressing to disguise personal identity, and attaching anti-State symbolism to their banners and songs. In recent years, major political and public unease has been expressed towards the neo-fascist practices and expressions of some *Ultras* groups, notably those following Lazio, Verona and Roma. To some extent, this reflects the intensification of separatist politics in Italy since the late 1980s, as illustrated at a recent Verona–Napoli fixture when home supporters wore surgical masks to 'protect themselves' from the 'health-risk' of visiting fans from the poorer, southern region.

Notwithstanding the semiotics of rebellion or cultural opposition, the *Ultras* cannot be simply labelled as 'Italy's hooligans'. Some groups certainly acquired pretty fearsome reputations. Notable here have been fans based in the richer north of Italy, thus contradicting some sociological arguments (such as those advanced by Eric Dunning and colleagues in *The Roots of Football Hooliganism*) which prefer to identify football hooligans as hailing from the poorest and 'least civilised' sections of the working class. The 'barbarian' Atalanta *Ultras* from the wealthy Bergamo area near Milan have long been viewed as particularly dangerous, while the Verona and Fiorentina

Ultras also gained notoriety for their violent expression of ancient civic pride. Conversely, *Ultras* who follow Italy's largest club, Juventus, and smallest 'big' club, Parma, have little reputation for punching their weight outside of the grounds. There may be something here in the particularly deep association of both these clubs with a dominant parent company – Fiat and Parmalat respectively – which perhaps overshadows the cultivation of a militant *Ultras* subculture. However, the main property of the *Ultras* is their militant, committed form of support, which may or may not be manifested through violence. It is a supporter subcultural style that came to prevail across southern Europe through the 1970s and '80s.

In Spain, *Ultra* groups emerged in the early 1980s. Politically, this came soon after the end of Franco and the establishment of a democratic state. Subculturally, however, the *Ultras* movements looked especially to Britain and Italy for their influences. Spanish *Ultras* are more prone to form only short-lived alliances with each other, often in opposition to the friendless *Ultra* groups from Catalonia or the Basque region. Spanish *Ultras* share a subcultural identity in terms of motivations, activities and levels of violence. While there are strong fascist undercurrents within some *Ultras* groups in Spain, as there are in Italy, there are anti-fascist or more socialist *Ultra* movements – notably those located in the Basque country or those following the working-class club of Rayo Vallecano in Madrid.

Through language and cultural exchange, the *Ultras* phenomenon came to share some spectacular and organisational commonalities with the '*Barras Bravas*' of Spanish-speaking South America. For their part, the *Barras Bravas* have their own complex genealogy: in Argentina, the phenomenon emerged in the mid-1960s, although in Lima there were equivalent groups back in the '30s. Like the *Ultras*, the *Barras Bravas* have a genuine degree of organisation and engage in very expressive forms of support inside stadia. The anti-State significations of the *Barras Bravas* have a deeper historical basis since during the various military regimes, as well as in more recent neo-liberal times, football crowds have been viewed with a mixture of contempt and anxiety by the violent security forces. Moreover, the *Barras Bravas* have possessed a significant political influence within clubs in South America, since the clubs are traditionally organised as private member associations and are thus 'owned' by those who are willing to pay a monthly or annual subscription. Office-holders are elected on an annual or biennial basis and it is here that the *Barras Bravas* can exercise influence, establishing a supporter base and 'getting out' the votes for their favoured candidates during these elections. Football politics is often a springboard into local electoral politics, so the *Barras Bravas* can be useful in this regard as well. Major concerns have been expressed about the corrupt and violent relationships that sometimes arise between the elites within the *Barras Bravas* and the elected office-holders, notably at the lower-class club of Boca Juniors in Buenos Aires. This provides the organisational and political background to the inter-fan violence that is subculturally embedded within the Argentinian game. Much of this violence has focussed upon the historical rivalry between Boca Juniors and River Plate, with some *Barras Bravas* groups even using guns, machetes and other weapons in recent years. An estimated 50 Argentinian fans have died since 1980, while the league programme has been suspended in recent years through strike action by players and judicial interventions, in both cases to protect players, match officials and fans from escalating levels of disorder.

In Europe, television coverage of English football, coupled with irregular visits by continental fans to English grounds, served to disseminate the UK supporter styles across European terraces. But the creole process, of UK to Europe, has not been all one-way. In an unconscious act of reciprocity, young English fans began to borrow and to reshape the general sport and menswear styles found especially on the continent, in order to create a hooligan identity, the 'casual' style, which dominated British grounds by the mid-1980s. Thus, the stylish designer labels to be found among habitués of a Parisian tennis club or strollers in an Italian piazza, were transplanted into the decaying Victorian ends of Britain's major and minor football clubs.

The exact origins of the casual style are difficult to document. Domestically, the style may have started with the recognition among the more violent English club fans that the stereotyped 'hooligan' look of the 1970s – visibly aggressive in bootboy regalia and bedecked in club colours – was impractical to evade surveillance and outdated as a youth style. Certainly, in the infamous 1978 *Panorama* documentary on Millwall fans, one mature member of the hooligan 'F-Troop' announces while en route to a match in Bristol, that they are deliberately eschewing the hooligan look of old, with its emphasis on club colours and avoidance of 'smart' or upmarket gear. This new approach, the lad asserted, was indicative of London smartness as opposed to the passé look of northerners or young supporters from the west of England. Alternatively, cultural commentators such as Steve Redhead have speculated plausibly that the casual style began with 'English shopping' abroad. As English clubs, notably those from the North and Midlands, dominated European competition for a decade from the mid-1970s, so their travelling fans would swoop on the continent's fashion and department stores without bothering to pay. Trips by the national team overseas – notably to Luxembourg and Italy – were bonuses. In part, through the Paninaro style, the youth in northern Italy and some other parts of the continent already had a stylish sibling to the soccer casual, but their links to the sport were not apparent. Upon arriving in England, the casual style quickly spread northward to Scotland, notably among Aberdeen and Motherwell hooligans to begin with, and then through northern Europe, primarily Germany, the Low Countries and Sweden by the late 1980s. The football-centred casual style also emerged in northern Italy, France, and the former Yugoslavia, but the deep subcultural roots of *Ultras* identity ensures that the casual style in southern Europe is something of a hybrid entity. The degree to which any one individual *Ultra* or pocket of *Ultras* pursues a primarily casual identity depends strongly on their respective knowledge of, or contacts with, football hooligan groups in the UK. For their part, UK hooligans have not made much of the supporter styles of the *Ultras*. Part of the casual style involves something of a cool contempt for overly expressive and decorative forms of support, particularly of the kind that can be carefully orchestrated as a package before television audiences. Thus, links with *Ultras* are more likely to pertain in a social, cosmopolitan manner, as individual UK-based hooligans develop personal interests in the cultural differences afforded by the *Ultras* movements and their internal rivalries.

The aggregation among English firms, to back England overseas, takes place on a scale that is not nearly matched by hooligan groups on the continent. On the continent, German and, to a lesser extent, Dutch hooligans have tended to represent the most significant opposition to England fans but there have been few confrontations at major fixtures in recent years. While Euro 2000 generated large numbers of arrests and confrontations with police, England fans appeared to encounter few problems from indigenous hooligan groups. Elsewhere, however, there are signs of some hooligan formations coming together to follow southern European nations. Lads from Real Madrid and RCD Espanol appear to be prominent in the emerging hooligan coalition in Spain. Among Italian fans, there is a developing formation, featuring some right-wing elements drawn from Verona, Roma, Lazio, Como and Bologna. This group came to some prominence at the 1998 World Cup finals in France when many of them were detained and sent back to Italy. At Euro 2000, they were involved in some incidents with immigrant groups in the Low Countries before around 150 of them gradually gathered prior to the final against France in Rotterdam; most were arrested after singing fascist songs and presenting Roman salutes behind the French end. Nevertheless, this inchoate Italian mob is still dwarfed by the more established 'Viking Italia' group – the official *Ultras* group which follows Italy and which eschews football violence on the grounds that it besmirches the national name. Looking further abroad, as we have noted, there are certainly hooligan groups within the *Barras Bravas* of Latin America and the various *Torcidas* that follow Brazilian clubs. But even with the inception of FIFA's World Club championships, there is no real opportunity for these violent South American subcultures to confront their European counterparts en masse at a major global tournament. Travel costs and internal club divisions would also prohibit large numbers of *Barras Bravas* attending major tournaments such as the World Cup finals in Europe.

At the national level, England's strongest rivals have traditionally been Scotland. In considering this rivalry, some solutions for repairing the reputations abroad of England fans might begin to emerge. Until the mid-1980s, the Scots' violent reputation and national obsession with defeating anything English would result in fixtures at Wembley being dominated by northern visitors. An English presence at fixtures in Glasgow was never really envisaged. The Scotland–England fixtures at Hampden in 1985, '87, and '89 changed all that, as English hooligans travelled north to try to debunk the hard mythology surrounding the Scots; a total of 250 fans from either side were arrested at the 1989 game, resulting in the world's oldest international fixture being suspended indefinitely. Yet throughout this time, the Scots had also embarked upon a parallel process, an image make-over as friendly, 'carnival' fans before a European and world-wide audience. This transformed public persona has been remarkably successful as Scots have won plaudits and awards for their gregarious, boisterous but apparently non-violent behaviour since the early 1980s. Accordingly, it is asked, with some exasperation, why can't England follow the Scottish example as reflected by other friendly supporter groups such as the Danes, the Dutch, even the Brazilians? There is no simple answer.

To begin with, reinvention of the Scottish fan identity has strong cultural roots in an anti-Englishness north of the border – not a violent anti-Englishness, but one that is more ironic and is manifested in schadenfreude. As a small nation the Scots have struggled to define themselves against the English before European audiences who are not versed in the vagaries of British pre-industrial history. In conjunction with their increasing use of distinctive 'traditional' dress, the Scots make the reductive point that they are not English because they are not hooligans. When England fans are tear-gassed in public squares, arrested en masse and deported from the continent, the Scottish response is one of exaggerated public indignation and barely suppressed celebration. To sustain their positive overseas image, the Scots need the English to retain their dubious reputation. What would become of Scottish fan identity if the English were indeed to be seen in a new light?

Secondly, this reinvention of the Scots' fan identity comes 'from below', from the 'lifeworld' of the supporters themselves. It was not imposed 'from above' by Scottish football's 'system' of corporate, political and sporting governance – the Scottish Football Association, the Scottish Office, club marketing men, leading media figures and so on. Though elements within the SFA and the Scottish Office claimed that legal and administrative measures (e.g. the 1980 Criminal Justice (Scotland) Act), had transformed the 'Tartan Army', it was the supporters themselves who voluntarily took on the extended, paternalist function of policing themselves, and engaging in amicable interaction with their hosts. To borrow from the German social theorist Jurgen Habermas, there did not appear to be a crude 'colonisation' of the supporters' lifeworld by the financial and political system that dominates the national game. The same, I fear, cannot be said for English football, and particularly the English national team. The English football authorities have sought to eradicate the xenophobia within England's fan culture by the following Home Office recommendations and overhauling the membership of the England Members' Club. This dubious policy might influence the identity of some England supporters within the ground, but it has serious flaws in ethical, technical and political terms. It smacks of an undemocratic and crude governmental exercise in social engineering. And, given the greater prevalence of ticket-touting and violence around football stadia at major tournaments, the policy might prove to be redundant because it does not affect the more disorderly elements within England's support. Such an administrative approach to transforming the fans' lifeworld might well meet with substantial resistance from the supporters because it has failed to enter into proper dialogue with the supporters themselves.

Thirdly, if we consider Scottish fans as a totality, we have to note that there is still a self-identifying 'hooligan' minority that will travel to international fixtures abroad if it's believed there is a hooligan opponent there to be challenged. Certainly, there are internal complications and divisions within this Scottish hooligan force. For instance some 'firms' (such as Aberdeen and a section of Hibs hooligans) refuse to participate in a 'National Firm' that combines Hearts, Rangers and a different section of Hibs casuals in particular. Nevertheless, in having hooligan elements following the national team, the Scots are little different from other northern European nations, notably Holland, Germany and Belgium. The point here is that any English policy endeavour to 'eradicate' hooliganism is not really practical. The more significant difference between the English case and these other nations is that the Scots, Dutch, Germans and so on can employ what I would term the 'Argument of Cultural Separatism' to protect their international reputation. They can keep their hooligans at a symbolic arm's length from the mainstream support, and present them as a minor and culturally separate entity to whomsoever they encounter. Perhaps more importantly, this kind of argument is also advanced voluntarily by the majority of non-hooligan supporters that follow these nations. Such an argument continues to be greeted with intense scepticism when presented in favour of England fans, but as an objective it is a good deal more practical than the official anti-hooligan policy of eradication or complete exclusion that one hears from English FA officials and British government ministers.

Fourthly, the world might have an enhanced impression of Scotland's international fans, but this does not preclude these supporters from performing traditional, masculine roles while overseas. Instead, cutting down on what might be seen as 'boorish' behaviour has served to improve greatly the Scots' chances of drinking in pubs throughout the night without the landlord calling the police. Hence, a supporter group does not have to comprise 'new men' to acquire a friendly identity that wins awards from international football bodies.

Fifthly, the Scots and their European siblings – such as the Danish 'roligans' – are routinely presented by the more powerful forces within the game (notably the various authorities and media spokespersons) as 'carnival' fans, in contradistinction to the apparently socio-pathic behaviour of England fans and other hooligan groups. However, this outlook reflects a rather partial understanding of what 'carnival' actually entails, particularly if we recall the original folk meaning of this term. Carnivals have their cultural roots in pagan rituals and festivities, but their closest line of descent is found in the traditional Catholic feasts that preceded the observance of Lent – festivals that are closely associated with merriment, riotous behaviour, and intoxication. During such events, the rules and norms of the wider society are typically mocked or turned upside down; possibility of social breakdown is always there. However, in modern times, 'carnivalesque' behaviour which is redolent of the tradition of carnivals has become increasingly controlled, orderly and sanitised. This is a deadening process that is often resisted by the potential participants in carnivals. Certainly, among Scots fans, there are expressions of opposition or alienation when the football 'carnival' is being over-policed, or manufactured by the corporate and media interests that dominate football tournaments. Viewed in this way, the disorderly behaviour of English fans abroad does not stand in historical opposition to 'carnival' culture. Rather, it is a more militant expression of the carnivalesque, a continuation of the riotous carnival cultural tradition in which *all* football supporters are implicated.

A final point, from a comparative viewpoint, is that England fans are unusual in that they may have access to the more peaceable and orderly 'carnival' culture of a kind that other national football team fans construct. However unlikely this may seem, the example of cricket suggests itself, most notably with the 'Barmy Army' fan culture that has attached itself to England's national team in the past decade. The social mores of this cricket culture are certainly analogous to those of the Tartan Army. I do not wish to suggest that the Barmy Army is comprised of frustrated football fans that have switched sports to experience a crowd culture that is more to their liking. But it is useful to observe that the Barmy Army provides an alternative space for a self-controlled carnival culture, one that may be considered and explored by English football fans in defence of their own variety of carnival activity. It is also striking to notice how fans of the English national team can engage in a cultural crossover, by easily changing their social practices and sporting outlook when they switch to following the English cricket team overseas. This is not necessarily good news for would-be reformers, since it is the very difference in spectator culture between football and cricket that serves to attract fans to one sport or to both and to behave in their different fashions. The same point may be made for the dance scene, which has often been forwarded as another apparent diversion from potential hooligan careers. The rise of ecstasy, acid house and the rave scene during the mid-late 1980s certainly decimated hooligan numbers over the long-term. But it does not need to be an either/or question. For there is surely little doubt that those involved in hooligan activities can adopt what some would call a 'neo-tribal' approach towards this other culture which is driven by music and drugs. That is to say, the lads may drift in and out of this latter scene, enjoying the emotional community that it contains, without it dominating their personal identity or jeopardising their participation in other subcultural activities. So, in a nutshell, an additional problem that reformers of English fans must face is the kind of cultural variation that disorderly fandom actually serves to offer young men within the spectrum of contemporary leisure culture. There are already opportunities to engage in 'friendly carnival' forms of popular culture, such as the Barmy Army or the club scene; the disorder associated with England abroad appears to offer a valued alternative cultural experience to young men, something different from other, more self-controlled leisure spheres.

The reinvention of English fan identity abroad cannot simply repeat the Scottish experience. There is no hooligan 'other' for the English to define themselves against; there are few signs of a genuine dialogue developing between England fans and the authorities; nor does there seem to be much political recognition that a more positive fan culture needs to be germinated largely 'from below', and that this may well contain forms of traditional (non-violent) male practices that are not manufactured for family viewing. In short, the English face a subcultural public sphere of hooliganism that the Scots did not have to deal with.

In the foreseeable future, the cultural flows between UK hooligans and those of continental clubs will increase exponentially, due to wider processes of Europeanisation and globalisation. Two particular factors are worth highlighting here. First, as the Champions League has become extended and institutionalised, so fixtures between top European clubs become a more regular occurrence. Whereas in the past Fiorentina fans might get the chance to visit the UK once every 7–10 years for a fixture, now those opportunities occur every year or two. On the field, particular rivalries may emerge between specific European players and European clubs, while off the field football fan subcultures (including hooligan ones) have greater opportunities to avenge prior insults or to cement friendships in the context of UK–European relations.

Secondly, perhaps more significantly, we have the information age to take into account. The Internet, e-mail and hooligan websites all serve to multiply the flows of communication among hooligans. Links between diverse European Lads are now established with routine facility. UK hooligan message boards regularly carry postings by overseas interlopers, keen to advertise their own crews and to cement ties with lads from other formations. Yet we should not succumb to a conspiracy theory here; that there is some highly orchestrated, subterranean hooligan network in the making – though doubtless there are the odd lads sprinkled across Europe who would fantasise about leading such a cabal. Rather, we should note that a friendly message from one *Ultras* group in Spain to a hooligan group in England is typically a one-to-one accord, and not a sign of a merger or formal alliance between the majority of hooligans associated with either side.

Within the hooligan group, a specific website for that group helps to work out its history and identity, to sharpen the collective memory of its participants. It provides a venue for 'Lads' new and old to debate the various statuses of other hooligan groups. It represents a social setting in which humour, stories and observations on football and life in general might be communicated and exchanged, without any immediate, intimidating 'pressure' from those who take a dissenting view. All of this takes place within a permanently accessible hooligan context, whereas in earlier times, due to other domestic and social commitments (notably work and family), physically meeting up with other lads during the week would not be viable.

Hooligan websites are opening up a whole new public sphere – one that is subcultural as well as exceptionally global. To develop this idea of a 'subcultural public sphere' among hooligans, we might borrow some terms and ideas from Jurgen Habermas. At the national level at least, a major problem for the informal hooligan network has been cutting through the 'bullshit' of boasting, misrepresentation, and plain mendacity that circulates about hooligan firms, their various activities and reputations. Hooligan websites represent the best setting to date for cutting through all this 'distorted communication', to get to more factually accurate interpretations about the capabilities or otherwise of rival firms, or to establish what contemporary hooliganism is all about. Thus, the web seems to resemble a kind of 'ideal speech' community for lads, where 'distorted' (false or irrational) forms of communication can be weeded out, exposed or discarded. 'Bullshitters' may be more easily detected when their claims are pushed up on the web, particularly on the major message boards. Those who have lost confrontations really struggle when hiding behind fabricated accounts to explain away their past failings. If limp excuses appear on a message board, they run a far greater risk of being discredited, and that in front of a potentially global audience. The same fate awaits those with more curious, or sadly, more popular, interpretations of fan violence.

Certainly, within this subcultural public sphere, there are issues in regard to who is able to contribute positively to debates on hooligan websites. Contributions are typically anonymous, but the identity of contributors using special web-names can be established over time by those who are 'in the know' within the hooligan scene. Contributors to hooligan message boards are typically wary in regard to their infiltration by police, particularly by attempts to draw out information (on individuals, on incidents, on relations with other mobs) that could be put to use in criminal investigations. While police officers and journalists have yet to prove particularly successful in this regard, there are regular complaints among website contributors that such external interlopers are too keen to post messages and are thus undermining the overall quality of dialogue. Additionally, one of the possible weaknesses of hooligan websites (like any 'ideal speech' community) is that they privilege the more articulate and resourceful elements within hooligan networks, possibly to the exclusion of relatively poorer, less educated or younger lads. Admittedly, insults exchanged between Lads can focus as much upon poor grammar and spelling as they do upon failings in the arts of pugilism or substance of argument. Like the rest of the web, hooligan message boards across the globe tend to privilege English speakers. However, as access to such technology becomes more established throughout all social classes, one would expect website postings from a wider social spectrum to occur.

A final point worth making, with regard to hooligan websites, is that they provide the wider public with some new insights into the subcultural universe of football violence. The postings are there for anyone with a computer to access. Sometimes, they point away from the kind of cultural identity that is assumed to exist among violent fans. Typically, English hooliganism is seen to be indicative of a wider malaise within the English cultural psyche: racist, xenophobic, lacking moral education, perhaps evincing a threatened sense of national identity in this era of British devolution and European integration. In short, hooligans are depicted as reflecting a deep cultural regression, a post-imperial identity crisis that permeates significant parts of English society. Comparatively speaking, this argument of cultural regression has all kinds of problems, not least since it cannot explain hooliganism in the wealthiest cities of mainland Europe. For example, rarely do we read of how Ajax's hooligan element stands accused of a post-imperial identity crisis. But, more factually, we need only look on the various hooligan message boards to confirm that many English hooligans do not live up to their stereo-typed reputation. Lads of some experience are less than likely to wander drunkenly into police traps in Europe's public squares, or to get themselves filmed singing 'No Surrender to the IRA' as an illustration of English jingoism abroad.

Overall, then, what we need is a more counter-intuitive and sceptical approach towards understanding England's hooligan fans. The lack of reliable, empirically-accurate knowledge regarding England fans is a noteworthy point. Twenty years ago, the book *Hooligans Abroad* by John Williams, Eric Dunning and Patrick Murphy promised to provide a research study of violent fans. But their research was undertaken on official tours organised by travel agents or football institutions, so they failed to engage with the hooligan fans themselves. That provides no adequate basis upon which to speculate on the possible causes or the nature of fan violence in England or any other nation. Latterly, writers like Gary Armstrong and Garry Robson have debunked much of the mythology surrounding English club-based hooligans through serious research, by actually engaging with these supporters and the broader, complex cultural lifeworld of which they are a part. However, at national level the lacuna in knowledge must be addressed before policy 'solutions' can be seriously contemplated.

Obviously the reputation of England fans abroad will not be reinvented over the short term. A long-term ambition for the English football authorities may be to achieve what other nations have effected. That would involve taking a realistic view of fan violence, allowing for its continuation, while firmly separating the dominant culture of these violent fans from that of the wider body of supporters. But this will not be achieved by attempting to transform England supporters *in toto* into embodiments of political correctness, by deadening their football carnival. Instead, perhaps like the Tartan Army, the transformation needs to be allowed to come from below, from the supporter body itself. The football carnival can comprise the more traditional libidinal pleasures of an escape overseas, and in greater volume and intensity if the supporter identity is a non-violent one. The only way towards encouraging that identity would be to enter into *direct* dialogue with these supporters rather than to impose a systematic policy upon them from above.

Acknowledgements

I am indebted to Jed Rosenstein for most of the information regarding Spanish football. My comments on Argentinian football draw in part upon the work of Vic Duke and Liz Crolley. My greatest thanks are due to numerous supporter groups at home and overseas for their invaluable comments and insights on football fan subcultures, some of them hooligan ones. My thanks as well to the editor Mark Perryman for very constructive, critical comments on a previous draft.

THE ORANGE PARTY

David Winner

I thought I'd made a decent effort to join in. I was wearing an orange T-shirt and a baseball cap with the word 'Holland' printed in black on the peak. But as soon as I took my seat among the massed Dutch fans for the group game against Denmark in Rotterdam, I realised I was embarrassingly, pathetically underdressed. As with every other Netherlands match in Euro 2000, the entire Dutch nation seemed to have put on fancy dress. Packed together in the stands, the local fans transformed the curved bowl of De Kuip into a bay of glowing orange. *The Observer* noted 'the almost Van Goghian beauty of the massed shirts of the Dutch fans, stippled and shimmering beyond the pitch.' Up close, though, the word 'stippled' barely begins to convey the spectacle.

A middle-aged couple had turned up in full evening dress: impeccably tailored tie and tails for him, elegant ball gown and feather boa for her, and all of it in luminous Day-Glo orange. Lots of men in orange lion suits. Blonde girls with fetching overbites wearing orange jumpsuits and a variety of elegant, inflatable, plastic orange headwear (footballs, windmills, crowns). Ridiculously tall Dutchmen with big beards (dyed orange) came dressed as traditional peasant girls complete with orange pigtails and painted-on freckles (guess what colour). In the seat in front of me was a man wearing an orange boiler suit. His face was painted orange, and on his head he wore a dreadlock wig, each strand woven from packets of orange condoms.

Holland's footballers ultimately failed on the pitch in Euro 2000. But if there were prizes for spectators, the host nation would have won the tournament at a canter. Not since the confetti-hurling Argentinians of the World Cup of 1978 has a football tournament's home fans made such an impression on the watching worldwide TV audience. But where the Argentinians got themselves noticed by the sheer scary intensity of their fanatical devotion, the party-loving Oranje Legioen, with their toeters (the oompah band which follows the team and leads the singing) inspired universal affection.

And it wasn't just fans with tickets who entered into the spirit. The whole country went (to mix a suitably fruity metaphor) orange bananas. Fountains in the centre of Rotterdam spurted orange water. Orange mechanics' overalls became high fashion items. Pets, including dogs, cats, hamsters and parakeets, were coloured orange. One farmer dyed his whole herd of dairy cows. Dutch TV carried pictures of a wedding where the bride wore an orange dress and the groom had orange hair. Near the Dutch team's training camp at Hoenderloo, the local townspeople were even sillier. In the style of Clint Eastwood in High Plains Drifter, where he paints the entire town red and renames it Hell, so Hoenderloo's residents daubed all their homes with orange paint, festooned their gardens with orange bunting and balloons, bought orange garden gnomes and renamed their village 'Oranjeloo'.

During Holland's matches, the streets emptied as the nation watched on TV. The atmosphere in pubs, bars and town squares was much the same as in the stadia. I saw Holland beat France 3–2 in a heaving pub near the Leidseplein with my friend Neil, a Brit who's lived in Amsterdam for four years. Beside us stood beautiful dark-haired twin sisters, students who claimed never to have watched football before, yet who knew everything about the team, its tactics and philosophy. Across the street, as the goals rattled in, a man evidently related to Ugly Naked Man from the TV show *Friends* stripped to his patriotic underwear and pranced in the window. After the game, a joyous street party erupted in the square. French fans in blue, passing tourists of all colours, nationalities and allegiances were swept up in the celebration and made to feel welcome and wholly included. These were the days, you'll recall, when, elsewhere in the Low Countries, belligerent all-male groups of English fans were seen on TV squaring up to riot police, singing 'No Surrender to the IRA' and insulting foreigners. The Dutch fans celebrated as sweetly and joyfully as their team played pretty football. As the party throbbed and swirled around us, beaming, bemused Neil seemed ecstatic. 'Brilliant! . . . just brilliant!' he kept saying. His eyes shone. He marvelled at the lack of hidden malice. But at one point something in the delirious, gentle happiness around us reminded him of its total absence in relation to the English national team. He turned to me with anguish in his heart and sadness in his soul to ask 'Why can't we ever be like this in England?'

Why indeed. Can English fans learn to throw a football party like the Dutch? Probably not. The orange carnival – a relatively recent phenomenon, historically speaking – seems to spring from deeply and specifically Dutch sources. For it is not only in relation to football that Holland dyes and tries to go to heaven. Almost any excuse will do.

Each year on April 30, the country celebrates Queen's Day, a curious festival marked by selling things on the street and drinking to excess. Again, everyone puts on orange clothes (often the national football shirt). Queen's Day is the only day in the year people are permitted to sell things in the street without a licence. The fact that the junk from one's neighbour's attic suddenly becomes available at a very reasonable price causes great excitement. For a couple of guilders you can pick up a rusty wok, old records by crooner Andre Hazes or a video recorder from the early '80s which almost works. Meanwhile, hundreds of thousands of orange-clad revellers descend on the centre of Amsterdam to party on the canals and get festive on an epic scale in the narrow streets. Queen's Day is increasingly marketed as one of the country's top tourist attractions and, from all the hype, I imagined it to be a tradition going back centuries at least and possibly even pre-dating the pyramids. In fact, the festival is an invented tradition. It was inaugurated by Queen Juliana in 1948 but was initially a stiff and formal affair. At the royal palace there were modest military parades and, elsewhere, until the '70s, children would be lined up in town squares to sing the praises of the monarch. Only in the last 20 years or so, in the wake of the social and cultural revolution of the '60s, did Queen's Day acquire its present character.

Perhaps the key word in all this is 'orange'. With the possible exception of the Irish green, no nation is now so identified with a single colour as the Dutch. The colour orange is, of course, the symbol of the Dutch royal family, deriving from the town of Orange in Provence, a possession acquired by the (originally German) royal house of Nassau. But whereas the symbol has been around for centuries, the phenomenon of the whole country painting itself orange is very recent. The colour was in evidence during the great celebrations which marked the country's liberation from Nazi occupation in 1945, but not on remotely the same scale as today's impromptu orange festivals. The current extraordinary, excessive Dutch use of orange surely carries some separate potent charge of its own. What, as old semioticians would say, does all this orange signify?

It must mean something. 'Colour is a means of exerting a direct influence on the soul', said the painter Wassily Kandinsky, who claimed to be able to hear colours as well as see them. 'Colour is a keyboard, the eyes, the hammers and the soul is the piano with many strings,' he declared. 'The artist is the hand which plays, touching one key or another purposively to cause vibrations in the soul'. Orange, said Kandinsky, 'is like a man, convinced of his own powers. Its note is that of the angelus, or of an old violin.'

Two hundred years before Ruud Gullit, one of the greatest stars of Oranje, as the national team is known, coined the phrase 'sexy football', the orange inspired Goethe to write an erotic poem:

Seest thou yon smiling Orange?
Upon the tree still hangs it;
Already March hath vanish'd,
And new-born flow'rs are shooting.
I draw nigh to the tree then,
And there I say: Oh Orange,
Thou ripe and juicy Orange,
Thou sweet and luscious Orange,

I shake the tree, I shake it,
Oh fall into my lap!'

'Lying between celestial gold and cthonian red, the primary symbolism of [orange] is that of the point of balance between the spirit and the libido', explains the *Penguin Dictionary of Symbols*. 'Acccording to traditions going back to worship of the Earth Mother, this balance was sought in the ritualistic orgy, regarded as bringing with it initiatory sublimation and revelation.' Dionysos, the Greek God of wine, madness and theatre was said to dress in orange. So too did the followers of Baghwan Shree Rajneesh, a guru best known for his teachings on sex and spirituality. Vietnamese brides traditionally wear orange as a sign of fertility. Orange is the colour of robes worn by Buddhist monks, of Masai warriors, of the Australian desert and aboriginal paintings.

But what on earth is it doing in such vivid abundance in a cold flat land beside the North Sea? I turned for guidance to Ann Lloyd, a colour consultant in London, who advises individual and corporate clients. Lloyd cheerfully admits to knowing little about Dutch footballers or their fans. ('I've heard they're quite good, aren't they?') Yet, when I ask her about their colour, she describes things that only someone with intimate knowledge of *het nederlands voetbal* could know.

There are, she says, identifiable orange characteristics, which are related, it seems, to the colour's physical properties. 'Different colours relate to different physical and spiritual energies, to different 'levels of being'" she explains. For example, red (orange's neighbour on the spectrum), has the strongest and longest wavelengths of all the colours. Red is the colour of raw physicality and primal urges. But at the other end of the spectrum, violet (which has a short and rapid wavelength) is the most 'spiritual' colour. Orange, meanwhile, is the colour of 'consciousness in the physical'. 'It is the first stage of awareness. While red represents blind instincts, orange is more social and elevated and involves conscious awareness of – and pleasure in – the body. With red, hunting, as a survival activity, is just killing and eating. With orange, the idea comes in that hunting and other survival necessities are better if they're done by people in partnership, or as a group. With red, sex is primal. It's just for procreating. With orange, sex is for pleasure and feelings.'

Hence Gullit, Goethe, orgies, etc?

'Well, orange is a very sexual, sensuous colour. It likes to express itself through its body. But if it's an unhappy orange, it will be rather sleazy. One-night stands, not getting emotionally involved, that sort of thing.'

Dutch footballers are renowned for their craft and playful artistry. Dutch fans are famously sociable. Lloyd traces both to the colour but points out that thing can go wrong when orange is not 'centred'.

When orange feels good about itself, its qualities make them sociable, friendly gregarious. They like doing things communally. I would think orange players are more likely to pass the ball than play as individuals. They'll enjoy taking risks, being spontaneous and revelling in their sense of adventure. For others, taking risks is frightening, but for orange it's fun. Actually, I don't understand why all football teams don't wear orange.

Lloyd says orange 'likes to express itself. It's a very creative colour, the colour of artisan creativity. There's a dextrousness with the hands and feet, a very physical expression. You'd see this in football, but also, for example, pottery and other crafts. Blue, its opposite colour, is more about ideas and imagination, Ideally you need the two together.' Orange is also a very insightful colour. 'Like Buddhism, it goes deep within to find the "being" reason for things. It doesn't think about things philosophically; it just knows. Orange's base is in the belly, so it's about gut feelings, deciding from emotions, a gut knowing, and trusting that.' Orange is also the colour of communication with a physical connection. 'It's not just communication, it's about communicating your being, expressing yourself from your truth. And it's communication with a physical connection.'

What about the fans' Dionysian revelries? 'Orange is the colour of bliss, of true ecstasy. It's about the sheer joy of being, very fun-loving, humorous, playful, party-going, sometimes endless party-going.' But there can be a dark side.

> A lot of things about orange are to do with the tension between individuals and groups. If you're uncomfortable with your own centre, you'll look for it in groups. For example, if you had an unhappy childhood, you might look for approval from others. Maybe you'd do drugs, alcohol, be a workaholic or become part of a team. Orange likes to feel 'linked'.

And of course, the Orange carnival is not always totally benign. In football, there have been dark overtones to the festivities when Holland played Germany, though the countries have not played each other in a match of importance for nearly a decade. And on Queen's Day in 2001, riots involving tear gas and much damage erupted near Amsterdam's Central Station after the sheer weight of numbers persuaded panicked railway officials to stop running trains.

Lloyd explains:

> Orange is very into groups. If it's an unhappy, un-centred orange, they'll want to escape from themselves, into drugs, perhaps, or parties or team jollity. Dependency and co-dependency issues come up a lot: they need others to make them feel good. Phobias and obsessions can also arise both

of which are dependencies on things or people outside of their own selves. In extremis, this could be a tendency towards fascism also. Orange can be manic depressive, either utterly happy with themselves or catastrophically down and depressed. If they're depressed, it's because they feel unworthy and unhappy in themselves. They get stuck and can't see a way out, can't see how to make changes. There's fear too: fear about survival, about not making it.

A lot of baffling things about Dutch footballers — their amazing technique and creative passing; their weird weaknesses in penalty shoot-outs; their tendency to lose to less gifted opponents — suddenly make a lot more sense.

Uri Geller, the paranormalist and football fan, thinks there's a problem with the Dutch fans. 'Orange is a very powerful assertive colour and Dutch supporters make a lot of noise, but there is something dead in them. There's no life, no spirit. If they had the spirit then they'd start winning. Maybe it's in the psyche of the Dutch people.' Something of this was apparent in Rotterdam in the game against Denmark. Despite their terrific costumes, the Dutch fans were, to my English eyes, oddly passive. Before the game and for the first hour, as Bergkamp, Kluivert and co. struggled to break the determined Danish defence, it was the relatively tiny group of Danish fans in the stadium who were making almost all the noise. Apart from a smattering of Father Christmases, the Danish outfits were relatively unimaginative. But with their mass swaying, relentless singing and chanting they generated an emotional energy which completely eclipsed the orange hordes. Only when the Dutch scored the first of three quick goals did the balance shift.

Cultural commentator Paul Scheffer, one of Holland's most stimulating writers on questions of national identity, suggests this may be because most of the Dutch spectators are not really fans in the sense that we in Britain understand the concept: 'There's a rather placid atmosphere around the game for many. Bill Shankly said football was more important than life and death. Here football is a matter of beer and laughing.' When Scheffer went to the World Cup in Italy in 1990 and France in 1998 he formed the impression that many of the army of Dutch fans simply weren't too bothered about the football.

> You might think it's strange to go all that way and not care about the game, but the truth is that in the stadiums they sometimes hardly watched the match. They were busy drinking and singing and showing their costumes and having their carnival. In fact, when you ask the people in the most outrageous orange costumes if they go to league games in Holland, they say: no, never! It's just a big party for them. They combine the World Cup with a holiday, take the whole family. They enjoy it, but it has more to do with the

surroundings than with the game itself. It's just an occasion to have a nice collective experience.

Of course, there are also plenty in Holland who care passionately about the game, people who, for example, cannot bear to watch images of Holland's Euro 2000 failure against Italy. Scheffer is one of these. But, he says, such people are simply not in a majority, especially when it comes to the national team.

Football is so important these days that a lot of people want to be associated with it. But in the really passionate football countries like England, Italy and Germany, you see how fans get behind their team. You have hopeful singing – 'come on England' and that sort of thing. But here, if the Dutch team is 0–1 down, total silence. Even when they're 1–0 up sometimes it's quiet. I think people who really love football would never come up with the idea of dressing up the way we do. You don't see this kind of carnival in Italy because Italians are much too nervous about the game to dress up in silly costumes. It takes a lot of energy to dress up like that. No. The Italians will put on a shirt, or carry a flag or a scarf, but not more until the game is won. Then maybe you can have a carnival. But when the Dutch do it, I'm sure it's for the occasion, not the game.

Gawi Keijser, a South African-born writer who lives in Holland, argues the orange carnival nevertheless has some very positive effects. 'There is something magical about sport. Even in America, a sporting arena is where, even if only for a short time, all social and economic differences are put aside, even if it's only for the duration of the game.' He compares the 'oranging' of the Netherlands to the healing, multicultural 'Rainbow Nation' idea which, relatively briefly, swept Mandela's post-apartheid South Africa during and after the country's 1995 Rugby World Cup triumph.

Euro 2000 was like that for the Dutch. The Netherlands is going though a big identity crisis, partly because it is becoming a multicultural society and also because of the EU. But Euro 2000 was one of the few moments when one can talk of national identity. In Euro 2000 the orange was everywhere. It hurt your eyes to look at it. It was a symbol of national identity, an abstract symbol for unifying people.

But he agrees with Scheffer's diagnosis of lack of passion.

Supporters here are much more docile than in England. The Dutch aren't passionate. In Euro 2000, they had their nice orange costumes. They sang their songs, but when Holland lose it's not a national crisis. Losing to Italy was forgotten the next day. When South Africa loses in any sport, the nation is in shock for weeks. In England, people are much more passionate about football than people are here. You have a tradition of boys going to matches with their fathers, of caring passionately about their clubs. We don't have that in the same way.

So just why do the Dutch need their Orange Carnival? The noted historian and expert of Dutch medieval literature Professor Herman Pleij of the University of Amsterdam, argues that it fills a deep emotional and cultural need which has nothing to do with football. He says:

> The Dutch are very self-centred. They live in their house and their house is their castle. It is a very difficult, complicated thing to be allowed to enter the home of a Dutch family. People from other countries often complain about this. We need this orange to compensate. We need to be able to come together, to feel together because we are also human. We need this kind of expression, this ritual expression of being members of the same family. And that's what we do with orange in sport and other festivals. It's an excuse for a party, for dressing up, for wearing funny clothes.

In the affluent, secularised, post-Calvinist, aprés-'60s Dutch cultural landscape the old ideologies have died and older traditions and rituals have been discarded.

> In the Netherlands, every group in society – the Catholics, the Protestants, the socialists, and so on – all used to have their own rituals. But this all disappeared in the '60s and '70s. There are no rituals left. But a society needs rituals to express feelings. There is a general lack in the Netherlands of feelings of togetherness. So we compensate for this with sport.

In Amsterdam it became popular to refer to the Ajax stars as *godenzonen* (sons of God). Only a generation or two ago, such talk would probably have been considered blasphemous by most in the Netherlands. And this adoration of sportsmen is all the more strange in a country where almost no other kind of hero worship is considered acceptable. But times have changed. Pleij says:

> We laugh at traditions in the Netherlands, and we do not look very much to the past. In fact, we laugh at heroes, so we have no national heroes. Sports heroes are the only heroes we are prepared to like because we think of them as normal boys and girls from next door. We like them to be simple. We pat them on the back, we praise them. But their careers are very short and, when they come back, they seem just like us. These are our only heroes and we

worship them in a very exaggerated way. It is a compensation for the lack of these kind of rituals elsewhere in our lives.

Although orange is notionally a royal symbol and Queen Beatrix is strikingly popular compared to her British counterpart, Pleij points out that current 'orangism' has little to do with the House of Orange. 'It's certainly not a worshipping of the royal house. We use the Queen and the royal family for something far more important.' Festive orangism, which started slowly in the '70s and '80s with football and seems to grow in intensity each year, has spread to other sports and has simply re-attached itself to royalty.

> Queen's Day is not a monarchist feast, not about loving the queen. We use the monarchy as an excuse. The orange carnival allows us to behave as if we are one big family, shouting, having fun, feeling that we share many things. There is a growing need to express these feelings of togetherness.

Meanwhile, Paul Scheffer is amused and slightly baffled that the Dutch have managed to convince the world – and themselves – that they are a perpetually fun-loving, tolerant people with a Mediterranean carnival sensibility. 'It's like the rather astonishing way Amsterdam is called the Venice of the North. Perhaps we are the Venice of the North, but we are certainly not the Brazilians of the North, although many people seem to think that we are, because we indulge in carnivalesque behaviour once in a while. Contrary to popular myth, he insists Holland actually has a 'rather boring, Swiss kind of society' as well as a prodigiously efficient workforce. 'Of course we are not completely Swiss or Swedish. But we do have rather disciplined and organised aspects.' He also challenges the popular image of Holland as a uniquely tolerant and relaxed society.

> I find that people much prefer to stick to looking at the surface. The image and message we convey to the outside world is that we are completely easy-going. When people think of Amsterdam, they think of our downtrodden 'coffee shops' where you can buy many things but not coffee. They think we are very tolerant and multicultural. But Dutch tolerance was developed in order to keep the peace, to avoid trouble. It has never been a laissez-faire tolerance. The Netherlands I know is a rather disciplined, conformist, society where everything tends towards the centre. Our tolerance is always in the context of something highly organised and on the theme of conflict avoidance. Tolerance is always in the name of consensus building. Dutch culture is about being separate from each other. We created cultural difference and separation where physical separation was not available. We should not confuse this tradition with the image of a free-floating, carnivalesque, open-minded society. Of course, the image is part of the reality too. But it's only a small part.

Meanwhile, the very extremity of the Orange Carnival reveals that it is more likely to be a way for the Dutch to let off steam than be evidence of an essentially freewheeling, fun-loving lifestyle.

> We live a rather orderly, nine-to-five life. Why are our roads completely full of cars between 7.30 and 9 a.m. and between 4.30 and 6 p.m.? Perhaps the carnival is an escape from our society rather than a symbol of it. Isn't carnival always like that? In Catholic countries, everything is very proper and serious, but for two days of carnival, everything explodes. and then things go back to how it was before. In Holland, we have our Calvinist Carnival. And it is more of an interruption of the flow of daily life than a continuous flowing thing which has deep roots in the way we live. The truth is that many aspects of Dutch life are more grey than orange.

LE FRANCAIS FEEL-GOOD FACTOR

Patrick Mignon

France has changed. The French people are more glad than ever before to be French according to a summer 2000 opinion poll published in *Le Journal du Dimanche*, the main French Sunday paper. A special issue of *Time* (12 June, 2000) praised 'a French renaissance' showing a country more economically dynamic, more confident in itself, culturally more open.

A number of reasons have been offered to explain both these changes in French society and how France is viewed overseas. It could be the success of Lionel Jospin's government's economic policy, France benefiting more than its neighbours from European integration or the result of three decades of improving living standards. Or why not the victories in the 1998 World Cup and Euro 2000? For France are champions at the sport and their dominant global media profile is unquestionable, with a team only Brazil can rival for cultural diversity.

For the French the team symbolises a progression towards a multicultural society, representing different waves of immigrants, each increasingly able to express themselves in different parts of the national popular culture. In the January 2000 annual poll of *Le Journal du Dimanche*, Zinedine Zidane was voted by readers as their most popular French personality, while at the same time numerous surveys have recorded increasing levels of tolerance by the French people towards immigrants, and a corresponding decline in racist attitudes.

It has therefore become increasingly difficult to divorce France's achievements on the football pitch from how these are used to explain a broader French 'feel-good factor'. But these positive changes often have a complicated pre-history, including decisions being taken as to where the stadia would be located in which France would eventually celebrate its World Cup victory.

Having secured the hosting of the Championships one of the key issues for the French tournament organisers, and especially when deciding to build the Stade de France in Saint-Denis, was the '*banlieues* issue'. *Banlieues* or suburbs are the areas on the edge of the big cities like Paris, Lyon, Lille or Strasbourg; some are wealthy, where since the nineteenth century the affluent have sought fresh air and an escape from urban promiscuity. But most of them are working-class or lower-middle-class areas, organised around factories and providing cheaper or more modern flats than in the inner city. Following 1960s urban growth and more recently de-industrialisation, these *banlieues* have become the symbol of economic, social and cultural decline and disconnection. The city of Saint-Denis is the heart of one of the most deprived areas in France, with high unemployment, the lowest average family income for the whole Paris area and record levels of delinquency. The local youth predominantly have low, or no, educational qualifications and the schools have the worst exam records. The area also has a substantial immigrant population. The siting of Stade de France in Saint-Denis was all about urban regeneration, but the victory, with the huge crowd on Champs-Elysées has been seen also as a sign of cultural regeneration: a multi-ethnic crowd celebrating the multi-ethnic team of a multi-ethnic France. 'La France blacks, blancs, beurs' as it was chanted: a France made up of people of African or West Indian, European and North African (*Beurs*) origins.

In reality, the French multicultural squad of 1998 was not such a new phenomenon. The line-up was just like previous French teams which ever since the 1930s had also been made up of players of different origins: Polish (Kopa); Moroccan (Ben Barek, Ben Tifour); Italian (Piantoni, Platini); Algerian (Mekloufi); Spanish (Amoros or Fernandez); Romania (Kovacs, the national coach of the early 1970s). Though now the team includes those of Portuguese (Pires); Algerian (Zidane); Tunisian (Lamouchi); Senegal (Ba or Vieira) and Ghanaian (Desailly) origins and also, of course, all the players coming from the French Antilles – Henry, Anelka, Wiltord and Thuram. The same levels of multiracial representation have for a long time been a feature of French athletics and boxing, or more recently in basketball. Former colonies, and different waves of immigrants have permanently transformed the face of French sport.

In part, this is a result of the principles of republican universalism which state that anyone is French who is born in France. This linked to the values of meritocracy, or republican elitism, which declare that anyone who has all the qualities required to improve themselves, provided they work hard or study to improve their various skills, should be able to improve their status in society. This is supposed to apply equally to education, careers and indeed sport. Some coaches, some fans, may think that black players are lazy, too individualistic or no good on a freezing winter's night, but the bulk of the managerial and coaching staff, and the vast majority of the supporters think that players can learn, improve themselves, dedicate themselves to their club or country's trophy-winning ambitions, whatever their colour or their origins.

According to the French ideals of republican integration, the State plays a vital role. Schools are mainly State owned or controlled. It's not very different in sport. Football's youth training system, set up during the '70s, is the new space where republican integration is carried out while republican elitism, the pursuit of excellence and equality, is celebrated with victories in international competition. For most of the twentieth century French republican law ensured that it is the State that is responsible for the improvement of the general well-being of citizens and for efforts to integrate all citizens into the nation. One law dating back to the 1920s obliges local authorities to offer sporting recreational facilities. While during the government of the Front Populaire in 1936–37, when the SFIO, the Socialist party, came to power, numerous stadiums were built and subsidies given to various sporting associations. In the early years of football professionalism, club presidents were instructed by their new governing body to ask the local authorities for finance to assist the local team in addition to any money that came from rich benefactors. During the 1960s, sports policy became an integral part of the Welfare State and was also aimed at gaining international success and prestige: sporting glory at the highest level and nuclear weapons were President De Gaulle's two central visions of national independence. To start with, the policy was mainly directed towards the Olympic Games, and therefore amateur sports like athletics or swimming, but gradually it encompassed football too.

The result was the State's intervention in the 1970s reorganisation of French football. In the 1950s, the French government had already created a category of civil servants known as the 'directeurs techniques nationaux' (DTN) to help sports' governing bodies develop their organisational infrastructures. This system included all sports, even professional ones, in the name of establishing a public service ethos within sport which was transferred from the State to the sports' federations. Consequently, sporting governing bodies represent a balance of power between individual clubs and the State. The DTN is the guarantor of good sporting development, nationally and internationally, while sports federations obtain State funding in proportion to their number of members and success in international competitions. In football, this public intervention led to incentives, in 1968, to organise new rules for players' transfers and contacts, the overseeing of coaches' qualifications, new cup competitions, the compulsory creation of training centres in every professional football club and the formation of a national football institute. All these reforms are the source of French football's current success and can be seen as an expression of the republican tradition where the State works for national prestige and social cohesion. For many members of the French government, the victory in the World Cup was also the victory of the French model of public services of policing, public transportation and urban policy. In contrast, the joy at winning the World Cup among a substantial part of the French population answered a fear that their principles of integration were failing in education, employment and the major cities, but at least it could still be said to be working well enough to become world champions at football.

Historically, in France, as in England, football players from immigrant communities excelled because, for them, the usual access to social mobility, through school and work, were closed. And in France sporting achievement was of no great concern, or status, for the French. In the '50s, Kopa became a professional player because, as a young Polish miner, he was not allowed to apply to further education to become an electrician. So he chose football to leave the mines. But for the majority of the French, football was no way to improve their social situation: between the wars and certainly until the '60s and '70s, they could become workers, employees or civil servants whether they were peasants, skilled workers or if they came from the unskilled working class. Football could be only a leisure activity for these workers, not a career, but for those from the new communities it was a chance to establish themselves.

What these players gave an earlier era of French football was the will to succeed and the desire to be recognised. Things changed slightly with the end of the '70s because sport in general became part of an explicit policy to achieve national success in big international competitions. But in football, the youth training schemes which have produced so many young gifted players continue to attract disproportionately the children of immigrant families because they are encountering more and more problems elsewhere in the education system. Problems which suggest issues of integration exist uneasily beside broader attitudes founded on discrimination. In France today, there is unquestionably a relationship between low expectations of achievement in school exams and high achievement, and correspondingly increased investment of time and effort, in football.

So how really satisfying is France's footballing feel-good factor? Amongst the crowds celebrating on the Champs-Elysées or those who watched the victories on the television different understandings coexisted of what the victory of the French team meant, along with different understandings of what France itself means. And what do we make of those who didn't join in the celebrations? They might have been grumbling about the players' high wages, or complaining there were too many Arabs or blacks in the team. These contradictory sets of feelings – celebration and alienation, are felt because football in France cannot be separated from the Republican State. Football, and politics, are both affected by the same crisis, they are indivisible.

For French football, one positive aspect has been the transformation of the Parc des Princes' Paris Saint Germain (PSG) crowd. Fifteen years ago, the Boulogne's end of the stadium, the 'Boulogne's *Kop*', was the territory of skinheads and racist supporters and the ordinary spectators at Parc des Princes were not typical of the population of Greater Paris. It was a mainly white – though immigrant – crowd, those who had been through an earlier phase of French integration. A lot of them were French Jews who had returned to France after the Algerian war and Tunisian independence in the

'60s and some of them had been involved in the birth of the club in the early '70s. There were Spanish and Portuguese and there was also a significant group of people from Martinique or Guadeloupe who have always considered Paris as their town. But there were no Maghrebians, no Africans, no young people from the younger generations of immigrants; in the suburbs, black youths wore Marseille's kits instead of PSG's. Today, it is different: PSG's kits are worn everywhere in the suburbs and the crowd is much closer to the composition of Paris. More young blacks and *Beurs* take part in this urban sporting culture. Part of the city of Paris – its football club – is becoming theirs. What is happening in football is also happening in music and film. Although the process is slower than in Britain or the United States, because the French idea of republican integration favours cultural universalism, and in Britain and the USA the importance of 'difference' which is central to multiculturalism is undervalued. Black immigrants may make a huge contribution to France's footballing victories but the real success of integration will be when judges, teachers, policemen, lawyers and journalists include a good proportion of young blacks in their numbers. This would mean that education, from the primary school to the university campus, had begun again to recreate routes to social mobility. France is not an idyllic, meritocratic republican society, and unity around the national team should not obscure the fact that many of our citizens, those the same colour and origins of many of our footballing heroes, remain excluded and discriminated against.

Why? Racism. The National Front (FN) has become, since 1980, one of the major political parties with FN Leader Jean-Marie Le Pen receiving 15 per cent of the vote in the presidential elections of 1995. Has the victory of Les Bleus substantially changed this situation? During the World Cup, Jean-Marie Le Pen made a speech stating that France could not be represented by coloured or foreign players, that the multi-ethnic team was a symbol of the decay of the true France. This speech was seen as a political mistake because of the increasing enthusiasm created by Les Bleus as the championship went on. The result of the competition, the crowd itself, and then the numerous polls showing the optimism of the French people and the splitting of the National Front into two parts, all seemed to mean that France had rid itself of at least the ugliest side of racism. But as the March 2001 local elections showed, the National Front and other far-right groups still appear attractive for a sizeable proportion of the electorate. In some areas, their candidates got more than 30 per cent of votes and several big towns in the South East of France still have far-right mayors. This support is especially strong amongst the unskilled, unemployed and socially excluded; those *petit* whites who lived in deprived *banlieues* close to large immigrant communities. And this support isn't restricted to older voters; it is also present among the under-thirties. It is also important to take note of the falling number of those bothering to vote. The turnout in the 2001 local elections was barely 60 per cent, another sign of the lack of faith amongst the most excluded and of a move towards traditional political values and a general feeling that there is a widening gap between those who have and those who have not. For the excluded Zidane or Henry represent those who have. For these non-voters, as for a proportion of Le Pen's voters, what motivation they might have is less focussed on race than on a personal sense of insecurity, based on not being noticed, by anyone. This prevents any sort of positive recognition of changes in French society, including progress towards multiculturalism.

Social and cultural exclusion is part of the experience of Black and *Beur* youth. After the World Cup and Euro 2000, there were several urban riots. Some of these were caused by police racism and violence; others by discrimination in school, in the neighbourhood or the workplace. Laws passed by the last right-wing government in 1995, have made it more difficult for immigrants to obtain French nationality. At the same time rising levels of unemployment have made integration more difficult. A general trend towards the demand for cultural identity has made African or Algerian youth more aware of how French universalism can undervalue, or discriminate. Football has in this context become a powerfully effective means of expressing the tension in French society about the way we define our national identity. This tension is most acute in the poorest parts of the big cities where the State, which was once the guarantor of integration, has less and less of a presence. The divisions around identity are made visible by the national football kits many in these localities choose to wear, or by the flags they wave. During the World Cup, in the first stage of the competition, youths in the suburbs wore the football kits of their origins: Portugal, Cameroon, Morocco – even Algeria who hadn't qualified. On the day of the final, Brazil's shirt was almost as popular as the French one among black and *Beurs* youngsters as an act of rebellion, and since 1998 Algeria's kit has seen more and more of a public presence.

For these young people from the *banlieues* neither Les Bleus, nor the Stade de France are seen as theirs. But as football is also part of their daily life, it remains a sign of hope of social mobility. Zidane is for them less a model of republican integration than a model of individual success.

Football is, undoubtedly, the most popular sport in France. It is played, according to the 2000 survey on sport and physical activities in France, more or less regularly by almost five million people. It has enjoyed this popular support for a long time but has always lacked the passion and excess that the sport has seen in England or Italy because the most intense local cultures preferred rugby; because of an enduring rural and provincial social geography which scattered football supporters in a mass of villages and small towns; and because an individual sport like cycling was more in touch with our sense of individual endeavour. And so French football crowds have always been smaller than in other European countries. No city has been able to support two teams and the ends occupied now by the *Ultras* seem empty compared to the *Kops* and curves elsewhere, and the French police could always testify that French hooligans were far easier to control than their foreign counterparts.

But French football has been enjoying increasing crowd attendances since the late '80s. During the 1987–88 season, it recorded the best attendance figures since the previous record, the 1950–51 season, with an average attendance of 12,000. In 1999–2000, the attendance reached new record levels with an average of 22,000 spectators per game – still below the German or English figures but French club teams now play to 50 to 80 per cent of their stadium's capacity and season-ticket holders are on the increase: 150,000 in 1998–99 rising to 211,000 in 2000–01.

The transformation of the crowds is also qualitative: the fans have showed a renewed passion in getting behind their teams. During the '70s, with the success in European competitions of Saint-Etienne, Bastia and Lens, France discovered noisy, passionate and partisan supporters, complete with their scarves, their chants and their banners. For most French people, this seemed to be the demonstration of an old France, the traditional working-class culture of miners in Saint-Etienne or Lens, or the normal eccentricity of the Corsican people, not a sign of the deeper changes a more metropolitan France felt more comfortable with and actively championed. Now, fans are returning to support French clubs because there is an improved level of football being played and because they are settled inhabitants of the major cities. Today in France identities of locality have a significance that once only politics enjoyed – right versus left, republican versus catholic – and so football has become a natural vehicle for this changing focus for loyalty. Collective and individual identities are being produced across French society in new forms, no longer defined simply by politics. Football fandom is just one sign of this change.

In terms of French fan culture itself, there are two kinds of supporters. The *'hools'* or *'independents'*, as they name themselves, influenced by the 1970s wave of English hooliganism and the Germans – and the *Ultras*, influenced by Italy. For a period, till the mid-'80s, there was a clear difference between Northern France, where the *'Kops'* could be found, faithful to what we know as an English style of football supporters, wearing club colours and chanting – and the South where huge flags were displayed, crowd choreography was set up and supporters were organised in groups. More recently, the tendency towards Italianization has been evident everywhere in France, but two sensibilities remain; one which is supposed to be more sober and internalised and the other more outgoing and more organised. Disorderly supporters can be found in both categories, but the mechanisms which drive some to violence are different.

At the end of the '70s and the beginning of the '80s, groups of supporters drawing their inspiration from British fan subcultures were seen in France organising themselves in the ends, traditionally called *virages* (curves), of the football stadiums, that they now christened *Kops*. These supporters, from Paris, Lille or Le Havre were well-versed in the English football and pop music learnt from their trips to London, where they appreciated the atmosphere of the stadiums, the pubs and the music venues they visited. This importing of British cultural goods is not new; the Beatles had been popular in France in the '60s. But during this later period, between 1975 and '80, the more significant exchange involved entire subcultures rather than simply the same bands topping the charts on both sides of the Channel. British rhythm-and- blues, pub rock and punk in turn became French music and influenced street fashion styles not only among a significant minority of young French people, but also amongst the country's football hooligans.

The development of these subcultures took place mainly in the bigger cities like Paris or Lille, with their large numbers of students and their attendant networks of cultural go-betweens. Thus it was in these two cities that the first skinhead and hooligan scenes appeared. It was in Paris that the adaptation of British subcultures coincided with the formation of PSG. Founded only in 1973, the club was desperately looking for supporters to fill the stands and this situation lasted till the mid '90s. But, during the 1978–79 and 1979–80 seasons, the club took a decision which has proved very important for Parisian fan culture. They offered very low ticket prices to attract young people: ten francs (one pound) for ten games (in 2001 the average price for a ticket to a *single* game is sixty francs). The result was that more and more young Parisian football fans eager to watch good football and to support a team of their own began to go regularly to the Parc des Princes, especially in the Boulogne curve which was christened 'Kop de Boulogne'. Also the club's initiative gave the new skinhead subcultures the opportunity to access a new status: it gave them a means of ensuring themselves the street credibility necessary in the stands to attract and to repel while imitating their Millwall, West Ham or Chelsea models. The first domestic hooligan incidents, outside of those provoked by English visitors, occurred from the 1978–79 season onwards, with flaunting the far-right symbol of a Celtic cross, Nazi saluting, chanting 'France for the French', and after the game chasing Arabs and blacks (more often than opposing supporters). These have all become regular routines at the Parc des Princes. Very quickly, and especially after the 1985 Heysel Stadium incident, these events attracted the media's attention and led to the erection of fences around the ground, the mobilisation of huge numbers of policemen and the implementation of specific laws against hooliganism. During the '80s, the skinheads became 'casuals', and now they are 'hools' or sometimes self-styled 'independents', accusing other supporters of being under the control of their clubs. What distinguishes them from other supporters is their special mix of extreme-right ideas, generalised support for racism and the affiliation of some of the fan-leaders to fascist organisations – but above all it is the taste for violence and for disorder, and the feeling of power created by their capacity to create disorder.

The most obvious difference between the 'hools' and the *Ultras* is the show the *Ultras* put on at every match, with orchestrated chants throughout the game, huge flags, choreography and pyrotechnic displays. The *Ultras* are organised. They have the whole week to prepare the show and there is a division of labour among the members. They have an official name, officially declared with a status, a president, a treasurer, and a secretary. They negotiate with the clubs, but also sometimes, as they did in Marseilles or Saint-Etienne, with the local authorities. Organisation is, for them, necessary and necessarily visible. They differ from the Kops' spirit, for whom the spontaneity is what matters, and the image of the mob or of the horde is all that is promoted.

The *Ultras* first appeared in the mid-'80s. One of the reasons for their success is that their model of action is spectacular; visible without necessarily being violent. Everybody can contribute something to the show during the game or the preparation in the week beforehand. And 'doing something' provides the content for a fan culture which, without the mass attendance of the English model, could never have acquired the shared meanings or common uses which basically define a culture. For during the development of French fan culture in the '70s and '80s, there weren't the massive crowds who were able to chant songs drawn from a long local, popular tradition, renewed by successive generations of football fans. Hooliganism is a form of competition between supporters, often attracting attention away from the game. This is the same for the *Ultras*, but theirs is a competition with more and more sophisticated effects – invariably visual – to react to. This is a realisation of the idea that being a supporter has became an end in itself; the fans' contribution to the match becomes as valid as the players'. Unity becomes very important to the *Ultras*, nothing must get in the way of them making the most effective contribution to the spectacle in the stands. In France this often means fans from left-wing and right-wing backgrounds working closely together in the same *Ultras* association. But, with the exception of those in Marseilles and to a much lesser extent in Lyon and Paris, *Ultras* are white, and their motivation is based on the experience of the 'poor, white suburban guy' who feels excluded by the evolution of society in general and football in particular.

The *Ultras* are not necessarily violent but they are a threatening presence. They are noisy and aggressive, and they don't bother much with the niceties, and the regulations, that govern crowd safety. They let off fireworks where they're not supposed to, and involve hundreds, sometimes thousands, in crowd choreography when the stadium authorities prefer fans just to sit and watch. The *Ultras* seek to influence decisions concerning their club. They criticise, organise and campaign, and are a type of protest movement. But they also seek to dominate their space at the stadium, in competition with *Ultras* from other clubs, and sometimes with rival *Ultras* from their own club. A similar competition over the control of space goes on in the streets surrounding the stadium. With each *Ultra* association building up a heritage of symbols, memories, and sometimes a financial investment in their enduring dominance too, the opportunities for tension, disorder and violence are obvious. The violence and criminal activity become part of the process of 'doing something together', producing memories and proof that the group still matters, in the process increasing the appeal of the *Ultras* to young men.

A fan culture certainly now exists in France. *Ultras*, their associations and their power to attract those who want to do something, have been playing an increasingly significant role. But there are others forms of fan cultures too, uniting both younger and older supporters. Often these are 'official' associations because they are integrated into the network of the clubs. Currently there are at least two supporters' associations at each professional football club. In the First Division, it is not uncommon for one club to have five or six associations. In Marseilles, there are ten or eleven and there are fifteen at PSG. The numbers and size of their memberships are constantly changing, depending on the clubs' results, any splits in the associations, and their various leaders retiring. Some of the bigger associations, at Lens and at other clubs where the *Ultras* have less of a presence, can bring together 6–7,000 members.

At Marseilles, *Ultras* account for 20,000 at a game and 15,000 at PSG. Because of their clubs' reputation, they each draw on a network of supporters to be found all over France. The organised strength of these supporters means that in the bigger clubs they represent almost a quarter of the attendance and the majority of supporters who travel away with their club. In total, in '*Ultras*' associations, there are 50,000 registered (paying their membership to an association) fans while a further 150,000 fans are involved in the *Ultras*' activities. Hardcore hools' number about 100 at PSG; about 50 at Lyon, Strasbourg, Lille and Saint-Etienne, and even fewer around clubs like Cannes or Nice. But the development of this fan culture has been rapid; it really only began to take any sort of shape in the early 1990s and the consequences for crowd disorder remain difficult to predict.

Why have attendances at football grown, and an attendant fan culture developed, since the 1990s? France has become an urban society. Those living in and around French cities (and before, this really only applied to Paris) think of themselves as living in the city, rather than identifying with their rural origins. Coupled with this is the rediscovery of local and regional identities, a process accelerated by broader tendencies towards political and social fragmentation. In politics, decentralisation, which started in 1982, has given much more power to local authorities and especially to the mayors of big cities. In economics, cities are increasingly in competition with each other to attract investments and a young, skilled workforce. For all these reasons, mayors and urban entrepreneurs have been very keen to help their local football club in order to give their city or region a profile that few other similar endeavours could provide.

The suburbanisation of the big cities means that the mechanisms of social integration have changed. Football, aided by local authorities and investors, has helped reinforce a sense of local pride, providing a means to participate in a shared routine, symbolised by spatial mobility within the big new metropolis. It means that allegiance to a club becomes a legitimate means of self-definition because of the competition between cities for economic growth, because of the competition between social and ethnic groups, and because trade unions and political parties are no longer in the position to express discontent or to share a vision of the future. To have our own space in a football stadium means being able to meet people, share the same social experience, have a good time together, fix regular meetings and mark out the week and places to go. For many, becoming a football fan creates a framework through which we can express, and give form to, emotions and needs which otherwise we might struggle to fulfil.

For a new generation of supporters, becoming, and remaining, a football fan is a product of the prolonging of this period in our lives called post-adolescence. The time we are likely to spend in some form of training, or in further or higher education is lengthening, and it is in these years that most of us become active fans. As the difficulties of finding a steady job grow and the refusal to 'settle down' mounts, the alternative attractions of football grow. Post-adolescence is linked also to the lightening of social constraints and to the increasing prevalence of youth values divorced from those of the adult world. These processes have meant that during the 1970s and '80s the experience of French youth had an increasing commonality with those of British and German youth. Social vacancy and mass popular youth cultures became international phenomena. During these two decades young people escaped from the strict controls of school and family, and a model of socialisation founded on identifying with the parental model was replaced by a model based on experimentation. For the young working-class male, as for the middle-class student, to be young no longer meant adhering to a course set by their parents' social position. Their ambition was no longer simply to reproduce their parents' careers, status and morality. Instead they increasingly sought a satisfactory definition of 'self' for themselves, with peer groups rather than parents as the key reference point. Fan culture is an example of the importance of peer groups in the socialisation of youth and the importance of the recognition of individuals' values by members of the peer groups and not by other adults.

In this context, mass popular culture (football for some; music, fashion, film and the like for others), has become an element of a shared experience and it provides a field to do this. Being a supporter, and for some being a disorderly supporter, is one of the ways to build a presence in society through anti-institutional attitudes. It constitutes a field of self-discovery and offers a space for experimentation through a search for differentiation and inclusion in something wider; a cause or a movement in which supporters can participate, with the young and true against the old and tame. Sometimes, the roles which are learnt within a fan culture can lead to to the acquisition of socially useful skills, like learning to manage groups, negotiation, enterpreneurship, as well as the experience of travelling across France and going abroad, participating in national and international networks. Being a fan provides the opportunity to develop status, and a reputation. Hooliganism and violence remain very much a minority experience for these fans.

What hooliganism does exist is almost exclusively at a club level, and not associated at all with the national team's support. For many fans the parochial appeal of following their club is quite sufficient but supporting the national team holds no special appeal. For *Ultras* and the 'hools' what motivates them in their different ways is their club loyalty. For some traditional fans the national team's supporters aren't 'real' enough, and for others supporting the national team is too close to supporting the idea of a multicultural France for their ideological comfort. Historically, there is no tradition of strong support for the French national team at international tournaments. No fans followed the French team to the 1958 World Cup in Sweden, nor to the 1982 World Cup in Spain. Hardly any supporters travelled to Euro '96, except the usual VIPs and football governing body representatives. Support hadn't even grown after the team's brilliantly thrilling performances at the 1982 and 1986 World Cups – nor following their lifting of the European title in 1984. The fans' enthusiasm had instead always been for their clubs: Reims in the '50s and '60s, then Saint-Etienne in '70s and latterly Marseilles. These clubs were seen as national representatives, a substitute for what were mediocre national teams. This took decades to change, notwithstanding the national team's improvements in the 1980s – followed though by the failure to qualify for the 1990 and '94 World Cups. It was only during the latter stages of the '98 World Cup that support started slowly to change from curiosity to the very real enthusiasm at the semi-finals and of course the national celebration that final victory turned into. It is as if football only acquires a formidable attraction when it reflects a key component of our republican values, the universal strength of the nation.

Today we have two football cultures in France. The fan culture which exists behind the clubs, with *Ultras* and some hooligans as their most spectacular and risky representatives; and the national team culture made up of the members of a broader footballing audience, favoured by those who give the sport its money, its sponsors, and those sponsors want to attract, the family and the female fans. But support for the national team is also in front of TV sets, in the bars and cafés, in town squares, homes and in the classrooms. France's international games attract a younger and more female audience, different from those who go to the live games or follow the Champions' Leagues. And here amongst this broader support, the diversity of cultural origins of the young fans matches the diversity of the players' cultural origins: Henry, Trezeguet and Desailly are pin-up characters competing for young girls' and boys' affections with rap bands like NTM or IAM (two of the major names on the French rap scene). Football players are now a key attraction for many of the young who find that something appeals to them in black culture. In the bars and workshops amongst the older fans, (except for those who are deeply racist) these young players prove that to be French you have only to show that you have worked hard and you are part of a team.

In this cultural landscape, Zinedine Zidane is pre-eminent. Like Pelé, his talent is indisputable. But he is also today the critical element in the multicultural symbol that the French national team has been turned into. Zidane represents the major line of division in French society: the contested status of people from North African origins and Muslims, but also old enemies from the 1954–62 Algerian war. For many he is the positive sign of the history of the relationships between Algeria and France: modest, hardworking, simply the best result of 150 years of interaction between France and Algeria. The negative sign is that Zidane is the only one of his kind in the team; Benarbia or Belmadi play with the Algerian team, although they were born in France. We have to wait for new players from Maghrebian roots who might ensure France a North African immigrant following. But this won't prevent the double allegiances we have already seen during the World Cup: Players playing for Cameroon, Tunisia or Portugal first, *then* France and so on. In May 2001, France, with Robert Pires of Portuguese origins, played against Portugal. Almost half of the Stade de France was Portuguese. In this case, double allegiance was not a problem for the media or public opinion. There are lots of French–Portuguese families, Portugal is in the EU, youths with Portuguese origins are not seen as a major social problem and French people have the same feelings towards Portugal as they would towards the Belgians or the British, or other European neighbours. But with Algeria it is different; the double allegiance is not so easily tolerated, understood and integrated within the national culture. Instead it is a source of discrimination, criminalisation and social division.

The 1998 World Cup said a lot about the state of French society. Far from a naive optimism which might make us think that all social ills could be solved thanks to a victory on the pitch, or that a multicultural team sealed the success of the French way of integrating cultural diversities, it showed simply that football in particular, and sport in general, has become more important than ever before in France. And by becoming so important football becomes a tool to help us to analyse, understand and to deal with – though not solve – many of our social divisions. But even this more modest achievement is not so readily accepted by all the French. For the ideas of republican universalism consigned sport to the role of a minor leisure activity, something which was good to strengthen the body and teach basic moral values but was of far less importance than high culture and politics. This attitude has helped frame not only an instrumental role for sport by our political elites, but also a contemptuous attitude to sport from radical intellectuals and academics who see sport – above all football and cycling – as a new opium of the people. Thinkers such as Jean Marie Brohm, a latter-day representative of the 'Frankfurt School' of critical theory, Robert Redeker, editor of *Les Temps Modernes*, the journal created by Jean-Paul Sartre, and others have written, before and after the World Cup, articles denouncing the 'cretinisation and depolitisation of the masses' by sport. They fail to see that our passion for sport and events like the European Championships or France lifting the World Cup are more complex than they like to think. Albert Camus, when he wrote that ' all that I know most surely about morality and obligations, I owe to football', was not claiming that football itself was moral but that it helped him to discuss moral issues. When we learn that the French philosopher Jacques Derrida dreamt of becoming a professional footballer when he was a boy, and remains a dedicated fan, we can reasonably imagine that his love for the game might help him to think through the limits, rules and the status of metaphysics. We can disagree with Jean Paul Sartre when he wrote in his *Critique of Dialectical Reason* that 'in football everything is complicated by the presence of the opposite team', because this exposes a peculiar conception by Sartre of otherness but it helps us to think of this otherness in quite different contexts from the ones we are used to, either as academics or football fans. And this works in the same way again and again through our ordinary experiences as supporters: football helps us to think about fate and chance, fairness and unfairness, offence and punishment, the individual and the collective, the local and the global, the particular and the universal. Being a fan is for us a way to take part in society, a position with which to express our point of view. It is another way to make politics. Some French intellectuals, sadly, have a nostalgic longing for their previous moral pre-eminence and find it difficult to come to terms with the fact that today for many French citizens, there is depth, thought and hope in what is 'only a game'. They simply don't understand how those who experienced that night on 12 July 1998 at the Champs-Elysées were part of a peaceful and joyous crowd, which became a space – duplicated all over France – where we no longer feared one another, where we were no longer alone. And in that moment – however partial or temporary we glimpsed at least the potential of a new society. On top of winning the World Cup, what a way to spend an evening.

HERE TO STAY WITH ST PAULI

René Martens

St Pauli has become a legend, but in a very different way and in a much shorter time than is normal in football. Other legendary clubs depend for their reputation on at least one footballer who becomes an icon by virtue of his skill or the character of his career, or by the club winning several championships – and in both cases it will take the club decades to create a legend which helps them to survive their lean spells. The most legendary clubs in German football, 1. FC Nürnberg and Schalke 04, achieved their status when they won nine and seven league championships respectively, mainly between 1920 and 1940. St Pauli needed only five years to become a legend, and its greatest achievement in that time, still unsurpassed, was a lowly tenth place in Germany's first division, the Bundesliga, during the 1988–89 season.

St Pauli's reputation is almost all due to the club's supporters, which is puzzling as St Pauli, during the 1960s and '70s, could only boast a hard core of around 3,000 supporters – and by the early 1980s not even this modest figure. But from 1986 onwards, at the club's ground, Millerntor, a new group of supporters became obvious, who began to combine their enthusiasm for the passionate and impetuous style of the team with left-wing politics, even turning this into a symbol of the club. The supporters developed a completely new conception of themselves as fans. They initiated anti-racist campaigns, debated the political aspects of football and began to get involved in the running of the club. In the summer of 1989, these new supporters founded *Millerntor Roar!* (*MR!*), the first anti-fascist and anti-corporate German fanzine. With their leaflets they called upon fans to take up the fight against racism in the stadiums and even convinced the team of St Pauli to support this. In the autumn of 1991, *MR!* were largely responsible for St Pauli becoming the first German club to adopt rules which banned supporters' racist chants or banners in the stadium. And in 1992, anti-fascist demonstrations in Hamburg were organised to follow immediately after St Pauli home games.

All this activity attracted more and more supporters who, until then, had felt excluded from football because of the anti-social attitudes that had become associated with it. Opposition to the anti-racist and anti-fascist campaigns was only expressed by a few unorganised individuals who preferred to keep politics out of football. 'Politics in our stadium? No thanks!' was, for instance, towards the end of 1990, a poster fixed to some trees around Millerntor. *MR!* responded, declaring that football was 'as apolitical as the production of an atomic bomb'.

St Pauli's traditional supporters, comprising until the mid-1970s quite a few workers from the harbour nearby, were too few to provoke a conflict between old and new fans. So, at Millerntor, the new combination of football with left-wing politics faced little or no opposition. It was not the same elsewhere: St Pauli and its supporters have, since the late 1980s, become hate figures for far-right supporters and hooligans from other clubs, especially at Hamburger SV (HSV). The situation became worse after the fall of the Berlin Wall in 1989 and the eventual annexation of East Germany. In this period the far right grew here. From 1992 to 1994, most of the St Pauli supporters didn't travel to away games to the East, fearing attacks from neo-Nazis. Their fears were justified when, in spring 1993 in Rostock, St Pauli supporters had to run for their lives when the police failed to protect them from an attack by 400 Nazi hooligans, armed with iron bars. In the second half of the 1990s, this hatred was turned into one of the most disgusting songs ever likely to be sung in a football stadium – the so-called 'Tube Song', full of Nazi fantasies of genocide:

> A tube, a tube,
> We're building a tube,
> From St Pauli to Auschwitz,
> We're building a tube.

In trying to explain the fan culture of St Pauli, we have to take account of different factors: the team's relative success (the legend developed during a five-year high in which the club progressed from Germany's Third Division to the First Division); the situation at St Pauli's rivals, HSV; social and cultural changes in the district of St Pauli; and the state of the far left in Germany. All in all, this particular fan culture couldn't have been developed at any another club.

A decisive change in St Pauli's fan base took place during the 1986–87 season, when St Pauli, just promoted to the Second Division, nearly secured a second successive promotion direct to the Bundesliga, only heroically failing in the play-offs. In that season, for the first time at St Pauli some very different football chants could be heard: 'Never again fascism! Never again war! Never again Third Division!', or: 'Who are the betraying rats? Social Democrats! Whose betrayal we will never see? Surely it is St Pauli!'. Previously the shouted answer to who would never betray the 'masses' was simply 'Anarchy!' now it was the local football club. For at least one section of the Hamburg left, something was clearly changing. Another chant which was very popular a few years later was: '*Wir sind das Olck*' ('We are the Olck'), a pun on '*Wir sind das Volk*' ('We are the people') the chant of demonstrators in East Germany shortly before the wall came down, and at the same time homage to the player Bernhard Olck, a 'terrier' of a defensive midfielder. These sorts of chants reflected the ironic humour of the supporters.

In the 1986–87 season there was an average gate of 7,500 people, 80 per cent more than in the 1984–85 season, when St Pauli had just been promoted to the Second Division. This increase can't only be explained by a change in loyalty of Hamburg's traditional football supporters, especially as HSV in the same season increased its average gate from 18,000 to 22,000, when the team won the cup and came second in the League Championship. In 1986–87, St Pauli, therefore, must have found a new set of fans to attract to their club who weren't tempted by the success of HSV.

Many of St Pauli's older supporters did start off as supporters of HSV. Not so astonishing, because between 1979 and 1984, HSV had its most successful period and St Pauli its worst. HSV, helped by Kevin Keegan who played with the club from 1977 to 1980, were three times German league champions, three times runners-up and were in the finals of the European Cup three times. In the European Cup, HSV lost in 1980 against Nottingham Forest and won in 1983 against Juventus, and in 1982 the team lost the UEFA Cup final against IFK Göteborg. At the same time St Pauli were playing in the Third Division.

But during the 1980s the atmosphere for fans became more and unpleasant at HSV's Volksparkstadion. The club became notorious for its fascist hooligans, and these drove other supporters away. In 1982, the first skinheads appeared in the stands wearing badges 'No More Foreigners! Vote NPD' (the NPD was for a long period after 1945 Germany's principal neo-Nazi party). In the same year, members of the far right HSV fan club 'Löwen' [Lions] murdered a 16-year-old supporter of Werder Bremen – the first such fatal assault on a supporter in the history of the Bundesliga. In the 1980s, we hadn't heard of 'hooligans' in Germany, but these HSV supporters, mainly working-class, many of them unemployed and with criminal convictions, were targeted by the neo-Nazi Aktionsfront Nationaler Sozialisten (ANS – since prohibited). The ANS leader Michael Kühnen, who lived in Hamburg, ordered his group to systematically recruit new members from the terraces. In 1983, the magazine *Der Spiegel* wrote: 'Football violence and the far right are especially interconnected on the West terrace of Volksparkstadion.'

Although the situation at Volksparkstadion has since changed for the better, there are still plenty of connections between hooligans and regional right-wing extremists. The readiness to use violence is still high: in 1998, during the World Cup, it was two HSV supporters who were involved in the attempted murder of policeman Daniel Nivel in Lens. And some months later, when St Pauli and HSV both played on the same weekend in Stuttgart (against Kickers Stuttgart and VfB Stuttgart respectively), HSV hooligans attacked St Pauli supporters as they left their train at the main station.

New supporters attracted to St Pauli rather than HSV were further encouraged by the fact that Volksparkstadion, due to its architecture, lacks any atmosphere and the view from the terraces is very bad indeed. Just the opposite, then, to the intimate feeling at Millerntor, an old-style football ground with 80 per cent terraces, spectators packed close to the touchline, and where, in contrast to most of the other German football stadiums, the whole ground, not only some blocks of spectators or one terrace, chants and sings. It was only in 1999 that HSV finally had a stadium the larger club could be proud of. Volksparkstadion was completely renovated, the athletic tracks were removed, and it is now a modern, family-friendly arena. Nevertheless, it still can't compete with Millerntor, not least because the Volksparkstadion remains located next to a cemetery and a refuse incinerator.

In the second half of the 1980s it was not only the crowd at Millerntor that changed, but life in the whole of the district of St Pauli. The area around the Reeperbahn, for decades only attractive for tourists looking for a red-light thrill, saw an upturn, due to underground clubs and bars opening up, inspired by Techno and House-music culture. Many establishments belonging to the sex industry went bust because of the fear of AIDS, so rooms became available at reasonable prices. At the same time, this formerly manual workers' district changed structurally and attracted students and artists to live there – quite different from the 1970s when the plight of the district simply represented urban decline. From 1970 to '85 the number of local inhabitants shrank from 31,000 to 22,000 and St Pauli was in danger of becoming a district of only elderly people. Since this low-point the population has grown to 32,000. First to move in were the students and members of alternative movements which in turn attracted the restaurant trade; this then lured companies from the creative industries and most recently from the new information technologies which brought even more restaurants and bars, and as quite a few of the original companies grew bigger, they attracted further companies. From 1997 onwards, St Pauli evolved into a centre of the multi-media industry. Millerntor now lies in the middle of the internet world, the head quarters of AOL-Europe are just a few hundred metres away.

The success of St Pauli and the growing attractiveness of the district is an important interaction. Worldwide, only a handful of other clubs can boast the same attractive environment near their stadium. There are 500 pubs, bars and restaurants within ten minutes' walk.

At the end of the 1980s, a terrace chant started being heard which for the first time showed the connection between the new supporters and their district: 'Hamburg without Hafenstrasse is like Bundesliga without FC St Pauli.' Hafenstrasse (Harbour Street), in the southern part of St Pauli, is a symbol of a small victory in the otherwise not very successful history of the West German far left. In October 1981, punks, anarchists and homeless people squatted in several derelict houses which all belonged to the city of Hamburg. Two mayors, readily supported by the local press, tried to evict the squatters, with countless police actions backed up by all the accompanying paramilitary hardware. But the houses and the residents are still there, symbols of a counter-culture, though the Hafenstrasse now functions as a conventional housing association.

In the media, during the 1980s and early 1990s, a 'Hafenstrasse-Bloc' on the second main terrace of Millerntor, just at the half-way line, was always being referred to. It made it sound as if these supporters all lived at Hafenstrasse – which was obviously not the case, but it was certainly true that most of them sympathised with, and identified politically with, the squatters. And on demonstrations in support of Hafenstrasse when, as regularly happened, evictions were threatened, there were always St Pauli supporters on the marches and at the rallies.

Quite a few left-wing activists felt attracted to St Pauli because the team had a perfect figure for them to identify with in the side: goalie Volker Ippig. Born in 1963, he had already made his first team debut in 1981, but his regular first-team appearances didn't start until 1986. In between he had put his football career on hold and followed other priorities: he helped to build a hospital in Nicaragua under the Sandinistas and he lived for a while in one of the squats at Hafenstrasse. Ippig became a cult figure amongst the fans. Today he is working as a goalkeeping coach at St Pauli. During his playing days he was immortalised on a T-shirt with the words: 'Volker Hör die Signale' ('Volkers, Hear the Signals') another one of those St Pauli puns, 'Völker, hört die Signale' (People, hear the signals) is the first line of 'The Internationale'.

Unconsciously, Ippig helped a lot of fans to project their desires on to the club; to believe that it might be possible in football, which already was heavily commodified, 'to give room to the other, whatever this other exactly might be'. These are the words of Volker Finke, manager of SC Freiburg, another club in the First Division which attracts, for different reasons, a similar fan culture to St Pauli's. St Pauli was an ideal focus for this projection of hopes and ideals because for most of the last 15 years Freiburg has had the status of an underdog. The stadium is small and partially decaying, so the club doesn't earn much and has to spend an increasing amount on repairs. And until recently, the club had always been managed very badly; the consequences of impoverishment and mismanagement and too many cheap players lacking too many necessary skills. At least some of the players, however, proved able, intoxicated by the atmosphere at Millerntor overcoming their deficiencies and proving themselves through fighting spirit and commitment. And it was exactly this that pleased the supporters – the style of play matched their social and political identification and what they wanted the club to stand for.

The image of the club thus corresponded with the image of the district. Many of St Pauli's inhabitants see themselves as underdogs, because the ruling classes of Hamburg have always discriminated against the district. In the seventeenth and eighteenth centuries factories were built in the area which produced an unbearable stench hanging over the district. They also needed space for expansion, invariably at the expense of the locals' homes. Today, in spite of the influx of jobs from the new information economy, 15 per cent of the district's inhabitants are still living on social security – twice as many as Hamburg's average. Some inhabitants think that choosing to live in this district itself is a dissident statement. 'St Pauli is the only possibility', reads the graffiti just opposite the supporters' shop in Thadenstrasse. The newspaper *Berliner Zeitung* calls St Pauli 'the last haven of the connection between popular culture and a political conscience'. In 1997 voter turnout in St Pauli for elections to the new city parliament was just 50 per cent, and of those who voted, the Green Party attracted 35 per cent; by far the biggest support.

No wonder, then, that the first organised action by the supporters of St Pauli stemmed from political as well as sporting unrest. In March 1989, fan activists asked the supporters not to support the team but just to keep silent during the first five minutes of the match against Karlsruher SC – a protest against the club's board which planned to build a 'Sport Dome', costing more than 500 million Deutschmarks. It was to be a combination of a multi-purpose hall with a sports stadium, hotels and lots of shops. If the idea had been realised, the rents in the district would have gone up enormously, and the traffic in the district, which covers an area of 2.6 square kilometres, would have come to a standstill on certain days. The protests against the Dome were led by football supporters who didn't want their beloved ground turned into a theme-park with a shopping mall attached and they were joined by residents opposed to the environmental impact of the development and not at all interested in football. Only in St Pauli could such an alliance seem feasible.

And it was successful! Two months later, the club withdrew the plans for the Dome and shamefacedly admitted that the project wasn't appropriate for the district. The success strengthened the fan activists' resolve to continue with their self-organisation. Out of the opposition to the Dome evolved a group of people whose influence would reach out far beyond Hamburg: the editorial group behind the fanzine *Millerntor Roar! (MR!)*. This publication impressed hard-core supporters as well as people who normally didn't bother with supporter groups or the administration of the club. Elsewhere in Hamburg though, some remnants of the far left criticised the St Pauli supporters for their appartent romanticism. But the critics' antipathy was based on media reports that were riddled with clichés, and not on any experience of their own fan culture. Then there was the 'Menotti Faction' which propagated a so-called left-wing football game which was beautiful and intelligent in the image of the Brazilian or Argentinian game. A kind of football, admittedly, which was not much played at Millerntor.

Soon it became clear that what was missing was a location where the supporters' activities could be co-ordinated. In 1990, the 'Fanladen' was founded, which remains to this day a unique organisational and communications centre in German football. Fanladen organises trips to away games as well as national supporters' campaigns, and sells fans' memorabilia, designed by people from the Fanladen, including the famous sticker with a fist popping out of the club's coat of arms and smashing a swastika. Two point three million of these have now been sold – a figure even the manager of the Manchester United Megastore would be impressed with.

The supporters' movement at St Pauli not only energised the fan scene with positions which were, at least in connection with football, fairly radical. It was humorous too. One high point was the campaign 'Books for Boller', initiated in 1992 by *MR!* This started with the answer striker Andreas 'Boller' Jeschke gave to a tabloid when asked which book he had read recently. 'I don't have any books,' Jeschke responded. So the fanzine appealed to their readers to send in some books for the philistine. Luckily, 'Boller' saw the joke and agreed to receive the books on the pitch before a home match. Some years later, though, he confessed to a local sports paper that all the books were still stored in his garage and that he hadn't got round to reading any of them.

In 1993 *MR!* folded, because there were different ideas about the line the magazine should follow. But this helped enhance the fan scene because both factions founded new fanzines: *Der Übersteiger* and *Unhaltbar!* The contents of the former might be described as 'football, fun, politics and punk-rock', whereas the latter (which closed in 1999) was more analytical and polemical. Shortly after both fanzines started they organised protests against the German Football Federation which planned two matches between the German and English national teams in Hamburg. On 20 April (Hitler's birthday of all days), a Senior International was scheduled to be played at Volksparkstadion, and on 19 April the countries' B-teams would play at Millerntor. But at Millerntor national anthems would have been treated as a provocation by a significant section of the St Pauli supporters. Even worse, there was a real danger that fascists and hooligans from both countries would have wreaked havoc in the district and marched together towards

Hafenstrasse. Luckily the plan was scrapped in December 1993, officially because of problems with parking space; in reality because of the opposition from the St Pauli supporters. Instead of Hamburg, Berlin was selected as location for the games – and it was only belatedly that the German Football Federation became aware that international opinion didn't think it was such a good idea – especially in view of growing neo-Nazism in Germany – to host an international on the day of Hitler's birthday, and the match was cancelled.

But as innovative as the St Pauli supporters' movement might be, sometimes there were signs that many of those who shouted left-wing slogans at Millerntor and at the club's away games didn't do it out of any deeply-felt conviction but because they felt it to be fashionable and felt it was all part of the fun. In November 1997, some days before a home match against Uerdingen, the club decided to sack manager Eckhard Krautzun, the worst manager at St Pauli for the last 30 years. The decision, long overdue, was only taken after the Players' Council spoke to the club president. The Players' Council consists of five players; it serves as a link between players or coaches and the club's management. Instead of supporting the players who had urged a necessary decision on to a weak President, the supporters, agitated by local newspapers, cheered for the sacked Krautzun and created a martyr out of someone who should have been a figure of fun. With banners reading 'Council of Players – Traitors' and 'Exercise on Your Own, You Wankers', some of the supporters didn't want to recognise that the Players' Council is an institution which allows at least a minimal representative democracy on the playing side.

During the second part of 1997, after relegation from the First Division, slowly but steadily regressive tendencies won ground on several levels. Or, to put this in a broader context, the shift in society towards conservatism – which had started with the government of Helmut Kohl and his 16 years of Conservative rule and from 1998 onwards was hardly reversed by Gerhard Schroeder's coalition government of Social Democrats and the Green Party – has not stopped at the gates of Millerntor. Hendrik Lüttmer, until recently manager of Fanladen, has observed that in the late 1990s many veteran fan activists retired from the scene (a normal enough development because at a certain age other things become more important). 'But our problem is that the old activists haven't been replaced by new ones', says Lüttmer.

> A gradual passivity is gaining ground. There are only 50 or 60 activists. Maybe for too long we basked in our good fortune of having splendid supporters and missed the chance to motivate younger supporters or to impart the spirit of the old times. Furthermore, we are hit by the recruitment problems of the fragmented left-wing political scene in general.

The most important reason for this development is that the new supporters are not comparable with the squatters and their sympathisers, with the left-wing activists who found a new home at Millerntor. Young people who are brought up with MTV have to be motivated by new means to get involved with the politics of football, all the more as involvement in fan activism doesn't promise the quick thrills they are used to.

Nevertheless, there is still some political activism at St Pauli. In December 2000 several supporter groups, website editors and the anti-fascist initiative 'Courageous Citizens' were forced to start a campaign against racism and sexism at Millerntor. With banners, leaflets and no fewer than 12 articles in the official club magazine (unthinkable at any other club, but then the magazine is incomparable because it is produced by contributors to an alternative daily, *Taz*), they denounced hooligans who had insulted black players as 'galley slaves' and who thought that the adjective 'queer' was appropriate in describing anything or anyone they didn't like on the pitch. The initiators of the campaign also picked up on a phenomenon which Hendrik Lüttmer calls 'action-orientated prevailing mood'. ('That's not hooliganism, it is not organised.') Lüttmer believes that the responsibility for a part of St Pauli's support becoming more aggressive lies with the police forces outside of Hamburg. 'We get the impression that there are quite a few policemen who use their uniform as an excuse to give full expression to their own violence,' says Lüttmer. How tense the atmosphere has become can be appreciated by looking at the attitude of St Pauli supporters towards other fans. In their best days they remained composed in the face of insults: they laughed or made fun of the slogans and chants. More recently, they have reacted by retaliating with their own insults.

There is an explanation for the growing aggressiveness by some supporters: they have had to put up with a deteriorating situation at the club, on the pitch as well as off it. For three years, from the start of the 1997–98 season until the end of 1999–2000, supporters of St Pauli have had to endure poor fare. The team played pitifully and were twice almost relegated to the Third Division. In the 1999–2000 season the club was only saved by a goal towards the end of the last game of the season. Sometimes it looked like the club would go bust. There were also fierce, nasty battles within the club.

The opposition supporters' group, AGiM (Arbeitsgemeinschaft interessierter MitgliederInnen), including some of those involved with *Der Übersteiger*, was becoming more and more critical of the policy of Club President Heinz Weisener, who, since taking office in 1990, had cultivated a sort of chaotic monarchy, while remaining, to the older supporters, a kind of saint. The conflict escalated in October 1998 when the club annual general meeting passed a motion proposed by the AGiM group to rename the stadium of the club. Since 1969 the stadium had been called after a long-serving president, Wilhelm Koch – but many supporters and members didn't find the name acceptable any more after it was revealed that Wilhelm Koch had been a member of the Nazi party NSDAP between 1937 and 1945. Now the stadium is again officially called 'Stadion am Millerntor'.

Some of the older supporters still idolised Wilhelm Koch, so for a while they held out against the re-naming. One of the club's highest-profile supporters, Hans Apel, a very conservative Social Democrat who had been Chancellor of the Exchequer and Minister of Defence under Prime Minister Helmut Schmidt, even resigned from his position on the Aufsichsrat (a monitoring body of six members to whom the board, consisting of the club President and two Vice-Presidents, are answerable) after the vote at the general meeting.

The mood at the club changed completely with the start of the 2000–01 season. Once again, St Pauli were the underdogs, because they started with the lowest budget of all 36 professional clubs and were prime candidates for relegation. But the young team stormed into a table-topping position in the Second Division, and secured promotion to the Bundesliga. They even scored more goals than any other team in the First or Second Divisions. In autumn 2000, President Heinz Weisener, no longer acceptable to the supporters, resigned at last and Tatjana Groeteke from AGiM took over as club secretary. The club also hired Sven Brux, former manager of Fanladen, as its head of stadium organisation and security.

'When, in the past, someone said FC St Pauli is a fantastic club, he sold an illusion. Only the supporters were fantastic,' explains Lüttmer. Now, everything has changed: 'We're missing younger fan-activists, but those formerly involved in the supporters' groups hold important positions at the club. Now if someone from a supporters' group wants to have an appointment with one of the officials, he or she gets it without problems, fairly quickly and directly.'

Tatjana Groeteke who, before becoming club secretary, had been a Chairwoman of the Aufsichsrat, sees the situation similarly: 'There is no strict border between the supporters and the club, even though the club is a business. But that is only possible because the club existed for a very long time without any professional structures.' This allowed for open spaces which were occupied by supporters.

AGiM did just that. The group first intervened in the politics of the club in 1996. The German Football Association ordered at that time that every professional club had to install a monitoring body ('Aufsichsrat') and must change the statutes accordingly. St Pauli's board missed the deadline, so the club needed to draft and agree new statutes in a very short time, otherwise it would lose its league status. Panic spread within the officials, allowing AGiM to convince them that they should be able to have a say in formulating the statutes. This was successful, firstly because the structures of the club were all too underdeveloped to manage this crisis on its own, and secondly, club officials had to rely on votes from the supporters' movement, because a change of statutes needs a general meeting majority of three quarters. The risk of losing the vote was too much for the president, because the new statutes were due the very same evening that the general meeting was to be held, at the German Football Association's headquarters in Frankfurt.

'We achieved a position of power which would not have been possible in any other professional club, because all the other clubs wrote their statutes in peace and quiet and without public ado,' explains Groeteke.

Originally, AGiM was formed to campaign that the amateur squad of the club, which commutes between the Third and Fourth Divisions, should be allowed to play at Millerntor. But the members of the group excelled themselves in offering a strategy to manage the entire club properly. Contrary to the critique of supporters in many other clubs who accused their officials of only thinking commercially, these supporters at St Pauli complained that their club wasn't functioning properly because the management didn't know how to do business properly.

AGiM achieved the right for all supporter's groups to have a say in the running of the club. They are represented on a committee which meets every two months and advises the club president. 'Nothing can be decided over the heads of the supporters,' maintains Groeteke, 'after all, it was the supporters who developed the brand name of St Pauli.'

This is best illustrated by the history of the most famous symbol of St Pauli, the skull and cross-bones. The website of the club (www.fcstpauli.de) recalls how a punk-rock veteran in Hamburg called Mabuse (named after a figure in a film by German director Fritz Lang) was responsible for it. Mabuse lived during the 1980s at Hafenstrasse and brought his pirate flag one day with him to the Hafenstrassebloc. Originally, the squatters honoured the memory of pirate Klaus Störtebeker who was executed in Hamburg in the year 1401 with the flag. Today, the skull and cross-bones is an unofficial second club badge. It is used in all the club's advertisements, in the official club magazine – and for the 2000–01 season, for the first time, it could be seen on the collars of the team's shirts.

This one example shows that football business has doubtless profited from critical, left-wing supporters. Tatjana Groeteke believes that it is possible to combine business with a critical conscience on a higher level: 'In the long run, we want to become an important club in the First Division, without losing what makes us special. What we will not allow to happen is to have a situation where all that remains from fan culture is just the fan.' Because the club needs money to realise this aim (which Groeteke calls a 'vision'), it plans its own fashion label, a bar on Reeperbahn and later maybe even a petrol station. Some supporters are already wondering if this kind of business can be reconciled with their hard-earned street credibility as St Pauli fans.

The eventual success of the struggle which began 12 years ago won't depend, though, on these commercial ventures. Rather it will be whether the politics and attitudes of St Pauli's supporters can successfully survive in such a 'modernised' environment. It is true that the fan culture at Millerntor still remains a bastion against hooliganism and fascism as demonstrated by the anti-racist campaign of December 2000. The club contributes to such an atmosphere. At the beginning of 2001 it joined the German foundation for compensation towards former victims of slave labour under the Nazi regime. So far, St Pauli is the only football club to do this.

It is not yet clear in which political direction the St Pauli supporters' movement will develop. In April 2001 several of the club's fanzines and supporter groups protested against fans who had organised a trip to an away game with the German airline Lufthansa. The reason for the protest − Lufthansa is involved in the deportation of 10,000 asylum seekers per year. So maybe the spirit of the old days is not as dead as some might like to think. But listen to the songs sung from the stands at Millerntor. As the fan culture became radicalised the chant went 'No one likes us, We don't care, Mayors come and go, But Hafenstrasse is here to stay', a football chant with a remarkably political edge. Today the fans sing, 'Players come and players go, But St Pauli is here to stay' − scarcely distinguishable from what could be heard at any stadium, anywhere in the German league.

Some pessimists fear that promotion to the Bundesliga will attract more of these apolitical fans and increasingly, as the media revitalise the myth of St Pauli, it will be reduced to a funny, romantic story of the eternal underdog − stripped of the politics.

And what about the optimists? They hope that everything at the club will change for the better following the euphoria of the promotion. And this euphoria is overwhelming. Indeed, promotion was achieved with an incredibly small budget of just seven million Deutschmarks (two point two million pounds). The decisive goal was scored 14 minutes before the final whistle of the last game of the season − almost one year after the team avoided relegation to the Third Division in the final minute of the last game of that season.

At the Saturday night celebrations of the promotion, just before the team took the stage, the English song 'Three Lions', was sung. It brilliantly summed up the mood of 20,000 celebrating fans who could still remember half a decade of agony: 'No more years of hurt, No more need for dreaming'. And the club has produced a T-shirt on which − good old irony − St Pauli's promotion is proclaimed as a world-shattering historic event, comparable to Germany's first World Cup win and that famous/infamous goal at Wembley. The T-shirt contains only three dates, one below the other: 1954 − 1966 − 2001.

Translation by Stefan Howald.

WAR IS OVER: BEYOND QUICK-FIX SOLUTIONS

ENGLAND, A SUITABLE CASE FOR TREATMENT

Patrick Barclay

At first I took the minimum of notice. If I considered him at all, it was to assume he was a harmless oaf, this Englishman yelling across the rather elegant space of a fine Italian restaurant in the Albanian capital of Tirana (if you detect a massive contradiction in terms in the past ten words, you haven't been to downtown Tirana lately). He was around 40 and not obviously aggressive. When it became clear that his message was directed at us – a few national newspaper journalists refuelling in readiness for the following night's World Cup qualifying match – we cocked an ear and quickly worked out the subject. 'Fucking twat' was one phrase that mingled with the soft music and tinkling cutlery, and 'Get your tongues out of his arse' a clear hint that the perceived villain-in-chief was the friendly face who had just stopped to greet us and have a chat on his way out of the restaurant after being entertained by Albanian football officials: Adam Crozier, Chief Executive of the FA. Since Crozier is a Scot and the footballing humour of the Englishman abroad often heavyhanded, we guessed that the verbal intruder was attempting to be funny and responded with smiles which we trusted would be terminal.

No such luck. The insults continued. So we tried smiling at the man's two companions. They were no help; they were leaner, with harder and more contemptuous faces, and clearly unconcerned by the prospect of disruption to a convivial evening. As the tirade continued, we reflected on the good fortune that caused only a few English diners to notice; the locals seemed to concentrate on enjoying their meals, sparing us from shame by association. But eventually impatience overcame my friend Joe Lovejoy of the *Sunday Times*, who strode over to the troubled table and demanded clarification of the vexed issue, which turned out to be Crozier's reforms of the England Members' Club (EMC). At length, while the man's pals walked silently out, he came to us, pulled up an uninvited chair and explained that it was felt Crozier was changing the EMC rules so that he and his like – loyal England fans who had not missed a match for decades – would struggle to obtain tickets.

He could not, however, explain why, except by bemoaning Crozier's supposed preference for families and hospitality junkets, and as he reeled away I was left with a strong impression that Crozier, if indeed he was trying to squeeze such followers out of the England entourage, was working along the right lines. That he has a big problem on his hands is obvious, and true in more senses than one. England have an exceptionally large support which can provide a thrilling addition to the spectacle of a major event – their dominance of the stadium in Toulouse during the 1998 World Cup, for example, and Charleroi during Euro 2000 was wonderfully vivid – but does not always add to the pleasures of the host community before and after the match.

You have to generalise and, while of course there can be thousands of exceptions, the general rule is that England fans are best avoided, liable to be a cut below their club-based equivalents from the same country. Cities that trust England fans – Malmo in 1992, Dublin in 1995 and so on – are let down. Cities that do not trust them and prepare for the worst, such as Rome in 1997, are accused of over-zealous policing. Yet I remember Rome in the hours before England played that 0-0 draw in the Olympic Stadium that sent them to the World Cup under Glenn Hoddle, the sneering expressions worn like badges by fans who roamed the streets, swearing noisily and insulting women. Having chosen an open-air restaurant in which to have lunch with Roy Hodgson, then manager of Blackburn, we realised he had been spotted and, shivering in the chillier atmosphere that suddenly descended, fled to somewhere more secluded. It was just another day, just another dolour; travelling with England can almost be relied upon to lower your spirits, to dilute the joys of a generally fascinating experience observing the universal game.

So much, then, for the gentrification of football. A myth, unfortunately. I believe strongly in the gentrification of football. In fact I believe in the gentrification of society and to this end, became disheartened at the fall from fashion experienced by socialism toward the end of the twentieth century. A large middle class, solvent and with a stake in society, is fundamental to my idea of Utopia. But in football, as elsewhere, a consequence of the spurt in prosperity enjoyed by the lucky ones in the 1980s and 1990s was that, commonly, they became even more crass and intoxicated as the Hooray Henry syndrome spread. In football, the Englishman's noise sets him apart. I refer exclusively to England, because the people of this country really do stand alone, to the extent – which would be comic in less distressing circumstances – of being blissfully unaware that they are louder than the rest. As for serious hooliganism, it is a subject I prefer to avoid rather than to study, but those in the know assure me that, since Heysel and Hillsborough and all those things that were supposed to have jolted us into a radical change of behaviour, the main change is that a lid has been applied by sustained and impressive police counter-measures with political support. Certainly the question that used always to be asked by those of us of a certain age and a certain type – 'they could take on the miners' pickets, so why can't they take on the football hooligans?' – has been comprehensively answered.

Only a fool would deny that hooliganism exists elsewhere in the footballing universe, and terrible violence, that there is racist abuse in Italy, there are stabbings in Holland, even shootings in Argentina but the purpose here is to address specifically those who travel to support their national teams and this is where the English stick out. Their reputation goes before them. It caused the organisers of the 1994 World Cup in the United States to exhale hugely with relief when Graham Taylor's team were knocked out the previous autumn by the Dutch; they immediately lopped fifteen million dollars off their 'security' budget, the amount set aside for, among other things, hush money to be handed to bar owners whose toilets and other fixtures and fittings were damaged. The Americans still feared trouble – after all, what did they know of football and its fans – but they were beautifully surprised, one of the off-the-field highlights of the tournament being a weekend in Orlando, Florida, during which the Dutch and Belgians mingled in drunken harmony with the Irish while battalions of tooled-up cops gradually relaxed, tipped back their caps and joined in the fun.

It was not untypical of what I have experienced in a dozen major tournaments. Football fans, by and large, are normal people who take a holiday mood into these summer jamborees. I have a dream of how football should be and, every couple of years, it comes true. It is not exactly Rangers versus Celtic – and the atmosphere at an Old Firm match is, I must confess, a prime example of how the unspeakable can thrill the senses – but there can be tremendous passion in the controlled tribalism that is exhibited when a vast crowd of self-policing celebrants make the atmosphere. Take the Irish. You can – you can take them anywhere – as was proved by the Republic of Ireland's unforgettable encounters with Italy in the 1990 and 1994 World Cups. So why, when such comparable congregations as the Irish, the Scots, the Danes and the Dutch can be eager participants, do the English need lessons in integration? I can't say for sure. All I know is that the Scots, among whom I was brought up, once did, forever being involved in rowdiness when they came to Wembley for the biennial match. Overseas they were fine. It was just that they could not resist the temptation to cock a snook at big brother. And more often than not things turned nasty as soon as they did so. Maybe that is how the English feel about Europe. Maybe it is now their turn to feel inferior, dominated, subjugated by another Union. Or maybe they just have a higher proportion of louts than the rest.

They certainly have a disturbing tendency to behave like soldiers in a raggle-taggle army. Outrageously, they steal the message of defiance to the IRA which better people than they, politicians included, have been brave enough to enact. When the louts claim to represent their country, though, it is only too true. They carry the flag for beach yobs and bar invaders who can ruin a pleasant holiday most weeks of a summer. When one of Crozier's predecessors, the late Ted Croker, told Margaret Thatcher that football's burden was 'your hooligans' he had a very good point. Which is not to deny that football has always borne a major share of moral responsibility for the cleaning of its own back yard – even if it has often failed to shoulder the implications. A terrible and profoundly selfish act, in my opinion, was instrumental in concentrating the poison on the national team's support. In 1985, when the atrocity committed by so-called Liverpool supporters at Heysel prompted the FA under Sir Bert Millichip, with Croker at his side, to withdraw English clubs from European competition, they seemed to forget about the English team whose supporters had the worst record of all: the national team. So, while the likes of blameless Everton and Norwich City shared the general punishment, England were able blithely to play on and the yobs expressed their gratitude by rallying to the cause, with predictable results – one of the first all too memorably scarring German streets in the European Championship a mere three years later.

By the time the EMC came along, in its earlier form as the England Travel Club, it was too late. And much too little. Time and again you gazed over at their enclosures and saw arms raised at Hitlerian angles. I mentioned this when, shortly after Euro 2000, I attended a meeting organised by the EMC's London branch at which fans interested in the forthcoming visit to Finland could learn about key cultural aspects of the host nation – mainly the opening hours of Helsinki's bars (most congenial, it turned out) but also art galleries and so on. The assumption that most who attended would be natural integrators, those at the opposite end of the spectrum from the yobs, proved accurate. There was a moment when two lads, after hearing I thought the 'No Surrender' chant had no place at an England game (many Scots, Welsh and indeed Irish people despise the IRA) thanked me and said they'd never considered it in that way; they would not chant it again. But when I brought up the subject of those raised arms one lad, to murmurs of assent, told me: 'You're getting it wrong. That's not a Hitler salute.' He demonstrated. 'Look. We raise both arms.' I asked why. He smiled patiently. 'It's natural,' he explained 'to raise your arms when you're singing the National Anthem. It just happens.' Nowhere else, mate. There are other anthems with cheesy sentiments. There are other peoples with much-loved songs about extending borders, ruling waves and all that sort of stuff. But most of them skip the gestures. They know where to draw the line. As I say, the FA have a massive job on their hands.

What they must do – and here I glance backward at the twisted faces in the Tirana restaurant – is, however long it takes, to keep working towards a time when the English can behave in a block as the Irish did in Rome 1990. Packed in behind a goal for the quarter-final against the host nation, they belted out their anthem but then not only went silent in anticipation of the

Italian anthem but lowered their flags in respect. Respect: the word that makes the difference. Having listened, they clapped. And then they roared and kept roaring until Toto Schillaci settled the match. The only problem afterwards was finding enough Guinness for them. Seven years later I travelled to the Eternal City with England, and was afflicted by the eternal gloom. There was no après-match to speak of – the atmosphere had been well and truly soured – except for a nice, long, late-night walk from the Olympic Stadium, necessitated by the local taxi drivers' understandable decision to head home early.

Now I have no doubt that many reading this will have formed the impression that I am little more than a curmudgeon, and anti-English to boot, that those lucky enough to earn a living by writing about a great international game are ill-advised to shrivel their noses at the thought of those, even the least attractive, who pay to support it. But I am not anti-English. I just suffer from occasional pangs of envy for the journalists who follow the national rugby-union team and can travel home from Paris with the fans, exchanging views with them, learning from them, getting even closer to the heart of a sport. I can't do that with confidence. Decent fans can't; when they go to places like Albania, they have to plan their itineraries carefully, not to avoid the local hoodlums but to circumvent areas rendered sensitive by the presence of compatriots. Yet the decent fans, in the fantasy I am led to believe the New FA share, are the future. There is nothing incorrigible about England. It is just that the combination of football and England has produced danger, a diseased heart. That the patient is a suitable case for treatment is beyond question. That Crozier and Soho Square are willing to help is encouraging. But the long-term cure can only come from within. Only then, when peer pressure becomes the police, can England's body of support be trusted.

FANS FOR A CHANGE

Dougie Brimson

If writing about hooliganism has taught me one thing, it's that the vast majority of supposedly factual information to be found which deals with it is based upon opinion, rumour or presumption. Often, it's nothing more than a combination of all three.

That's nothing unusual of course. The worlds of astronomy and archaeology for example, are littered with individuals who have forged astonishingly successful careers by seemingly doing nothing more than stating the blindingly obvious or formulating ideas based on a combination of guesswork and hearsay. And whilst in most instances, the consequences of such 'research' have little or no impact on the real world, occasionally they do. And the results can be catastrophic.

This has never been better illustrated than with the issue of football hooliganism. When the problem of crowd violence began to exert a major influence over the game in the early '70s, the sociologists, anthropologists and criminologists immediately began searching for reasons. Inevitably they focussed in on class, intelligence and family. Later, politics was to be added to that list, plus alienation and even rebellion, until eventually, the theorists came to the conclusion that most hooligans were right-wing, poorly educated products of broken homes searching for some kind of belonging. Of course, the fact that these theories were delivered by 'Doctor' this or 'Professor' that gave them enormous credibility. So much so that for the most part, they were accepted without question by those in authority and as a result, helped form a strategy and policy to try and combat the growing threat. However, they were wrong. At least in part. For whilst it was true that the majority of people involved in hooliganism were working class, that was simply because football was the working-class game. But many were reasonably well-educated and in decent, stable employment. More importantly, very few, if any, were searching for anything other than a good time. And that was exactly what hooliganism was providing. Week in and week out.

In reality, this was at the core of the entire issue. But in their quest to apply rational reasoning to an irrational problem, it was the one factor that the theorists missed, with the result that the starting point for the policy makers was wrong. As a consequence, the end product of these policies has been negligible. Indeed, other than handing the police ever more draconian legislation, it is debatable that they have had any effect at all. A point surely proven by the fact that almost three decades later the culture of hooliganism has become so entrenched in the game that authority has all but given up trying to cure it and instead, seeks ever more complex ways to suppress it.

Yet astonishingly, despite this obvious failure, in certain circles those theories still dictate thinking. And when you have people making decisions who are so blinkered to the realities of a situation, how can you ever hope to move forward? Thankfully, there are signs that things are changing. For those with the power to bring about a solution to the hooligan problem are finally waking up to the reality of the situation they have inherited. And however this has been brought about, be it by a grudging acceptance that it has been handled badly from the outset or a final realisation that legislation on its own is all but worthless, it is a sign that deserves a belated welcome. Yet the most interesting thing will be what happens next. For if we are ever to see any kind of permanent solution to the problem of football violence, then it is going to take a few major and very brave steps.

But no one should be under the illusion that we will ever solve this problem. We won't. Football, by its very nature, is a confrontational sport and no matter how hard you try and how much work you do, where you have two sides competing you have the potential for some degree of friction. That will never change and in truth, I for one would not want it to. For that edge is what makes watching football different from watching any other sport. However, what you can do is to change the nature and consequences of that friction; mould it into something positive instead of something negative. That really is possible. But it will require a degree of reflection – not only on what has been tried before but also what hasn't. For despite years of 'study' into the peculiar nature of football violence, one of the most important aspects of the issue is one that has received little by way of examination: why do individuals involved finally give it up? Given that so much time, effort and money has been poured into providing futile deterrents, I have always found this rather odd. But having spoken to hundreds of former combatants personally over the years, from hard-core lads to hangers-on, it is a certain fact that the vast majority give up not because of any outside influence, but because they themselves decide the time is right. That might be down to age, boredom or even one close shave too many, but ultimately, the decision is one made through personal choice.

To me, this leads to two obvious conclusions. First, outside deterrents are all but useless and second, the resources poured into these ineffective deterrents would be better utilised by providing the motivation for those individuals to make that personal choice earlier in their hooligan career.

This approach might not be well received in certain circles, but there can be no doubt that the tactic of trying to isolate the hooligans and force them out and away from football has failed miserably. What we have to do therefore is to provide them with a more attractive alternative, one which retains the passion and the pride but which removes the anti-social elements of intimidation and violence. But most importantly of all, it must be something that doesn't marginalise them, but instead, actively involves them, not as thugs, but as fans. We have to create something that not only replaces a hooligan culture that is an integral part of the English, if not the world, game, but which actually retains some elements of it.

I'm not talking about creating anything artificial here; there has to be room for the humour and commitment that is unique to the English game, but what I am talking about is something akin to what which we see in Italian football. Fair enough, they have their own hooligan problems but the sheer spectacle of a major Serie A game makes the hairs on the back of your neck stand on end. This is created by the fans themselves and if they can do it, why can't we? The answer of course, is that we *can*. We have the tools, we have the will, we just have to pull it all together and do the work. And to see just how successful we could be if everyone set their minds to it, we need look no further than how the issue of racism has been dealt with.

I make no apologies for saying this (mostly because it's about time someone did), but football in this country has done an absolutely phenomenal job of combating the cancerous racism that infected almost every single ground in the early 1980s. OK, it's still not 100 per cent, and there is still much work to be done away from the insular world of the Premier League, but compare what we have today with 20 years ago when entire ends would be making monkey chants and throwing bananas whenever players such as John Barnes or Luther Blissett ran out on to the pitch. Those days were horrific, but they have been banished forever and unlike some of our European neighbours, we have put our game in the position where on the rare occasions someone does shout out something they shouldn't, more often than not someone, anyone, will either front them up or report them. That in itself is astonishing progress but more importantly, those abusers will already know that their words and actions are both wrong and unacceptable. That awareness alone has been a major and very positive step forward in race relations. And the reason for this success is simple: peer pressure. The 'Kick Racism out of Football' campaign realised early on that true power lay with the silent majority. So what it did was to involve them in the removal of something that even back then was becoming increasingly regarded as unacceptable. But equally, it gave the majority a platform to show their dislike for what was going on. And it worked. To such an extent that the only colour anyone is interested these days is the colour of the shirt on a player's back. We have to build on that success and alongside 'Kick Racism', give fans the incentive to create an environment where intimidation and excessive aggression are shown up for what they are – bullying. And given the opportunity, it could be done. Indeed, it has to be done. But we have to involve everyone and get them pulling in the same direction. And that includes FIFA and UEFA downwards. For it is incredible to me that English football is treated so appallingly by the game's supposed governing bodies whilst supporters from other European nations routinely force abandonments or major public order problems and nothing is done to punish them. If action is going to be taken, it has to be taken across the board. And it has to be seen to be being done.

Yet whilst FIFA and UEFA must lead internationally, domestically the FA must be the driving force. It is their role to administer the game and hooliganism is one aspect of it they have been allowed to avoid for far too long. The first, and most important thing they must do is to turn everything on its head. Right from the start, the hooligan debate has concentrated on those who cause the problem. It is a tactic that pandered to this minority primarily because in its misguided attempts to re-invent itself under the shadow of Hillsborough, football allowed its natural fear of crowd violence to dictate the shape of any change. This would have been fine if, alongside that, they had done something to counter the existence of the culture that causes the problem in the first place, but they did not. As a result, the decent law-abiding majority have become saddled with everything from blanket CCTV to early kick-offs, whilst hooliganism has simply evolved to keep ahead of the changes, festering and growing on the edges of the game to such an extent that many people have become blind to the consequences that the threat of it brings to every single competitive fixture within the professional game. That has to change. The majority deserve better because the match day experience should be something defined by their hopes and needs rather than one that seems on too many occasions to be something dependent on the all-powerful whims of the local constabulary worried about a few idiots.

Therefore, the FA and Football League have to go on the offensive by putting pressure on the clubs to force them to deal directly with their own less savoury elements. The authorities know who the offending individuals are because the police and stewards have been keeping an eye on them for years so the time has come to confront them and tell them that enough is enough. Step out of line again and out you go, never to return. Remember, no one has a divine right to walk through a turnstile. Not even someone who travelled away to Stockport on a cold December Tuesday night back in 1973.

Faced with a possible loss of income and the prospect of having actually to communicate with some of their own support, the clubs may well fight such a suggestion but they should have no choice in the matter. The control of their supporters, be it home or away; inside the ground or out, has to be their responsibility. And if they refuse to comply, tough. Hit them where it really hurts. One point deducted for every supporter convicted for anything related to violence on a match day should be as good an incentive as any – something that would also encourage the supporters to police themselves.

Alongside the clubs, the media must be forced to be less inflammatory when dealing with this issue and in particular the travelling England fans. There are signs that this is beginning to happen but just in case, the FA should wield some of the immense power they have at their disposal and warn the boys from the back pages that they too are under caution. Responsible reporting is one thing, but the sensationalist, blanket coverage that accompanied the events in Charleroi during Euro 2000 is something else. Any more of that and the worst offenders in the press should be left in no doubt that their access to the international side would be withdrawn for a few months. Can you imagine the impact on sales that would have?

Similarly, the police must take a step back from the almost despotic stance they have taken at some clubs. I don't want them to abandon their role altogether but instead, change their tactics a little. They have to stop playing the cat-and-mouse game with the lads at their respective clubs and should send them the direct message that this time round the police really do mean business. If that means paying them a visit at work or at home and telling them it's all over, then it should be done. Then, if they step out of line again, either inside or outside a ground, out they go. And if they show their faces the next week, stick them in the back of a van and hold them for a few hours. Do that every week for a couple of months and you'd be amazed how soon someone would get pissed off.

But the most important people are the fans themselves. Since the formation of the Premier League and the involvement of BSkyB, almost every aspect of the game has been altered except the role of the people who walk through the gates and hand over the money. Clearly, when even at Old Trafford the atmosphere is becoming less intense, that has proven to be a huge mistake and it must be addressed. But that can only happen if the fans themselves are involved collectively. They are the only ones with the power and ability to create an environment which, whilst noisy and passionate, is one where even the merest threat of violence is regarded as not just unacceptable but unimaginable. The football authorities have to give them the responsibility, and the opportunity, to do that job. Key to this has to be a return of the true supporters' clubs rather than the ticketing and travel agents we've ended up with. They are the perfect way to involve fans directly in their clubs but equally, they would provide a true forum for dialogue to make sure we're all pulling in the same direction.

Away from the individual clubs, supporters need a single, properly funded body to represent their interests and that body must be both vocal and, when necessary, militant. Because the truth is, what we have at the moment is simply not strong enough. The Football Supporters Association is regarded by far too many people as nothing more than a lobby group of well-intentioned individuals whilst other groups such as the National Federation of Football Supporters Clubs are too anonymous to have any kind of credibility. That isn't good enough either. The football authorities have to understand that if they worked with the fans instead of alienating them, everyone would benefit.

Furthermore, supporters have to become involved with agencies such as the FA and in campaigns like 'Kick Racism' and must redefine what being a football fan is all about. But more importantly, we have to define what it isn't. For example, it's one thing telling a section of England fans not to sing the *Dambusters* theme or 'No Surrender to the IRA'; it's quite another to encourage the rest to find more positive songs. Surely there is an anthem that celebrates Englishness and the English game in the same way that 'Flower of Scotland' does for those north of the border. If so, let's have it!

It is vital that such work begins within the domestic game, but it remains equally important that changes are made on the international front, because there can be no doubt that the historically negative image of England fans causes far more problems than the modern-day reality. All too often, the misguided fear of English hooligans means that decent law-abiding supporters face the prospect of travelling to places where they are in serious danger. That is a scandal. The Scots fans are no less passionate than the English and they are certainly as vocal. Yet when they travel, they are positively welcomed. They not only have fun, they create fun; a situation replicated by the 'Barmy Army' who follow English cricket. More importantly, no one around either group ever feels threatened.

Yes, of course the local police must be ready for the possibility of trouble, but the FA must go on a major public relations exercise and tell the host nations that what trouble there may be will come from a tiny minority and not the majority. Furthermore, that majority should be protected by the rule of law and not be fearful of it. Nor should they be left to fend for themselves when abused or assaulted by local youths. That is simply unacceptable and government has an equally important role to play here. Sitting back and doing little or nothing while English citizens are rounded up and deported simply for being English is outrageous. Especially when such treatment is undertaken arbitrarily and is proven to be so. Treat people as you would expect to be treated is the accepted norm in this country and we should expect the same courtesy when we travel abroad. If we don't get it, the very least we can expect is that our government asks why we haven't. For such mistreatment creates an atmosphere of tension which in turn, breeds anger. And if you have anger, you have the potential for disorder.

However, it is fair to say that concerned as I remain, for the first time in years, I have also begun to feel some signs of optimism that the desire to find a solution actually extends beyond the need for retribution. Certainly both the British government and the European Parliament have begun to take a fresh look at the problem. They have done this primarily with a view to developing ways of encouraging a more positive fan culture around the England national side – something that the FA is also taking a keen, if long overdue, interest in. This has begun to extend to the media too, who, after decades of anti-England fan rhetoric, have finally begun to realise that in many cases, the truth is somewhat different from what they have been printing. As a result, they have begun to give more balanced and honest coverage of violence involving English supporters abroad – something that has a knock-on, and positive, effect in terms of the mood amongst those same travelling supporters.

We can only hope that these first moves are more than mere gestures. But I have no doubt that if we can keep the momentum going, we will reach a solution of sorts. And when we do, it isn't only the supporters who will benefit, so will football.

BORO'S NUMBER 007

David Shayler

When I was released from La Sante prison, in Paris in November 1998, some people accused me of showing a lack of judgement for wearing a Middlesbrough away shirt as I took my first steps of freedom for nearly four months, to face the British media. I think it was one of the best things I ever did, for a number of reasons. First, I wanted to thank all the Boro fans who had written to me in prison, particularly Andy Smith and Geoff Vickers from the fanzine *Middlesbrough Supporters South* and Dave Carter who had organised a campaign to support me on Teesside. While I was doing time, they kept me up to date with all the unexpected madness that us hardened Boro fans have got used to over the years, like Paul Merson-ary taking the Villa-nous bribe; Gazza appearing to self-destruct once again; and us winning two away games on the bounce in the top flight for the first time since former Chairman Charlie Amer and his son were helping themselves to bricks from Ayresome Park.

Second, I wanted people to know that I'm not the monster and so-called traitor the right-wing press has tried to make me out to be. I'm just a bloke who likes his beer and footie (particularly the Boro), who found himself in the extraordinary circumstances of being privy to corruption and murder on the part of the British state. Nothing wrong with that, you might think. But on reflection, I'm pretty sure it counted against me in MI5. Not only was I – horror of horrors – an ex-journalist but I was also a northerner and a footie fan.

Third, I wanted people to know that I'm proud of being a Boro fan and it matters more to me than all their stupid court cases, Official Secrets Acts and extradition hearings.

But it wasn't an easy decision to make: to wear or not to wear a Boro shirt to the final hearing, which could on the one hand free me that very evening and on the other consign me to a year's incarceration in HM Belmarsh, a high security prison. The night before the judgement, I thought about wearing my Boro top under a proper shirt so I could pull it off, à la Superman, in front of the British media outside the Palais de Justice, if I was released, to reveal the gleaming Argentina-style away shirt underneath. But I chickened out. I chickened out because of good old-fashioned superstition. I mean, let's face it, given Middlesbrough's record of snatching defeat from the jaws of victory, would you feel that wearing a Boro shirt was likely to enhance the chances of things going right for once? So the night before the release, I decided that wearing the Boro top was out. But when the decision came the following day, I was sent from the Palais de Justice back to prison to pick up my belongings. With the delight at my release came the knowledge that I could walk out of prison in my Boro away top – away because I was away from home, of course. The result was amazing. On seeing the television coverage, Boro fans bombarded the switchboard of the local paper to ask if I was a Boro fan. Other footie fans suddenly became sympathetic. They realised that I was not the monster the press made me out to be because I did what they would have done in the same circumstances. I advertised my allegiance. I stuck with my tribe. That said, I had already received a letter from the Manchester United fans campaigning against Murdoch's attempt to take over the club because they had heard I was, as they put it, a 'smog chomper'. They even had the cheek to ask me if I was a johnny-come-lately-glory-seeking Boro fan because I haven't got a Teesside accent. Imagine that: being accused of being a glory seeker by Manchester United fans. I think that shocked me more than my arrest, imprisonment and subsequent release put together did.

I've supported the Boro for 27 years although I don't think 'support' is really a strong enough word for what I've put into this relationship. It's been like the worst kind of tempestuous, unrequited long-distance love affair imaginable. I mean, let's face it, I would never have devoted nearly 30 years of my life to a girlfriend who tempted me and tempted me or promised so much but never let me go all the way – and I certainly wouldn't have made regular 500-mile round trips to see her. Take the 1997 Coca-Cola Cup final, for instance, when we were 1–0 up in extra time. With five minutes to go, my toes were peddling, my heart was palpitating. In fact, 27 years' worth of pent-up frustration and disillusionment was about to explode into teeming, unbridled ecstasy. But it turned out to be premature expectation all over again.

I first became aware of the Boro when I was about seven or eight years old. I'm sure I would have got into them earlier but we moved south for the first time when I was six and, as we all know, southerners are big softies when it comes to the beautiful game. So when we rather surprisingly moved back to Teesside 18 months later I was already behind my classmates in the footie fanaticism stakes. But not for long. My first specific memory of the Boro was the 8–0 thrashing of Sheffield Wednesday in April 1974 in a game which was meaningless as we had been virtually promoted by Xmas. I seemed to have timed my run into the box just right. The Boro were back in the old First Division for the first time in 20 years. I had the Second Division Champions poster that May. And I can still name from memory the players that Jack

Charlton turned into an efficient if uninspiring unit: Jim Platt, John Craggs, Frank Spraggon, Peter Brine, Stuart Boam, Willie Maddren, Bobby Murdoch, David Mills, John Hickton, Alan Foggon and Spike Armstrong (with Malcolm Smith and Billy Woof on the subs bench) – oh yeah, and Graeme Souness. Although none of them were rewarded with full caps (while they played for the Boro), a good number of them could have drunk for their countries judging by their beer guts. Years later, when Bobby Murdoch, who died recently, was sacked as Boro manager, my auntie and uncle bought his house in nearby Eston. I'm not joking, it took them a week to clear away the empties.

On the morning of 21 September 1974, my dad just announced he was taking me to see the Boro against Manchester City. The first thing I asked him was whether I could take a 'casey' along for a kick-around because he had only previously taken me to watch rugby at Acklam Park. I don't know whether he was at the time planning to get me interested in rugby because it was more middle class and he was rising through the ranks of the Taylor Woodrow Constuction, or whether it was just an excuse to get out for a pint on a Saturday afternoon. Either way, I saw it as a chance to have a kick-about when I got bored, which wasn't long given the awfulness of the oval-ball game. Despite my dad's success at work, he was still the same old working-class bloke. The Boro had been the method by which working-class Teesside fathers like him had bonded with their sons over the years. That first match at Ayresome Park was therefore a real rite of passage. I was eight, the same age as my dad was when his dad took him to his first Boro match in 1947. As we reached the top of the steps and walked out onto the East End terrace, I just stopped and gazed in wonder. I had never seen so many people together in one place – if memory serves me correctly there were 35,000 at Ayresome that day. As I stood surveying one of the best pitches in the country, verdant and lush in the late summer sun, I had never felt so small. In the thick atmosphere of baccy smoke, stale beer and adult male sweat, I had never been so aware of my immaturity in comparison with the adult male. We won 3-0 that day, but I have only one clear memory: Willie Donachie punching John Hickton, followed by nearly 35,000 people rising as one to snarl: 'Off, off, off . . . ' as they pointed to the players' tunnel. I don't know whether this experience scarred me but since then I've always thought that a good sending-off livens up any match.

At some point after that game and before our sixth failed attempt to win an FA Cup quarter-final later that season, the Boro became more important to me than just about anything. Twenty seven years on, with me approaching the age my dad was when he first took me, I still haven't cured myself of this obsessive, unrequited love. I say 'unrequited' because I often think I put more into this relationship than they do. I mean, one trophy or a European place would seem just reward for my dedication.

Like some mysterious tropical fever I don't know how I got it in the first place but the debilitating symptoms really first showed themselves when we lost that quarter final 1–0 to Birmingham in 1974. The Boro being joint top of the league at Xmas 1974 may even have brought it on. Looking back, I wish I had appreciated being top of the First Division – today we'd call it the Premiership – more but at the time I could never have known what a rare experience that would prove to be. I became more deeply aware of my reverence for all things Boro when I was walking home from the Avenue School in Nunthorpe one day. There was this bloke cleaning his car, which was an unusual sight at three o'clock on a weekday afternoon as all the dads round our way had full-time jobs. As I got closer I recognised the slightly balding forehead and straight straw-coloured hair . . . It couldn't be but it was. I was sure, yes, the bloke was John Hickton, then the Boro number nine and leading scorer at the club for the best part of a decade. I rushed nervously past. Over the next few months, I must have seen him virtually every afternoon pottering around his house but I never dared speak to him once. Perhaps, I thought, it might break some spell, narrow the gap too brutally between my status as a mortal and his as a god. At the age of eight, I had some sort of excuse for this behaviour.

Last Christmas at the age of 34, I finally had my first conversation with a Boro player. It went something like this:

'Hi there, Dave,' said the tallish, dark figure in a tentative Irish brogue, 'how's it going?'

'Fine, Keith,' I replied, trying to make it sound like I'd just bumped into an old mate in our local. We were in fact in the Union Tavern at the Middlesbrough Supporters South Christmas party. More embarrassingly, I was at that very moment standing about two yards from Robbo and a few other Boro players, urging myself to go and talk to them but paralysed with fear. Of course, I hadn't intended it to happen like this. They weren't supposed to recognise me and approach me before I could prepare some kind of rudimentary script.

'When are you gonna be back in the team?' I asked because I couldn't think of anything else to say.

'Soon (Pause). I've been injured, y'know.'

'I know(Pause). I read it the paper,' I replied.

Of course I knew Keith O'Neill was injured. I'm a Boro fan. But what should I say next? I thought about mentioning a possible mutual friend, a mate of mine called Graham who covers Norwich City, O'Neill's former club, for the *Eastern Daily News*. But I didn't. Suddenly, the pause ceased to be merely pregnant. In fact, it would be fair to say it was well into labour, contractions coming thick and fast.

'Keith, do you realise this is the first conversation I've ever had with a Boro player?' I asked to fill the screaming silence, 'apart from when Nicky

Mohan hit me with a stray shot during the warm-up at Luton in April 1994 and he said: "Sorry," and I said: "No problem" but I don't suppose that really counts.'

'Er . . . no', said Keith, edging away from me and suddenly looking for autographs to sign. 'Cheers. See you later.'

With that hasty valediction ringing in my ears, he was once again part of the throng of the Christmas party. 'Cheers,' I half-said. George, the ten-year-old I was with, depressingly a Manchester United fan there to collect the scrawls of our better known (ex- Manchester United) players, came running up to me. 'I've got Incey's autograph,' he shouted several times over, waving a bit of paper bearing the Secrets of Tutankhamen or some other equally impenetrable hieroglyphic.

'No one will believe you. It's just a load of scribble,' I replied, angry at my tongue-tied, strangled conversation with the Boro number 23 – and worse still at my jealousy. I mean, why did he get to merrily go around the Boro players picking up autographs when I couldn't? I've met household names in the field of light entertainment. I've actually interviewed people like Howard Kendall and Terry Venables (although long before he was at the Boro). I've sparred verbally with *Newsnight* presenters. Yet, I was too nervous to conduct a conversation with a 25-year-old wingback, who is not even a regular for a provincial club which has won nowt in 125 years. I turned to my brother, Phil, one of IBM's international sales force and as nutty as I am about the Boro, to share my inadequacy with him. But he was standing there open-mouthed and silent. Even though he could argue his case with the Chief Executive of IBM UK, like me, he was traumatised by the prospect of a conversation with one of the chosen few, our chosen few.

In 1974–75 when we finished seventh and missed out on Europe by a place, I could never have known this would remain our best league placing to date in my lifetime. In 1975 we moved south again to Buckinghamshire and that exile seemed only to deepen rather than relieve my obsession. I used to drag my dad along to all Boro's London games. When back on Teesside visiting relations, I would get to see the odd few games a season at Ayresome Park. I suppose some kids would have switched allegiance but I kept with the faith, even though being the only Boro fan among my mates meant I had to bear the brunt of their inevitable piss-taking all by myself. It's a wonder I never grew disillusioned, it really is. After all, the Boro have never been good away from home. They are also the kind of unfashionable team who are cheated on a regular basis by London referees; the most obvious example I suppose of the north/south divide. Plenty of people don't mind QPR. In one of his end-of-season videos, Danny Baker compares them to a 'maiden aunt', just *there* and harmless. I have a less charitable view. I despise them for a series of dodgy penalties awarded against us whenever we played them in the 1970s. In fact, the worst example was repeated in the mid-'90s on one of those football nostalgia shows. I hadn't seen the footage since I first saw it on that Sunday's *Big Match* in 1975 (and that after being at the game). When it came to the dodgy penalty incident, I once again leapt out of my chair to complain, even though I'd had 20 years to come to terms with it.

I suppose what kept me going was the belief that we could win a trophy or qualify for Europe. Even at the age of ten, it was patently obvious to me that all the Boro needed was to invest in one or two more quality players and we would be lifting trophies. So why couldn't Chairman Charlie Amer see that? Every season we'd promise so much. Every season I would finish up bemoaning our mediocre, mid-table finish in the top division. For the last 21 years, I've craved that sort of mediocrity, cursing myself for taking it for granted in the first place. Socialists often tell us that the rich fail to be aware of their own privilege while the poor are only too aware of their own lack of it. The same is true of football. You don't know how privileged you are until you've spent a wet afternoon at Gillingham watching a 0–0 draw where you actually become convinced that you really could do better than the team on the park.

In 1976, we reached our first League Cup semi-final, against Manchester City. I didn't go, for the same reasons I didn't go to any of the four FA Cup quarter-finals we played between 1975 and 1981: my dad wasn't as fanatical as me. This meant I couldn't afford the train fare, the match ticket, and God knows what other expenses on twenty pence-a-week a week pocket money. But I still felt the pain of defeat just as badly. In fact, it pains me even to write about them now. The heartbreak of the 1975 FA Cup quarter-final defeat at Birmingham was all the harder to bear as we had beaten them 3–0, twice, in the league that season. When we drew Liverpool away at the same stage of the competition two years later, I never gave up hope even though Liverpool were virtually invincible at the time, partly because we'd miraculously won 2–0 at Anfield a season or two before. We were on holiday in Stratford that weekend but I refused to go out sightseeing with my family. Instead, I watched *Grandstand* for the updates. It was 0–0 at half-time and I was just starting to believe we could get them back to Ayresome where we could beat anyone. *Grandstand* was showing the rugby international Wales against Scotland in the days when Wales were still good. It was the match when Phil Bennett scored that try where he runs the length of the pitch beating every Scottish player at least once before planting the ball underneath the posts. The second after he did it, that day, live, *Grandstand* flashed up 'Liverpool 2. Middlesbrough 0'. I've seen that try repeated many times since and each time I half expect that scoreline to appear again. It may, in fact, be one of the reasons I hate the oval-ball game so much.

And then there was Orient, or Leyton Orient as they are known now. This time, with us at home, and in the top ten of the top flight while Orient languished in the lower regions of the old Second Division, I thought, our time had come. There are images that people take to their graves. And one of mine, I'm sure, will be the sight of Billy Ashcroft, scuffing a shot from six yards out straight into the arms of the keeper. Not just because it was his death or glory moment and every Boro fan would have forgiven him everything if he'd put that ball in the back of the net. But because someone actually went to the bother of painting that scene. With the perversity we so often have to put up with at the Boro, the painting adorned the front of each matchday programme for an entire season. After losing the replay 2–1, I think we'd all just about given up. But a season later in 1981 we drew Wolves at home in the quarter-finals. Bizarrely, we all thought, Wolves would be easier than Orient as they were a struggling First Division outfit at the time so the Boro would be under less pressure against them. But we were always behind, always chasing them. Eventually, we lost the replay in extra time.

And then just as I reached 16, the age where I had the money to go and see games further afield from London, we fell apart. We sold the best team we ever had and used the money to build a sports centre which we never used or Charlie Amer's new house, depending on who you believe.

I don't suppose you can fault the following 19 or so seasons in terms of excitement. Every season from 1982 onwards (apart from 1995-96) has gone to the last week in terms of play-offs, relegation or promotion. And even that all palls next to that harrowing broadcast in 1986 that told us all that Boro were dead: ' wound up by the Official Receiver'.

I must admit, I nearly lost the faith in the seasons after that relegation in 1982. It may have been my age: booze and birds loomed large for the first time in my life, and in 1984 I went away to college. Despite applying to Durham, Leeds and Sheffield (Teesside Poly didn't do English Lit, I checked) I had to take a place at Dundee which was just as far from Middlesbrough as London so I'd still only get to Ayresome Park two or three times a season, usually by breaking the 500-mile trip home at the end of term. But the Boro never stopped mattering to me, even though we were dreadful and I now spent my time discussing The Smiths, Lloyd Cole, Camus and Sartre rather than Phil Boersma and Stan Bowles. In those days football wasn't the media-luvvied, yuppie-friendly game it is now. So, come 4.45 p.m. on a Saturday, I'd sneak off to the TV room in my hall of residence for *Final Score*. I once confessed to my student friends what I was doing. Judging by their reaction, I'm sure it would have been less embarrassing to tell them I was going for a wank. I had further heartaches while at college. They used to hold the May Ball, the social event of the year, on the last day of the football season. So in 1986, 1988 (when we failed to get a promotion place proper and had to go into the play-offs) and 1989, I spent the Ball being berated by girlfriends for getting so pissed, after spending all that money on a ticket, as I tried to blot out the misery of our latest failure.

After college, I thought I'd be able to see the Boro whenever I wanted but

I got a job on the *Sunday Times* where I had to work Saturdays. At one point, I was even working in the sports department covering the old First Division matches. Friends would say, 'You've fallen on your feet, a football fan like you.' But the truth was I hated it because every Saturday I knew I wouldn't be watching the Boro. The *Sunday Times* came up trumps, though, on one occasion. I managed to grab a press pass for the ZDS Cup Final, Boro's now-forgotten first-ever Wembley final in 1990 (and where we began our now regular feat of losing to Chelsea at the 'Venue of Legends'). The *Sunday Times* job barely outlasted the 1989–90 season, though, and I found myself in Scotland again and still without enough money to see the Boro regularly.

Then in November 1991, I got the job at MI5, where minor public school culture is still very much dominant. There were organised cricket and rugby matches against MI6 and GCHQ, but never football. That said, there were enough people interested in football to want to have a semi-organised kick around the park at lunchtime or after work.

I was still in London but now I had the freedom and the money to go and watch Boro as often as I liked. I was also without that footie fan's perennial handicap – a girlfriend. I saw 25 matches in 1991-92 and then I was moved to the counter-IRA section. Although I was still based in London, a good deal of my work after that was done in the North-East. From August '92 to February '93, I saw every Boro match. I only stopped because I had to be in Northern Ireland for work the night of the Sheffield United match on 8 February. I still saw 39 out of the 47 games we played that season, often having to get up before six in the morning to get to work at MI5 on time and not use up my holiday entitlement. Because of my Jesuitical zeal, everyone in MI5 got to know I was a Boro fan, doing a 500-mile round trip for every home game. Most MI5 staff – who frowned on passion, no matter from what quarter it came – thought I was a total idiot.

My actions did though bring other people out of the closet, so to speak. A lot more staff started owning up to going to football. In my work outside the office, football had always served me well. I mean, what else was I likely to have in common with a 59-year-old copper from Weston-Super-Mare, apart from an interest in the beautiful game? But football was to prove particularly useful when I visited Special Branches (SB) in the North-East. I remember the first time I went to a regional conference up there. I sat down with some coppers from Cleveland SB – or 'polis' as they are known in the local vernacular. The conversation went something like this:

'Are you all Middlesbrough fans?' I asked.

'Yes,' they agreed.

'I've seen all the games this season.' I replied.

'Oh, which team?' they asked, half-interested.

'Oh, Middlesbrough.' I replied casually.

'Oh aye,' you could see them thinking, 'We've got some bloke here with

a southern accent saying he's a Boro fan to try and win our confidence.'
After answering questions on the Boro ranging from 'What was David
Armstrong's nickname?' to 'What club record did he set?' to 'How many
consecutive games was it?' (answers: Spike; the most consecutive games; 385),
I managed to convince them. As a result, I built up strong working
relationships not just with Middlesbrough SB but with all the other North-
East SBs because just about every bloke in the North-East is mad about
footie. Indeed, more professional footballers are born in the North-East than
any other area of the country, compared to population. I remember going to,
for example, Northumbria SB, which is obviously split between Newcastle
and Sunderland fans; fortunately though the head of Special Branch there
was a Boro fan, who coincidentally was in charge of crowd control the night
Boro were promoted in 1987.

Towards the end of the 1992–93 season, the Boro played a small but not
insignificant role in getting me and my current girlfriend, Annie, together. I
used to go out for drinks with colleagues in MI5, of whom Annie was one,
and entertain them (they may not have seen it that way) with stories of the
Boro in an attempt to convert them into Boro fans. Annie steadfastly
detested all things football. One day, she told me she'd 'like me so much
more' if I didn't go on and on about football and, in particular, the Boro.
Paradoxically, I took this to be the green light to ask her out. People don't
make statements like that to work colleagues, particularly not in the stuffy
environment of MI5, unless there's something in it. As a result, we started to
go out at the end of the 1992–93 season and our relationship deepened
when I convinced her that any bloke who could devote 20-odd years of his
life to a football team who'd done bugger-all must be the loyal, faithful type.
I suppose she timed her run into the box as well. She started to go out with
me just as we got relegated, followed by our most mediocre season in living
memory, 1993-94. She was with me at the last game at Ayresome Park, which
I watched with a perpetual lump in my throat as I felt I was leaving an old
friend. I think I might have burst into tears if towards the end Jamie Pollock
had converted his one-on-one with the keeper and made the last goalscorer
at Ayresome Park, and in front of the Holgate, a Teesside lad.

When the Boro moved to the Riverside, I went to the first match there.
I then became a season ticket holder, although I pine for the Holgate and the
madness of bouncing up and down while either humming 'My Angel is the
Centrefold' or chanting 'Let's go fuckin' mental'. Until August 1997 when I
went on the run, I was still going to between 15 and 20 games a season,
including of course all those cup-ties and finals.

I think the best Boro match I've ever been to was the FA Cup quarter-
final against Derby County in March 1997 – yes, better than that season's
3-3 semi-final thriller against Chesterfield. I mean how can your favourite
game be a 3–3 draw against a Second Division side? More importantly, the

victory against Derby laid to rest all the ghosts of those four earlier quarter-final defeats. I can still remember the sensation as Ravanelli let fly with his left foot in the last minute and we all watched the ball whizz – but in slow motion – into the back of the net, before going 'fuckin' mental'. I remember being as high as a kite as Boro players who'd never even heard of Middlesbrough at the time of those cup defeats stood in front of us arm in arm knowing they'd just made history. I was as happy then as I was despondent two minutes from the end of extra time in the Coca-Cola Cup final, when Emile Heskey equalised; 43 seconds after the start of the 1997 FA Cup final, when De Matteo scored; and at the end of the 1998 Coca-Cola Cup final, which we lost. Mind you, it would have been typical if we had won the latter and picked up our first major honour when I had absolutely no chance of being there because I was on the run from MI5.

Just before I went on the run, I saw the first game of the 1997–98 season, home to Charlton. I didn't know at the time it would be three years before I saw the Boro live again. Two weeks later, while I waited for my article to hit the streets, I kept flicking up Ceefax from the safety of a hotel room in Holland. When we eventually lost 0–1 at home to Stoke, I became convinced I had done the wrong thing. Fortunately, the season picked up and I managed to keep in touch with the Boro results on the Net. In fact, my first faltering steps on the information superhighway led me to news about Anthony Ormerod's injury at the time. Strangely, thanks to all the Net information services and an e-mailed Boro newsletter, I was better informed about the Boro in a farmhouse in the middle of nowhere in France than I had been ever before. I caught some games on Sky, even though it was a nine-hour round trip to my nearest bar which had satellite TV. And I watched the Coca-Cola Cup final in a bar in Amsterdam, despite Annie's worries that I would be recognised by other Boro fans and shopped to the police. Ironically, I was arrested after watching Boro–Empoli on Sky in a bar, in the JD Cup – a meaningless pre-season tournament. It was a blow because I'd arranged to be at my first Boro game in a year in Den Haag the following weekend.

When I returned to the Riverside in August 2000 we were top of the league, even if our record was Played 2, Won 1, Drawn 1. Because I am superstitious about wearing team colours to a game, I wore my *Philosophy Football* T-shirt bearing the Albert Camus legend: 'All that I know most surely about morality and obligations I owe to football.' But, as the BT Cellnet Stadium – once famously described as resembling Space Station Alpha – loomed out of the rain-soaked Tees, I was reminded of that less famous football quote by Camus: 'When I am in a football stadium, I feel like a child.' As I got nearer the ground, Boro fans came up to me and shook me by the hand. Everyone was so supportive. If any of them disagreed with what I had done, they were certainly keeping their counsel to themselves. And it wasn't just the odd person. All in all, I think nearly a hundred people must have approached me – not just to wish me luck on a personal level, but to impart to me their fervent wish that I gave the intelligence services what for because it was about time someone did. I was particularly touched as a group of Boro fans mobbed me and started singing: 'There's only one David Shayler.' In fact, I nearly cried. I hadn't really recovered before I finally pushed through the turnstile. With that in mind, I thought that the Boro might for once come good and beat Leeds just for me. But the football fan's love for his team is seldom requited. By half-time, I was – as they say – gutted, Hamilton Ricard was as bad as he had been when I left three years earlier. But one line from earlier in the day summed up for me the warmth and cleverness of the Teesside wit. Just before I went in, one wag jokingly accused me of being a fair-weather fan.

'Typical of some people,' he said. 'They only turn up when we're top of the league.'

Note: An earlier version of this chapter first appeared in the fanzine *Middlesbrough Supporters South*, www.mss.org.uk

GOLDEN GOALS TO GOLD MEDALS, FOOTBALL'S OLYMPIAN LESSONS

Alan Tomlinson

The Olympic Games and football's World Cup share the global spotlight in the international media's sporting calendar. Both are special events in two ways. Firstly, they are quadrennial, not annual. Secondly, they involve the vast majority of the world's nations. So whilst some other major spectator sports can lay claim to more sustained audiences and followings – athletics, whenever it's sufficiently well-organised, and the Formula One motor-racing circuit, for example – the specially rationed nature of the Olympics and the World Cup preserve a sense of expectation and aura around the events.

For the Olympic movement, the Los Angeles Games of 1984 were a turning point, bringing Hollywood-style design principles to the production and presentation of a Cold-War fuelled extravaganza. Jimmy Carter had dragged the USA out of the 1980 Moscow Olympics, in protest at the Soviet Union's invasion of Afghanistan. The Soviet Union and most of its allies responded tit for tat in 1984 and the way was clear for the USA brazenly to politicise the Olympics on a scale unsurpassed since the Berlin Nazi Olympics of 1936. In 1936 huge audiences were mobilised in a perfectly executed and ruthlessly organised political pageant. LA followed suit almost a half century on. These were the first Olympics presided over by the International Olympic Committee's new top man, Juan Antonio Samaranch, who would expand the business until he stepped down in the summer of 2001.

The LA lore followed hot on the heels of the successfully expanded football World Cup finals in Spain in 1982, the first to line up 24 finalists. This fulfilled a pledge given to Third World countries by the Brazilian João Havelange, boss of football's world governing body, FIFA, who had taken over in 1974 and was to dominate global football business until his retirement after 24 years – at France '98, the first 32-team finals. Between them, the Olympics and the World Cup have gobbled up billions of revenue for television rights and hugely lucrative sponsorship packages, and have fuelled bidding rivalries between cities and countries across the world keen to get in on the PR act and promo show that modern sport's highest profile events must now be. All this is based upon the belief that these events fire the imaginations of millions of fans and billions of viewers.

Sydney 2000 was the Bumper Summer Olympics. It welcomed more than 11,000 athletes, several thousand officials and coaches, and as the 16 days whizzed by estimates of the number of mediafolk in town reached 21,000 – although official estimates had been initially put at around 15,000. Athens 2004 plans to cater for 18,000 media. The Main Press Centre at the Olympic Park was vast, and the International Broadcast Centre was dominated by US broadcaster NBC, who'd paid $705 million for the rights, and mobilised a workforce of more than 2,000. More athletes, more sports, more professionals. Bigger, bigger, bigger.

How *do* we watch sport? You have a choice. Go to any English football ground and you can see it now, clearer than ever. All-seater stadiums have zoned the fan culture. We couldn't see this nearly as vividly when the crowd was a standing, swaying mass of upright individuals. Now we sit among the singers and the chanters and the ranters. We can see what they're wearing, tell them to sit down – if we dare – so that some of us can watch the football. Those who stand up are led not by the flow of the contest on the pitch, but by the dynamics of the interaction with the rival fans. Two recent renditions by Burnley fans flaunted the deep roots of homophobia and racism in the traditional constituencies of the people's game in England. Winding-up Watford's absent Chairman Sir Elton John, Burnley fans in the singing sections of Turf Moor bawled with a grinding regularity, 'If you're queer as fuck, stand up'. So excitedly was this grunted (it would be a decimation of English usage to say 'sung') that many grunters jumped up on the second line. Repressed expression of sexual complexity, or post-modern irony? 'Town full of Pakis, You're just a town full of Pakis', chanted many Burnley fans at the local derby game at Blackburn Rovers' Ewood Park ground. You can sit among this category of traditional fan and see and hear a frothing regional jingoism and racism that wouldn't be out of place in the meeting halls of the Ku Klux Klan. Yet a few blocks away will be old men in trilby hats or ratters (peaked cloth caps), recalling the days when the action on the pitch had more cadence, when the main abuse directed to the referee was to call him 'four-eyes', when the Bovril was cheaper, the meat-pie choice was less stressful, and the world was a simpler place. Among them will be some younger fans, keen to distance themselves from the aggressive element, their deep-seated affinity for the club expressed in more hesitant singing styles or loud one-off opinions. And a few rows down from the desperate, racist Neanderthals there will be family groups, kids-for-a-quid admissions encouraged by clubs to join the football family, to see in their local club a place for a party. 'Mum, what does "queer as fuck" mean?'

On the other side of the world at the Sydney 2000 Olympics, the cabby in Melbourne corrected me. I'd just been in the ABC studio doing the breakfast show, talking about Olympic sport and the commercialisation of global sport, and I was on my way back to my hosts at the University of Melbourne, who'd invited me down to give a public lecture on the state of world sport. It was good to be able to talk about the Olympics and the football tournament in the Olympics. Most of the city of Melbourne had something else on its mind that week, the Grand Finals of Aussie Rules, a mini-tournament of the top teams that drew crowds of 90,000 to 100,000, and took place between teams representing different areas of the city. The cabby was a football (or, for Australians, soccer) man and we were talking about the forthcoming Olympics match at the MCG, the Melbourne Cricket Ground, between Australia and Italy. It was a sell-out already, and I remarked that it must feel great for him to be able to see a few of his favourite Italian players in the Italian line-up, and cheer on his home nation. Speaking with the strongest of Italian accents he put me in my place, saying that he and all his five children would be rooting for the 'Roos. He was an Australian and he wouldn't pass over such a chance to reaffirm this, with and for a new generation, at the game.

I didn't manage to get to that game, but South Africa versus Brazil (in the men's tournament), at the BCG (Brisbane Cricket Ground), seemed a reasonable alternative. And Norway versus Germany was shaping up as one of the semi-finals in the women's tournament. Walking over to that game from my base in Sydney might be a good chance to mingle with the Olympic football fans. Brazil strolled carelessly towards defeat, by 1–3, in Brisbane. The young South African players were elated, and back at their hotel base, the Novotel, they looked as if they still couldn't believe it. Perhaps they never quite came down to earth, following up this result with a mediocre performance that kept them out of the next round. But it was the fans that were interesting. There weren't many Brazilians on show, and scarcely any visible presence of South African fans. So who was there? It was expatriates, one generation removed perhaps, with a lineage soaked in football commitment – like the young man walking back through Brisbane's spectacular riverside arboreal gardens, in his Blackburn Rovers shirt. With football taking a higher profile in Australia, and English Premier League action relayed back to his old country by Murdoch's global initiatives, the world history of the game could be injected into the bloodstream of the embryonic fan culture of this most multicultural of nations. I asked him why the Blackburn shirt? It was status as much as history that inspired him, Blackburn having been champions of the English league when he'd started following the game in the early years of the Premiership. But he'd stuck with them, since their fall from these heights. And families were there. There were fathers with daughters, mothers with sons; admen's whole dream families. Not always in the Juventus, Manchester United, Real Madrid or Brazil shirts either. In the half-time snack queue – Hunter Valley Chardonnay here, a nice change from Boddington or Thwaites back in North-East Lancs – I asked one father about his. Another cultural misreading. His was the strip of a suburban team in the Brisbane area. He wore his local team's shirt proudly, mingling with the England, Arsenal, Liverpool, Juventus shirts and the rest.

The women's semi was back in the heart of the Olympic event. Sydney was strange. Strategically, I thought, where might you meet fans an hour or two before an Olympic football semi-final? A big pub on a main junction ten or fifteen minutes' walk from the stadium seemed about right. There was no sign of a world sporting event in there though. Pokies (the ubiquitous upmarket one-armed-bandit machines catering to the Australian gambling fixation) whirred away. Telescreens showed pony-racing and offered odds and commentary on that. Throughout the pubs and bars of the city, life went on as if the Olympic football was happening at the other side of the world. Maybe I'd picked the wrong spot, though a party of mildly carnivalesque Norwegians came in, had one or two drinks, shared a few droll exchanges and trudged on stadiumwards. At the ground it was the same as Brisbane, but even quieter. Cocktail party chatter rather than terrace chants. This was the semi-final of one of the two biggest tournaments in world women's football. The ground was nowhere near full. The football flowed fitfully. The German centre-half set Wagnerian bells ringing, looping by with a backheader, a harmless upfield punt over her oncoming goalkeeper, sending the band of Norwegian fans into a restrained jig of delight. Most of the crowd was quiet and comprised family groups and – though by no means in an obvious majority – women. It was a nice walk back towards Sydney Central and the city, like coming out of the Opera or Sadler's Wells – satisfied consumers, rather than rabid fans. There was something missing, some edge or other just not there. But it was better than being leaned over by riot police on horses or snarled at by trained killer dogs, as I would be at Bramall Lane in Sheffield, nine months later. 'You're worse than the Stasi, you lot', observed my brother.

'Is that right?,' responded a rattled riot cop in full operational mode, shielded and armed, ready for action, but bemused by this verdict in cross-cultural studies.

The opening match of the Euro 2000 football championships took place at the King Baudouin Stadium, at Heysel, on the outskirts of Brussels. This was the biggest game in Brussels since the tragic encounter at the same stadium between the Italian side Juventus and England's Liverpool, in the final of the European Cup. There was much to prove and there were searingly painful memories to transcend. In the first game Belgium took on a subdued Swedish side, winning despite a nervy start. The opening ceremony was more memorable than the football, as much for its arcane symbolism as anything else, inspiring writer Harry Pearson to wonder out aloud in the next seat to me how the hell he was going to write anything coherent or interesting about it for the Monday morning *Guardian*. At least he made it for the next issue of *When Saturday Comes*: 'Someone has just broadcast the news that the opening ceremony will only last 11 minutes. There is a palpable sense of relief ... The finale comes when a giant humanoid form is wheeled onto the field and kicks a white football straight into the air. Hard to know what it was all about ... ' Thanks, Harry. Around the stadium – well served by underground, trams and buses – the fans were polite and patient, the police were restrained. It was only later in the centre of the city that tensions would explode, as stand-by police played chase with mainly Belgian revellers. It was like a magnified weekend night in any English town from Harrow-on-the-Hill to Hull.

The friendly little ground at Bruges was a bus ride from the town centre and the railway station. The world champions France had just cruised past an an over-respectful and ultimately insipid Danish challenge and soon the horns on the Viking headgear of the Denmark fans looked like mere bravado. But the fans knew that they were outclassed by a team in its pomp, and they weren't going to let mere defeat stop the party. 'Well-played,' I ventured to some red-shirted, horn-wearing, battered-looking Danes as I settled in for a pasta on the edge of the old town. I couldn't decipher the reply but the looks said it all: 'Don't patronise us, you English git. We were crap.' Younger Danish fans filled some of the liveliest and most fashionable bars in Bruges, where they drank, chatted and danced with the French fans and with the Belgian locals. There was no trouble whatsoever to be seen, and no observable police presence. 'Yes, we're going to Ibiza, yes, were going to have a party' they sang along in the late bars in Bruges, confirming the Club 18–30 spirit of the evening after the game.

Many said that a football World Cup in the United States would be a disaster. But it wasn't. If a US audience knows that it's watching the best thing in the world of its kind, whatever the expertise or the feat, serious or trivial, there's the likelihood of a respectful and captivated – albeit ignorant – audience. This was the case in USA '94. Except there had been a huge sigh of relief among the international football community when England failed to qualify, happy that its largely troublesome fans wouldn't be flooding across the Atlantic. Los Angeles – or more accurately, Pasadena's Rosebowl – simply saw the World Cup final as just another, but rather parochial, big sports game.

World Cup final eve was quite the party. We were based in Santa Monica, the Brighton of California, where the cheapest pier and seascape is available for the quick location shot by the movie industry. The Brazilians and their fellow travellers brought a taste of Brazilian carnival to Santa Monica's streets and promenades. The bars, restaurants and night clubs were seething with people mostly bedecked in the gold-dominated colours of Brazil, mingling with a sizeable minority sporting the Mediterranean blue of Italy. Most of those whose teams had been knocked out in previous rounds adopted Brazil as their favourites. Third World first here, as devotees of the world's most popular game rushed to be associated with its most dashing cavaliers. As the bars emptied into the streets in the small hours of Cup final day a noisy, but peaceful, face-off ensued between fans and adopted fans of the two finalists. Amidst much flag waving, swaying and dancing, orchestrated alternate chants of 'BRAAA . . . ZIL, BRAAA . . . ZIL, EETAL . . . YAH, EETAL . . . YAH' rang out into the clear California night sky. The partygoers were women as well as men, youngish cosmopolitan consumers. This was a shared celebration of respective national identity and friendly international rivalry. Both sets of supporters were in good voice and good humour. There was no chance of any trouble between them and the greatest threat was posed by policemen and policewomen lurking in the shadows. They had never experienced anything like this before at a sports match. The cops stood off 20 metres, nervously fingering their riot sticks and wondering.

FIFA and the US soccer federation were delighted by the lack of hooliganism. Ironically, the most disruptive element came from another nation which failed to qualify, France. But even the French hooligan fringe was limited to one troublemaker, who, when he was not fighting with security guards, was roughing up opponents in the midfield at Old Trafford. Napoleon, dumped on the beach on Elba, could not have struck a pose more full of Gallic indignation than Eric Cantona's after he had been ejected from the Giant's Stadium for thumping an official. For the fabled 'true' English supporter who had travelled to the USA simply to soak up the atmosphere of the World Cup finals, the absence of his national team engendered mixed feelings. We met a group of Lancashire lads who were combining the World Cup with an American holiday and they expressed the dilemma eloquently. 'It's those cockney bastards who spoil everything' explained the car salesman in his replica Blackburn shirt. 'If England had qualified they would have spoiled it, causing trouble wherever they went. It's sad that England aren't here, but it wouldn't have been the same. There would have been a few who wanted to fight and we'd all have been tarred with the same brush.'

The walk to the ground had a dream-like quality. The sunshine and heat, the brightly coloured, happy, noisy crowds, the sprinklers watering the extensive gardens of the millionaires' houses which surrounded the stadium, the bumper-to-bumper traffic, the big, yellow buses and the black-and-white highway patrol cars, and the street vendors – hundreds of them selling T-shirts, flags, balls, hats, bottled water and cold minerals – and the ticket touts doing a brisk trade with tickets marked up at around eight hundred dollars.

On the way into the ground we had formed orderly lines to be searched before reaching the turnstiles. As we were funnelled towards our entrance we found ourselves shoulder-to-shoulder with a man wearing a Brentford FC shirt. 'Fair play to you, pal, it takes guts to wear that in public.' He did not respond at first. Then he looked towards the sky, made a barely audible whistle and said to nobody in particular, 'Of all the gates in all the world –

I've travelled three and a half thousand miles to get stuck in the queue with a fucking Scouser!'

We sat with Tony (originally from Belfast, now with a small business in New York) and a few seats away there were three more Ulster men from Coleraine. They held aloft between them a large Ulster flag, the red cross of Saint George against a white background with the red hand of Ulster and a gold crown at the centre. They were here to support any team that had beaten the Republic of Ireland and had celebrated long into the night when the Dutch repeated King William of Orange's victory at the battle of the Boyne in 1690, by knocking the Irish and their mercenaries out of this competition in Florida. The final presented them with a real problem because both teams represented devoutly Catholic countries. They resolved this problem by supporting nobody, sitting stoically and silently for the duration of the game. These silent, sombre, sad and sinister figures were the exceptions. For the rest of the world gathered in the Rosebowl it was carnival time. Flags, replica shirts and painted faces emblazoned across one of the largest cosmopolitan gatherings of all time.

Football generates extraordinary levels of commitment and passion. Footballers can be the butt of jokes, the object of adoration; heroes one moment and villains the next, in an unremitting soap opera of hope, despair and refuelled hope.

The World Cup and the Olympics attract two very different sorts of fan. For a start, football fans follow their teams on the national trail as an extension of their support for clubs. This carries with it a draining baggage of expectation. Players at international level know that they face pressure from a public that is potentially hostile and abusive, and that if they underperform in the national shirt, they could be vilified and abused. Olympic sportsmen and women are in a different, lower league of celebrity and prominence. The odd truly global superstar may emerge on the Olympic scene, affecting generations world-wide. At the 1972 Games the Russian gymnast Olga Korbut was iconic in this sense, an image or what we now call a role-model, having major influence on the way in which the Olympic spectacle is staged, and on the activities and aspirations of generations. But apart from the professional athletes in the classical athletics disciplines, or those with the potential to make professional careers such as boxing, Olympians often come and go, living relatively low profiles between the events themselves. Who remembers the gold-medal winning clay-pigeon shooter or yachtsman? Olympic competitors also represent the UK, in the Great Britain Olympic team. Only Steve Redgrave and his team won gold in Atlanta in 1996, and the gradual benefits of lottery funding showed in the UK medal tally in Sydney – 11 golds, and up from 36th at Atlanta (hot on the heels of Ethiopia) to 10th (one place behind Cuba) in the overall medal table. But it was a roll-call of Olympic winners of whom only specialist minorities within the British sporting public would have heard. This might change afterwards for some. Returning as medallists, they would be fêted and sometimes courted by the media and the sponsors. But many of them would be opening supermarkets rather than listening to offers from *Hello* magazine, doing good grass-roots school work and proper sport development rather than boosting up personal fortunes helped by hustling agents. Sydney gold medallists – boxer Audley Harrison, heptathlete Denise Lewis, and rower Steve Redgrave – have been used by the FA to promote football, appearing on the pitch just before the England–Germany game after Sydney, and participating in the draw for the FA Cup tournament. Some Olympians will sustain national profiles. But for most Olympians, it is a fundamentally different relationship between follower and performer than that between the football fan and the football star. It is a less volatile relationship, a special date rather than an ongoing passionate relationship.

In the eyes of the public a European Championship or a World Cup is just one more event in a crowded cycle of ambitions and expectations. It's special of course because the eyes of the watching world might be turned your way, and it's a bit of a lark to brandish your banner, if you're from Rochdale or Brentford, in front of an audience of millions, product placing your local roots at the England game. You don't see many Union Jacks at England football matches – too much Scotland and the rest in that one. You see the revitalised stark image of the flag of St George, an obstinate-looking throwback to some vague myth of national superiority – or maybe a cultural separateness coming out of its shell in a post-devolution UK.

At the Olympic Games it's the Union Jack on display, that's waved by the flag-carrier in the opening ceremony, raised when there's a medal triumph, and carried by the fans. There may be thousands there from the UK, but they're there for a lot of different sports. And of course so that the four UK football associations don't get their special status at FIFA questioned, there are no Great Britain football teams entered in the Olympics. So no football fans, or Barmy Army cricket fans. Olympic spectators are more discriminating and heterogeneous.

Nationalism is at the centre of Olympism. Although the modern Olympic Games were founded – by French aristocrat Baron Pierre de Coubertin – to create what he called a free-trade of the future, and to champion peaceable internationalism rather than war, they inexorably stimulated nationalist trappings. This happened right from the beginning in the first modern Olympics in Athens in 1896, when Greece used the event to boost national sentiment and bolster a fragile monarchy. But tempered in appropriate ways, the nationalism of contemporary Olympism can be subdued. All nations are on display in the parapahernalia of nationalism, and all countries can participate in at least some of the action. The myths and rhetorics of Olympism play down the intensely anatagonistic undercurrents of Olympic sport. The athletes might not be able to stand the sight of each other, but unless they are on such a prima donna level of mega-stardom or the organising committee bends its rules for its own, they on the whole live in the athletes' village together. And there, real internationalism can certainly come into play. There was a daily condom allocation to all athletes – men and women – in Sydney. The Cuban team was reported to be the first to ask for more, the Oliver Twists of the youthful hedonism truly at the heart of the Olympic theme of the unity of youth.

The Olympics can be like a giant playground, with things going on all over the place, for journalists as well as fans. In Sydney all the journalists were chasing a story, and yet always had one eye on an event elsewhere, like celebrity spotters at a socialite party. Conversely, the football event is concentrated and intense. It has the pattern of the sexual encounter, the build-up, the encounter, the locked passions, the climax, and the come-down. In the Olympics there's another set of dynamics across the village or down at the waterfront. Next to the relational intensity of the football event and the World Cup, the Olympics is like a series of teasing flirtations. The spectator body moves on, to another line-up, another queue, another thrill, like punters at Disneyland.

In the most intense of Olympic moments – and these are usually in the Olympic stadium itself – a global dynamic can sometimes be almost tangible. In such cases the individual champions can transcend the narrow nationalism of nation versus nation. Cathy Freeman, the Aboriginal Australian 400 metres champion did precisely this in the Sydney Olympics. Standing, too, for women as well as her race, she lit the torch at the opening ceremony and so enhanced the universalism of her image. The world then all but willed her to her individual victory in the second week of the tournament.

Beneath the manipulated and orchestrated surfaces of Olympic ceremony and spectacle nationalist currents run strong. In order to build up momentum as the Australian team, confident of successes, chased its target of 60 medals, the Games organisers scheduled the swimming events in the first week, putting its ace swimming team centre-stage right from the start. There were even rumours that the pool at the Olympic Park was designed to favour Australian techniques such as its turning strengths. The US team felt provoked by this, and early Australian successes. The international press salivated at the US team's gloating prediction that it would smash the Australian men's relay team like guitars. When the Australian men won, they mimed the playing of their unsmashed guitars. The seats were scarcely full of the hoi-polloi –not at those ticket prices, and with the high-profile political and cultural figures in the best seats – and so this could be defused as high spirits rather than provocation. In the big-screen outdoor live sites of Sydney itself, cheers accompanied the Australian victories, from groups of individuals rather than fan cultures. They gathered – women alone, family groups, all ages – with their picnic blankets and supplies, waiting for the Freeman race or the Ian Thorpe swim, drifting off immediately after the outcome of the contest. The infrequency of the event, and the transience of the fan base, meant that nationalist passions were not channelled or built-up in any sustained way, not really *deeply* aroused.

During the Sydney Olympics the Australian media were narrowly nationalist in their concerns and coverage of the events, puffing up Australian hopes and picking out glamour figures from the pool, including the women water polo champions, the track, the beach volleyball. This was matched by the crowds at events and viewing sites. In the boxing hall, anything Australian – the bout referee for instance – would get a loud home cheer. The loudest jeers and boos were reserved for anyone American, closely followed by anyone from Great Britain. So this playful expression of nationalist resentment and hostility was directed at the old imperialist oppressor – whose Union Jack flag, ironically, adorned every Australian honour tucked away in the corner of the Australian national flag – and at the new global oppressor, at least culturally, the US. But in the end it was all friendly and harmless stuff, on home soil, cheer-leading rather than rabble-rousing.

Without a doubt football is tribal. This is not meant in any atavistic sense. It refers more neutrally than that, to the collective and divisive nature of football loyalties. We know that football can be a marvellous global calling-card, an Esperanto of the body. Football is a pretty simple game and fans world-wide understand it. Whether it's with a cabby in Brighton or Australia, or a stranger in a Manhattan urinal, football can launch you into the most unexpected of conversations. But for most fans it is essentially excluding of others, assertive of local collective identity. Local derbies and the fierce partisanship expressed by neighbours are the most compelling cases of this feature of football and fan culture. Football fan cultures based on place as the main source of distinctiveness testify to the fragility of claims about the overall globalisation of the contemporary world. And despite the gentrification of football and its European glitzification in the English Premier League, other European domestic leagues, and the Champions League, the football tribe has at its core a traditional set of values – tough, working-class masculinity. In no Olympic city or around any Olympic event will a set of sports fans capable of the excesses of this traditional rump of football culture be present. But there's a hard-edged, class-influenced, hard-man xenophobia and racism that still colours parts of the traditional football culture, and especially so in the English case.

Sports in the Olympics offer a completely different basis for the fans. The extended agenda of Olympic contests in Sydney covered 28 sports, and athletics with all its disciplines and events was just one of these. Aquatics covered swimming, synchronised swimming, diving and water polo, and swimming itself of course is subdivided into a range of specialist events.

Sydney introduced two new sports for their Olympic debuts, tae kwon do and triathlon. And two sports that first appeared at the Atlanta Games, softball and beach volleyball, were again featured in Sydney. So the Olympic events are watched in a multitude of ways. If you can't get a ticket for one event or your favourite sport, you can find a ticket for something else, just to be there. At Bondi Beach the beach volleyball attracted lager-swilling lads, as well as family groups. There wasn't much discussion of team tactics in this audience. It was a good-time crowd, oblivious to the niceties of the sport, animated by a DJ master of ceremonies. Without taking anything away from the athleticism, dedication and commitment of the players, it was staged as a cross between a beauty contest and a television game show.

The Olympics can look like a bloated beast, but one grain of optimism as some of us try and salvage some positive values from the debacle of consumer excess, organisational scandal and jingoistic nationalism, is that the proportion of women competing at the Games has risen dramatically. The old Soviet Union and other East European states always knew how to win lots of medals: pick obscure sports, people with some physical aptitude, train up on drugs and dedicate lots of resources to esoteric activities. Do this with your women athletes too and most of the West's hopeful beauties won't stand a chance. China's followed the formula well too, with its women athletes and swimmers. So has Australia, with strong lobbying by sportswomen in its corridors of policy-making power. There it was argued that the general profile of women's sports, and the country's position in the medal table, would rise if more women's sports appeared on the programme. So the Australian Olympic Committee supported, prepared and sent loads of impressively athletic and fearsomely competitive women to the Games. And it makes an interesting counterpoint in Australia to the nation's top four team sports – rugby union, rugby league, cricket and Australian rules football – all male sports and not on the Olympic programme. Nor should we forget the major Australian sport for women and girls, netball, again not featured in the Olympics.

There is something about the national holiday at the Olympics, with international guests thrown in. This is mildly carnivalesque at times, but has more the innocent character of the family day-out that goes well, or the school sports day. It's an unthreatening joy in seeing the country have a go (and, in the Sydney case, do unprecedentedly well to boot) and for a home nation to demonstrate that it can put on a good show. British sports fans cheering Steve Redgrave's row into immortality were not a lot different from earlier generations cheering on the record-breakers of the amateur era. This was an Englishman cheered on for Great Britain. Stephanie Cook would be cheered to her modern pentathlon gold by similar proud and non-aggressive fans. It's the old distinction – a keen patriotism and pride in national achievement, rather than an aggressive nationalism. At the Olympics the Great Britain achievements were in some senses a renaissance of amateurism – performers on sabbaticals, supported by funds and grants from the national lottery. They were cheered to success by spectators and supporters worlds and cultures apart from the male-dominated ranks of the England football fans.

The big football event always has an edge. The European Cup final of 2001 between Bayern Munich and Valencia filled Milan's San Siro with the red and the orange of the respective teams, and an incredibly sustained and infectious chanting from the fans. Before the game, almost a hundred black-clad performers from La Scala reaffirmed the staged meeting of the high culture with the popular, prompting star UK journalist Hugh McIlvanney to splutter 'what's the fuck this got to do with football?' A dramatic penalty shoot-out went the German club's way. The disappointed fans of Valencia trooped out of the stadium as soon as they could, leaving the Bayern fans rapturous in their triumph. The squares and streets of Milan were not littered with the debris of hooliganism or riot. The Spanish side and its fans took defeat with dignity. The German victors and their followers were rapturous but not triumphalist in the bistros of the gallerias and plazas. The Italian police looked relaxed and Mussolini's monuments weren't molested or defaced. There's always an edge in these orgies of passionate nationalism. But, thinking of the twentieth-century history of the three nations involved, I'd leaned over to my colleague in the press box at the game and noted that this was a hell of a lot better than fascism.

The edge is at its tensest when England fans are in the picture. Top IOC man Dick Pound, runner for the IOC presidency in the summer of 2001, had, unprompted, asked me a couple of days before the San Siro match, 'What are you – England – going to do about your followers and your hooligan fans?' He was dismissive of the position of the sports authorities and the government on this question. This is a world-wide perception and seriously hampers aspirations to bring more sporting spectacles to England and the UK. There is one solution and one only to the high-profile minority for whom continuing hooligan wars have so much attraction. It is not a pleasant or a comfortable solution for democrats or libertarians. It is to continue to seek to identify those England fans for whom the cocktail of toughness and nationalist posturing proves irresistible, and to deny them access to the sites of football's greatest spectacles. The Sweden fans singing in the bars of Brussels's central square at the heart of the city – like the Danes in Bruges – were partying energetically, singing lustily, and downing innumerable lagers. But without a hint of menace. England's hooligan wars will not be solved by cosmetic changes to the administration of the sport spectacle; nor, long-term, by the control of individuals' movements across national borders. It is a much more cardinal issue than can be blamed upon football organisations. It is a question of whether a deep-rooted English masculinity, often traditionally working-class and xenophobic, can be disassembled, and an alternative formulation of national pride and collective passion articulated on football's greatest stages. It is possible, as vignettes of cosmopolitanism and audience diversity from events at LA '94 and Sydney 2000 in particular reaffirm, to have passionate crowds meet in intensely competitive circumstances and settings, with no sub-text of aggression or violence. But it is usually less possible when England is on the march.

Note: When you go behind the television screens and get up close to the two biggest media events in the world your interpretations will inevitably be selective and impressionistic. But what else is there? If we're honest about these things we have to make our observational interventions, linking these to a sound historical understanding and a context provided by (quite as selective) macro-research, on audiences and consumption for instance. The section on LA '94 in this chapter is drawn from John Sugden and Alan Tomlinson, 'One day in LA', *Leisure Studies Association Newsletter*, 1995. The University of Brighton has given me consistent support in getting up close to the big events, and I remain grateful for this. My brother John Tomlinson and my sister Jill Connors have given me extensive help and understanding in much of my time following Burnley Football Club.

RESOURCES OF HOPE

READING, CONTACTS AND CAMPAIGNS

Hooligan Wars is intended to be an intelligently accessible read through a subject of considerable importance to all who care for the future of football. Neither ducking complex questions nor serving up simplistic solutions can be a difficult balancing act. Contributors have been asked to offer their argument, analysis or account uncluttered by detailed references, numbered footnotes or lengthy quotations. This 'Resources of Hope' section is therefore provided for those who would like to follow up further some of the matters raised in the individual contributions. The section is organised in rough chronological order to match the sequence of the chapters. Most of the books cited should be available from any well-stocked bookshop or library. Failing this try *www.sportspages.co.uk*

England fan culture is a largely uncovered topic. Mark Perryman's edited collection *The Ingerland Factor: Home Truths from Football* is the most comprehensive attempt yet to explore what the ways in which we follow the national team say about the state of our nation. Subjects covered include the cult of nostalgia, tabloid excesses, the fate of the English male, football and music, with authors including Billy Bragg, Pete Davies, Dominik Diamond and John Peel.

Supporters committed to a positive passion and the separating of the pride from the prejudice are at the core of the relaunched England supporters organisation, *englandfans*. Run by the FA, there is a commitment to developing a constructive dialogue between fans and the football authorities, with backing given to fan-led initiatives to isolate the violent minority, information and advice for those who travel to away games, plus priority for overseas match, World Cup and European Championships tickets. Details can be found on the FA website: www.the-fa.org

There are a growing number of websites that promote the potential for an anti-violence, pro-passion fan culture. Visit www.philosophyfootball.com for a weekly newsflash, argumentative opinion space, and the full range of T-shirts from the fabled 'sporting outfitters of intellectual distinction'. From the British Council, no less, the excellent www.footballculture.net showcases not only the best of domestic fan culture and all matters football, but a global roundup of fan culture too. A good general fans' website full of message boards, news, and a comprehensive mediawatch is www.onetouchfootball.com which is run in association with the monthly football magazine *When Saturday Comes*.

The Football Supporters Association is a membership-based organisation that campaigns on all fan-related issues, as well as pioneering the 'Fan Embassies' that seek to provide an information and support service for England fans at away matches and tournaments. Further details from The Football Supporters Association, PO Box 11, Liverpool L26 1XP. Kevin Miles, who ran the Football Supporters Association Fan Embassies at Euro 2000 has written up his account of life as an England fan at a major championship in *An English Fan Abroad*.

The key books from the late 1980s debate on football violence were co-authored by Eric Dunning, Patrick Murphy and John Williams. *Hooligans Abroad, The Roots of Football Hooliganism* and *Football on Trial* remain essential introductions to the subject.

Kick It Out is the football anti-racist campaign. Fan-led, supported by The Football Association and The Professional Footballers Association, plus most league clubs and hundreds of fanzines, this initiative has successfully marginalised most of the racist chanting and abuse that once was so common at any football match. For up-to-date information on the campaign and to access a wide range of anti-racist resources visit www.kickitout.org.uk. One of the best books ever written about the complexities underpinning racism in football is Dave Hill's *Out of His Skin* which is centred on the career of John Barnes. A new and vitally important book on football's various formations of race and identity is *The Changing Face of Football* by Les Back, Tim Crabbe and John Solomos. *Race, Sport and British Society* edited by Ben Carrington and Ian McDonald looks not just at football to reveal how racism remains a pervasive influence across many aspects of sport in Britain.

For a comprehensive introduction to the work of Dorothy Rowe visit www.dorothyrowe.com.au Her latest book *Friends and Enemies: Our Need to Love and Hate* develops many of the themes in her chapter. Clifford Stott is a writer and researcher helping to develop a remarkably original social pyschological understanding of crowd trouble connected to football, read his 'How Conflict Escalates: The Inter-Group Dynamics of Football Crowd Violence' co-authored with Steve Reicher in the academic journal *Sociology*, 32, pp 353-77, 1998.

Goliath: Britain's Dangerous Places by Beatrix Campbell is one of the few books to relate public disorder to gender relations, though it doesn't do this in the context of football, rather the urban and housing estate riots of the 1990s. *One of the Lads* by Anne Coddington recounts the particular experience of women in football – as fans, employees, mothers, wives and journalists. Liz Crolley's chapter in *The Ingerland Factor* 'Lads Will be Lads' links this exclusion to the emergence of new Laddism.

For a greater spatial awareness of the football stadium there's no better place to start than Simon Inglis' *Football Grounds of Britain*. His personal account of the cultural, artistic and social significance of some of the world's most famous stadiums, *Sightlines: A Stadium Odyssey* is an entertaining must-read. *Hillsborough: The Truth* by Phil Scraton is a distinctly sobering investigation into the causes and aftermath of the Hillsborough disaster. Treat yourself to a great photographic record of what the places we watch football in represent, with a slow flick through *The Homes of Football* by Stuart Clarke or visit Stuart's web-site at www.edirectory.co.uk/homesoffootball.

The presence of fascist groups is a constant allegation whenever football violence explodes, while football hooligans are often named as the most likely supporters of marches and demonstrations organised by the British National Party and the National Front. The single most authoritative source on this subject is *Searchlight* magazine, the international anti-fascist monthly, their website address is: www.searchlightmagazine.com.

Engaging with football as an international sport and with varied fan cultures around the world, Richard Giulianotti's *Football: A Sociology of the Global Game* is essential reading. Edited by both Richard Giulianotti and Gary Armstrong *Entering the Field* opened a series of books that they also co-edited, including *Football Cultures and Identities* and *Fear and Loathing in World Football* that cover a huge variety of national football cultures, creating an incredibly interesting study of both commonalities and discontinuities.

On French Football *Le Foot* edited by Christov Ruhn is a good introduction, and for the background to, and long-lasting significance of France's hosting of the 1998 World Cup, read *France and the 1998 World Cup* edited by Hugh Dauncey and Geoff Hare. There's no better book on Dutch football, and not many books that are better on *anything* connected to football, than David Winner's *Brilliant Orange*. It is illuminating, incisive and an intellectual read that will have any reader chuckling as soon as they start turning the pages. The official FC St Pauli website is at www.fcstpauli.de Independent St Pauli fan sites include www.uebersteiger.de plus www.karo-family.de and www.kiezkicker.de and probably the funniest www.diefeuchtenbiber.de A St Pauli fan site which is available in both German and English is www.west-brigade.de

Football Hooligans by Gary Armstrong is a vital addition to the analysis of football violence and its causes and effects. Breaking ranks with much of the academic work that preceded his own, Gary Armstrong's book combines detailed first-hand research into the fan group that follows Sheffield United, 'the Blades', with a determination to expose the authoritarianism that lies behind most attempts to police fans. Dougie Brimson's terrace classic *Everywhere We Go* was co-authored with his brother Eddie Brimson and it was followed by their *England, My England, Capital Punishment* and *Derby Days*. Dougie Brimson's latest is *Barmy Army*. Details of all these books, with a large amount of valuable background material, can be found at www.brimson.net.

For a comparison of England fan culture from north of the border read Ian Black's *Tales of the Tartan Army*. To compare England fan culture across sports visit the England cricket fans' site www.barmy-army.com

How FIFA seek to manage football as an international sport, and the role of World Cup organisation within this is extensively covered in two books written by John Sugden and Alan Tomlinson, *FIFA and the Contest for World Football* and *Great Balls of Fire*. Contrasting the 1996 Olympics and the 1998 World Cup Alan Tomlinson makes some very interesting points in a short article 'Staging the Spectacle: Reflections on Olympic and World Cup, Ceremonies' in the journal *Soundings*, 13, Autumn 1999.

If reading *Hooligan Wars* has made you think you'd like to study the causes and effects of football violence, and related subjects in the sociology of sport further, there are a wide range of courses available at a number of different levels of academic and time commitment. The pick of these is the following: the early summer evening class Football Culture and Society run each year by Birkbeck College in central London (details from: Football, Culture and Society, Faculty of Continuing Education, Birkbeck College, 26 Russell Square, London WC1); and the MA Sport and Leisure Cultures at the University of Brighton (details from: MA Sport and Leisure Cultures, Area B Administration, Chelsea School Research Centre, University of Brighton, Trevin Towers, Gaudick Road, Eastbourne BN20 7SP.) or visit: www.bton.ac.uk/edusport/chelsea/html/research.htm).

NOTES ON CONTRIBUTORS

Patrick Barclay is a football columnist on the *Sunday Telegraph*. He has covered every European Championship since 1980 and every World Cup since 1982 for a range of newspapers.

Dougie Brimson is the author of *Barmy Army* and *The Geezer's Guide to Football*. He is the co-author, with Eddie Brimson, of the terrace classics, *Everywhere We Go, England My England, Capital Punishment* and *Derby Days*.

Beatrix Campbell is a feminist author, journalist and broadcaster. Her book *Goliath: Britain's Dangerous Places* is a pioneering analysis of gender and generation, policing and politics.

Vivek Chaudary is the Sports News Correspondent of *The Guardian*. In 2000 he was highly commended by the Sports Writers Association for his reporting, particularly from Euro 2000 and the Sydney Olympics.

Adam L. Dawson had never had any of his writing published before being asked by Beatrix Campbell to collaborate on her chapter in this collection. Currently unemployed, Adam is a season-ticket holder for Manchester United, a club he has supported since childhood.

Richard Giulianotti is the author of *Football: A Sociology of the Global Game*. He co-edited, with Gary Armstrong *Entering the Field: New Perspectives on World Football* which was followed up by *Football, Cultures and Identities* and *Fear and Loathing in World Football*. Richard is Senior Lecturer in Sociology at the University of Aberdeen.

Simon Inglis wrote *Football Grounds of Britain*. He is editor of *The Guide to Safety at Sports Grounds*, is an exhibition curator, broadcaster and stadium consultant and his latest book *Sightlines: A Stadium Odyssey* ensures a stand will never again be thought of as a place simply to watch a game of football from.

Nick Lowles is co-editor of *Searchlight*, the international anti-fascist monthly magazine.

René Martens is the author of two books about FC St Pauli, *Verloag Die Werrkstatt* and *Kiez Kult Allta*.

Patrick Mignon was a contributor to *France and the 1998 World Cup: The National Impact of a World Sporting Event*. Author of *La Passion du Football*, he is the Director of the Sociology of Sport Research Centre at the Institut National du Sport et de l'Education Physique, Paris.

Mark Perryman is the editor of *The Ingerland Factor: Home Truths from Football*. He was a member of the England Members Club National Consultative Committee and the Home Office Football and Disorder Working Group. In 1994 Mark co-founded the self-styled 'sporting outfitters of intellectual distinction' *Philosophy Football*. He writes regularly for *When Saturday Comes, Total Football* and the *New Statesman*. Mark is a Research Fellow at The Chelsea School, University of Brighton.

Emma Poulton is a lecturer in the Sociology of Sport at the University of Durham. Her doctoral research was based on the construction and representation of national identity through the media coverage of football.

Dorothy Rowe is one of the world's leading clinical psychologists. Researcher, writer and lecturer, her books include *Friends and Enemies: Our Need to Love and Hate* and *Depression: The Way Out of Your Prison*.

David Shayler is a former MI5 intelligence officer. Having escaped to France following his exposure of illegal activities by the security services he returned to England in 2000 to face prosecution under the Official Secrets Act.

John Sugden is the co-author, with Alan Tomlinson, of *Great Balls of Fire: How Big Money is Hijacking World Football* and *FIFA and the Contest for World Football*. He is Professor in the Sociology of Sport, The Chelsea School, University of Brighton.

Alan Tomlinson is the co-author, with John Sugden, of *Great Balls of Fire: How Big Money is Hijacking World Football* and *FIFA and the Contest for World Football*. Alan is Professor in Sport and Leisure Studies, The Chelsea School, University of Brighton.

John Williams is the co-editor of *Passing Rhythms: Liverpool FC and the Transformation of Football*. With Eric Dunning and Patrick Murphy he wrote the hugely influential *Hooligans Abroad, The Roots of Football Hooliganism* and *Football on Trial*. He is director of the Sir Norman Chester Centre for Football Research at the University of Leicester.

David Winner is the author of *Brilliant Orange: The Neurotic Genius of Dutch Football*. A freelance journalist living in Amsterdam and London he co-translated *Ajax, Barcelona, Cruyff : The ABC of an Obstinate Maestro*.

INDEX